UNION COMBINED OPERATIONS IN THE CIVIL WAR

Union Combined Operations in the Civil War

Edited by
Craig L. Symonds

Fordham University Press
New York 2010

Copyright © 2010 Fordham University Press

All rights reserved. No part of this publication may be reproduced, stored in a retrieval system, or transmitted in any form or by any means—electronic, mechanical, photocopy, recording, or any other—except for brief quotations in printed reviews, without the prior permission of the publisher.

Fordham University Press has no responsibility for the persistence or accuracy of URLs for external or third-party Internet websites referred to in this publication and does not guarantee that any content on such websites is, or will remain, accurate or appropriate.

Library of Congress Cataloging-in-Publication Data

Union combined operations in the Civil War / edited by Craig L. Symonds.
    p.   cm.— (The North's Civil War)
  Includes bibliographical references and index.
  ISBN 978-0-8232-3286-4 (cloth : alk. paper)
  1. United States. Army—History—Civil War, 1861–1865. 2. Combined operations (Military science)—History—19th century. 3. United States—History—Civil War, 1861–1865—Campaigns. 4. Generals—United States—History—19th century.
  I. Symonds, Craig L.
  E491.U4817 2010
  973.7′3—dc22

2009047898

Printed in the United States of America
12 11 10 5 4 3 2 1
First edition

Contents

List of Figures — vii
List of Abbreviations Used in the Notes — ix
Acknowledgments — xi

Introduction, Craig L. Symonds | 1

1. Burnside When He Was Brilliant: Ambrose Burnside and Union Combined Operations in Pamlico Sound, David E. Long | 10

2. A Thorn, Not a Dagger: Strategic Implications of Ambrose Burnside's North Carolina Campaign, David C. Skaggs | 23

3. "Very Crude Notions on the Subject": William B. Franklin's Amphibious Assault at Eltham's Landing, Mark A. Snell | 32

4. The Union Attack at Drewry's Bluff: An Opportunity Lost, Robert E. Sheridan | 44

5. Union Combined Operations on the Texas Coast, 1863–64, John P. Fisher | 56

6. Assailing Satan's Kingdom: Union Combined Operations at Charleston, Francis J. DuCoin | 74

7. Grant Moves South: Combined Operations on the James River, 1864, Craig L. Symonds | 87

8. Closing Down the Kingdom: Union Combined Operations Against Wilmington, Chris E. Fonvielle Jr. | 96

9 "The Absence of Decisive Results":
British Assessments of Union
Combined Operations, Howard J.
Fuller | 115

10 Union Combined Operations in the
Civil War: Lessons Learned, Lessons
Forgotten, Edward H. Wiser | 135

List of Contributors   152
Index   155

Figures

Coast and Sounds of North Carolina	18
Southeastern Virginia	34
Coast of Louisiana and Texas	59
Charleston Harbor, 1862–63	78
Road Between Bermuda Hundred and Enemy's Line of Intrenchments	90
Approaches to Wilmington, North Carolina	98

Abbreviations Used in the Notes

OR *Official Records of the Union and Confederate Armies in the War of the Rebellion.* 128 vols. Washington, D.C.: Government Printing Office, 1880–1901. All references are to series I unless otherwise indicated.

ORN *Official Records of the Union and Confederate Navies in the War of the Rebellion.* 30 vols. Washington, D.C.: Government Printing Office, 1894–1922. All references are to series I unless otherwise indicated.

Acknowledgments

"Coast and Sounds of North Carolina" in Chapter 1, "Map of Southeastern Virginia" in Chapter 3, and "Approaches to Wilmington, North Carolina" in Chapter 8 are reprinted from *The Official Records of the Union and Confederate Navies in the War of the Rebellion*, volume 8.

"Coast of Louisiana and Texas" in Chapter 5 is reprinted from *The Official Records of the Union and Confederate Navies in the War of the Rebellion*, volume 17.

The map of Charleston Harbor, 1862–63, in Chapter 6 is by Bill Clipson and is reprinted with permission from Craig L. Symonds, *The Naval Institute Historical Atlas of the U.S. Navy* (Annapolis: Naval Institute Press, 1995).

"Road Between Bermuda Hundred and Enemy's Line of Intrenchments" in Chapter 7 is reprinted from *The Atlas to Accompany the Official Records of the Union and Confederate Armies* (New York: Crown, 1978).

Union Combined
Operations in the
Civil War

Introduction

Craig L. Symonds

Despite the number of operational studies on the campaigns of the American Civil War, the subject of combined or joint operations is one that has been largely overlooked. Only one book devotes itself to the subject, Rowena's Reed's *Combined Operations in the Civil War*, first published in 1978 and reprinted in 1993, and it is flawed by Reed's infatuation with what she deems the strategic genius of George B. McClellan, whom she describes as "a thoroughly 'modern' young soldier of seemingly inexhaustible energy and talent." One of the most notable things about McClellan was that he apparently had the kind of personality that made perfectly reasonable people fall under the spell of his charm. Evidently his ability to cast this spell continued after his death, for there is no other explanation for Reed's startling conclusion that "had McClellan's brilliant strategy been fully implemented, it would have ended the Civil War in 1862." Of course, it is worth noting that if the Civil War *had* ended in 1862, slavery would have remained intact, leaving its solution to another time and perhaps another war. Because of her sympathy for McClellan, Reed accepts her hero's argument that it was interference from the central government, and in particular meddling by Winfield Scott, Henry Halleck, and others—including Abraham Lincoln—that prevented Little Mac from achieving this brilliant strategic accomplishment. Though Reed makes a number of valuable points, they are overwhelmed by her determination to portray McClellan as the military genius of the war. Other than this one volume, there is no full-scale study of Union combined operations.[1]

Contemporaries as well as historians were guilty of overlooking the role of combined arms. The tactical manual used by all but a handful of the West Point graduates who fought in the Civil War was William Hardee's *Tactics*, which did not even mention joint operations, and the most widely read text on strategy, Antoine Henri Jomini's *The Art of War*, noted only that such operations were "rare" and "among the most difficult in war."[2]

Another problem was that there was virtually no protocol for effecting the efficient cooperation of army and navy forces. The Navy Department and the War Department were completely separate from each other; almost like a boundary, there was a bright line separating Neptune's domain from that of Mars. Officers of one service were under no obligation to accept orders from an officer of another, regardless of the difference in their rank. They could choose to cooperate, of course, but such cooperation was entirely at their discretion; and because each service tended to be jealous of its independence, requests for support had to be couched deferentially, and could be easily (though almost always politely) refused. Because army and navy leaders were unwilling to subordinate their own service goals to the greater goal of Union victory, Union forces experienced a number of lost opportunities. Successful combined operations were therefore not only more often the exception than the rule, they were also subject to misunderstanding, confusion, and subsequent bickering.

According to the Constitution, the only person in the Union government who had direct command authority over both the army and the navy was the president of the United States. It was, of course, impractical for Lincoln to act as the on-scene commander in chief for all combined operations, but an instructive example of how effective combined operations might have been with a single commander in charge occurred in the spring of 1862 when Lincoln visited Hampton Roads, Virginia. The vast army that McClellan had assembled and successfully transported to Fort Monroe had stalled on the lower peninsula in front of the Yorktown fortifications, and Lincoln hoped to prod his reluctant general into action. He took along both Edwin Stanton, secretary of war, and Salmon P. Chase, secretary of the treasury, and they traveled by sea on the small revenue cutter *Miami*. It was Lincoln's first voyage on Neptune's element, and almost the moment the *Miami* entered the Chesapeake Bay, he fell victim to seasickness. He spent most of the trip stretched out on a locker in the ship's tiny cabin.[3]

Once the *Miami* arrived in Hampton Roads, Lincoln transferred to the much larger, and more stable, steam frigate *Minnesota*, where he met the navy's squadron commander, Flag Officer Louis M. Goldsborough. From the deck of the *Minnesota*, Goldsborough pointed out to Lincoln the pertinent military features of the roadstead, including the scene of the already-famous duel between the ironclads that had taken place two months before, and the location of the rebel batteries on Sewall's Point on the southern edge of the roadstead. As Lincoln studied the enemy fortifications across the water, he asked Goldsborough why the navy did not undertake a bombardment of those batteries. The flag officer had no good answer to that, and he agreed to organize a "demonstration"—essentially a reconnaissance in force—to test them. Lincoln had come to Hampton Roads to see if he could prod his reluctant general, but he saw that prodding was likely to be necessary in other quarters as well.

While Goldsborough went off to set things in motion for the demonstration, Lincoln and his party visited the little *Monitor*, already famous as an icon of naval warfare because of its duel with the Confederate ironclad *Virginia* (which the Federals continued to call the *Merrimac*) the previous March. He shook hands with the officers and inspected the crew, which gave him three cheers when he left.[4]

That afternoon, Goldsborough organized a naval bombardment of the Sewall's Point batteries. To observe it, Lincoln took a boat out to the Rip Raps—a man-made island not quite half way between Fort Monroe and Sewall's Point. The battery there had originally been called Fort Calhoun, but after the war began had been renamed Fort Wool after the seventy-six-year-old Union general who commanded the garrison at Fort Monroe. From there, Lincoln had the rare experience of watching a military operation that he had set in motion personally. The navy's big ships drew up their anchors, steamed toward Sewall's Point, and opened fire. The bombardment provoked the big rebel ironclad *Virginia* to sortie, though it did not come out beyond the entrance to the Elizabeth River, and after not more than an hour the rebel batteries at Sewall's Point were silenced. Lincoln may have wondered why, if the navy's guns could so easily silence enemy batteries, Goldsborough had waited until now to do it. But he did not say "I told you so" or anything else to Goldsborough besides extending congratulations.[5]

This little success was gratifying, but rather than bask in it, Lincoln sought instead to seize the moment and expand on it. En route back to the *Minnesota* from an inspection of the troops ashore, he ordered the tug's skipper to put him alongside the *Monitor*. There he deferentially asked the *Monitor*'s skipper, William N. Jeffers, if "there would be any military impropriety" if he got his ship underway without orders from Flag Officer Goldsborough, and if not, would he mind conducting a quick reconnaissance of Sewall's Point to see if the batteries there had been completely abandoned. Once back on the *Minnesota*, Lincoln then suggested to Major General John E. Wool that if the works ashore had, in fact, been abandoned, might it not be possible to land an armed force there to approach Norfolk from the rear.[6]

Wool was hesitant. There was no satisfactory landing site; the *Merrimack* was still a threat; and he had no orders from General McClellan. Lincoln had by now become accustomed to hearing reasons from his commanders why operations were either unwise or impossible. It probably did not surprise him that a few officers even suggested that it would be better to send army troops to Burnside in the North Carolina Sounds in order to approach Norfolk from the south. Very likely, it seemed to Lincoln that all his officers—of both services—

were suffering from McClellanism, favoring an indirect approach when a direct approach was available.

That same afternoon, however, Secretary Chase came back from a cruise about the roadstead on the little *Miami* to report that he and General Wool had found "a good and convenient landing place" just east of Sewall's Point. The news provoked Lincoln to call for a chart of the area and, after conversing with a local pilot, he identified another possible landing site even closer to Norfolk. He told Chase that he "wished to go and see about it on the spot," and thus it was that the president of the United States and two of his cabinet members, accompanied by about twenty soldiers and sailors, went out in a small steam tug to conduct a reconnaissance of the enemy coastline. He returned with information about a second landing site, and Wool agreed that the operation could go ahead, though he preferred to use the beach he and Chase had reconnoitered.[7]

Just as Lincoln had embarrassed Goldsborough into attacking the rebel batteries, he effectively embarrassed Wool into launching an amphibious assault. Moreover, it was a true combined operation as the navy's warships escorted scores of small canal boats across the roadstead from Hampton to the landing site and covered the landing while the soldiers scrambled ashore. Lincoln went too. A soldier in one of the canal boats recalled seeing the nation's chief executive on one of the ships, "rushing about, hollering to someone on the wharf." The landing was a bit haphazard, as was to be expected in such an ad hoc operation, but by that afternoon all the forces were safely ashore. Once there, however, no one seemed to be quite sure what to do next. Lincoln stayed aboard ship, but Secretary Chase had gone onto land with the troops and, appalled by the disorder and chaos, questioned Wool rather forcefully about what he saw.[8]

Wool declared that the confusion was because the officers were worried about violating the chain of command. Characteristic of combined operations, no one knew who was in charge or who was senior to whom, and as a result the men milled about on the beach looking for something to do. Fed up with such punctiliousness, Chase ordered one of the generals "in the name of the President of the United States" to take command and march toward Norfolk. That, apparently, was all it took. The column started out at once, and a few miles short of the city it met a delegation of civilians, headed by the mayor of Norfolk, who had all come out to surrender the city. Only later did someone figure out that the extended surrender ceremony had been arranged in order to allow the last of the evacuating rebel soldiers to get away.[9]

So Norfolk fell to Union arms. It fell, in fact, to a combined operation of the army and the navy, an operation that would not have taken place at all if the one man who had joint control over both services had not happened to be there to insist on it. Lincoln found that by taking the lead and showing how progress could be made, he could inspire his commanders to be more assertive with the enemy and more cooperative with one another. In a letter to his daughter, Secretary Chase wrote that if Lincoln had not come down to Hampton Roads, Norfolk would still be in rebel hands, and he was very likely correct.[10]

The loss of Norfolk led directly to the loss of the *Merrimack/Virginia* as well. Without its base, the *Virginia* could not survive, and the day Lincoln left to return to Washington, the rebels blew it up. A navy movement had cleared the beach for an army landing; and the army landing had deprived the rebel monster of its base, resulting in the destruction of the navy's greatest foe. This was the way combined operations were supposed to work: one hand washes the other.

It worked, however, only when the commander in chief was there to make it happen. Even then it was sometimes not enough. While McClellan was employed in a leisurely pursuit of the retreating Confederates to Williamsburg, he sought support from the navy for his left flank. Eager to help, Lincoln called for Goldsborough to see what could be done. The answer, according to Goldsborough, was not very much. McClellan wanted Goldsborough to send a squadron of vessels up the James River, but when the assistant secretary of the navy, Gustavus Fox, asked Goldsborough if he might temporarily place himself under McClellan's command for this emergency, Goldsborough replied that "he would never under any circumstances place himself under the orders of an officer of the army," though he did agree to cooperate voluntarily.[11]

Even when the president himself asked Goldsborough to advance up the James River, Goldsborough hesitated. He told Lincoln he would first have to bring ships around from the York River to ensure his continued naval superiority in Hampton Roads. Seward, who witnessed the conversation, lost his temper and told Goldsborough that he was to do as he was told and do it at once, never mind the excuses. Goldsborough naturally bristled, and Lincoln, playing (as he often did) the role of peacemaker among his quarreling subordinates, said quietly that the mission was an important one and that he hoped Goldsborough could find a way to make it happen. He shifted the conversation by asking Goldsborough who he thought might command such an expedition, and after some thought Goldsborough named John Rodgers. Lincoln thereupon sent for Rodgers and they began to discuss not *whether* to do it, but *how* to do it. In this way, Lincoln managed to get a naval squadron up the James River on McClellan's left flank during the advance on Richmond. The ships got as far as Drewry's Bluff (see Chapter 4) but failed to achieve a breakthrough.[12]

The success of combined operations in Hampton Roads did not, however, establish a model for future operations. Lincoln could not be everywhere at once, and in his absence combined operations along the rebel coast suffered from precisely the kind of impediments he had encountered in Hampton Roads: generals and admirals were wary of one another; like Goldsborough, they refused to accept orders from officers of the other service; and though they often agreed to "cooperate," such cooperation tended to fall apart as soon as difficulties arose. Lincoln himself never wanted to assume a leadership role in coordinating the two services. He wanted officers who would take charge, work together, and achieve the mission. He didn't know it yet, but he was looking for Ulysses S. Grant and David Farragut. Until they emerged, however, he stepped in and did it himself. It was the unprecedented character of the American Civil War, and the absence of a clear protocol for combined operations, that compelled him to do so.

The ten essays in this volume are case studies of combined operations in the Civil War, all of them by Union forces, and most of them fraught with the kind of difficulties suggested above. The essays are arranged in chronological order, though this is not intended to be a comprehensive narrative of such operations, for not all combined efforts by Union forces are included. Rather, each operation illuminates some aspect of combined operations during a time of changing technology and doctrine. Nor do these essays cover all aspects of combined operations, for none focus on the river war in the western theater, which was burdened by its own set of bureaucratic and operational difficulties. Instead, the essays herein cover the war along the rebel coast: the operations in the North Carolina Sounds in 1861, the Union thrusts up the York and James Rivers during the Peninsula Campaign in 1862 and 1864, and the various Union efforts to seize rebel seaports from the Texas coast to Charleston and Wilmington between 1863 and 1865. Two of the chapters evaluate the impact of Union combined operations on subsequent doctrine in both the United States and Britain. All these essays save one were first presented at a March 2008 conference at the USS *Monitor* Center, part of the Mariners' Museum in Newport News, Virginia.

It is important to note here that the phrase "combined operations" was the one used by contemporaries to describe cooperative efforts involving both the army and the navy. Today, operations that involve more than one service, such as the kind of army–navy–air force operations that have characterized the wars in Iraq and Afghanistan, are called "joint operations," while the phrase "combined operations" generally refers to those conducted by more than one country. The Allied invasion of Normandy, for example, was both a *joint* operation (involving army and navy assets as well as the army air corps) and a *combined* operation (involving, among others, American, British, Canadian, and Free French forces). In the nineteenth century, however, the term used to describe campaigns involving both the army and the navy was "combined operations," so that is the term adopted here.

Today the importance of such operations is clearly acknowledged. The nation's war colleges are dominated by constant calls for "jointness" in order to overcome traditional service loyalty. The chairmanship of the Joint Chiefs of Staff rotates among the services, and officers who are especially sensitive to the importance of joint planning and joint operations are called "purple suiters," which is supposedly the color you would get if you mixed army and marine corps green with navy blue and air force light blue into a single uniform. Today a navy admiral can command a theater with authority over army and air force assets. But in 1861 the idea that officers of one service would be placed under the operational command of an officer of a different service was not only new, it was for most professional officers an abomination. To be sure, officers could choose to cooperate, but voluntary cooperation was a slender reed amid a hard-fought campaign. Though orders to field officers and squadron commanders often enjoined them to exercise "the most cordial and effectual cooperation between the officers of the two services," those orders also decreed that "no officer of the Army or Navy, whatever may be his rank, can assume any direct command, independent of consent, over an officer of the other service." In other words, though cooperation was encouraged and even expected, it was not mandated, and in the end, all officers were held responsible and accountable for their own actions. It depended a great deal, therefore, on how well—if at all—the personalities of the cooperating commanders meshed. When they did, it often meant success; when they did not, it generally meant inefficiency and failure, with consequent finger-pointing and self-justification.[13]

Several of the essays in this volume refer to, and use as a starting point, Rowena Reed's 1978 book. Because of her conviction that combined operations constituted a lost opportunity for Union forces in the Civil War, she emphasized—arguably overemphasized—the importance of George McClellan's strategic plans to use combined operations to cripple Confederate transportation. It was McClellan, Reed argues, who recognized that "bludgeoning the enemy to death" was not only unnecessary but also foolish, and who instead sought to use combined operations "as part of a comprehensive plan to paralyze the South from within." As she noted, "Only General McClellan envisioned the use of combined operations as the foundation of a comprehensive plan to paralyze the South from within."[14]

Today few scholars of the Civil War era endorse such views. Whatever the merit of McClellan's vision of combined operations, he lacked both the steadfastness necessary to manage them effectively and the drive to see them through. He did outline a comprehensive plan to use army and navy forces to disrupt the Confederacy's internal communications network and dispatched his friend Ambrose Burnside to the coast of North Carolina in pursuit of that. As David Long points out, Burnside conducted himself with skill and energy in this assignment, but McClellan did not follow through. As David Skaggs and Robert Sheridan show in their essays, McClellan's unwillingness to weaken his main field army to support these combined thrusts properly was a major cause of their failure. In his essay on the Union amphibious move to Eltham's Landing, Mark Snell demonstrates that when combined operations did work, it was less because of leadership or direction from the top than because some mid-level officer on the scene took it on himself to ensure that both proper planning and necessary preparations took place.

In the Union effort to capture or close the major Confederate seaports at Galveston and Sabine Pass on the Texas coast, at Charleston, South Carolina, and at Wilmington, North Carolina, cooperation was sometimes present, but not unified command. John Fisher, Francis DuCoin, and Chris Fonvielle Jr. show how service jealousy as well as poor communication kept Union forces from achieving their goals, or achieving them quickly with minimal losses. What these studies suggest is that in the conduct of combined operations, the whole can sometimes be considerably *less* than the sum of its parts.

All wars offer lessons, for winners and losers alike. Howard Fuller and Edward Wiser examine the lessons that British and American war planners took from considering combined operations in the Civil War, as well as how they applied those lessons, or failed to do so, in the years that followed. Perhaps the most remarkable thing to note about the lessons of Union combined operations in the Civil War is that it took another eighty-two years, and two world wars, before the United States finally unified the services in the National Defense Act of 1947.

I am grateful to all the contributors for their work, and to the Mariners' Museum, which hosted the conference at which most of these arguments were first presented and debated. The USS *Monitor* Center at the Mariners' Museum is a model of an exhibit that is both historically significant and exciting to visit. It will stand for many years as the prototype of both a user-friendly museum as well as a center for the study, preservation, and conservation of naval artifacts.

Notes

Portions of this chapter are adapted from Craig L. Symonds, *Lincoln and His Admirals: Abraham Lincoln, the U.S. Navy, and the Civil War* (New York: Oxford University Press, 2008), 146–56. © 2008 by Craig Symonds.

    1. Rowena Reed, *Combined Operations in the Civil War* (Annapolis, Md.: Naval Institute Press, 1978), xv, xviii.

2. William J. Hardee, *Rifle and Light Infantry Tactics* (Philadelphia: J. B. Lippincott, 1855); Antoine Henri Jomini, *The Art of War* (Philadelphia: J. B. Lippincott, 1862), 248–52. See also Scott W. Stucky, "Joint Operations in the Civil War," *Joint Force Quarterly* 6 (Autumn–Winter, 1994–95): 92–105.

3. Chase to "my darling Nettie," May 7, 1862, in Chase, *Inside Lincoln's Cabinet: The Civil War Diaries of Salmon P. Chase*, edited by David Donald (New York: Longmans, Green, 1954), 75–76.

4. Frederick F. Keeler to "Dear Anna," May 7, 1862, in Keeler, *Aboard the USS Monitor: 1862*, edited by Robert W. Daly (Annapolis, Md.: Naval Institute Press, 1964), 107.

5. Chase to "my darling Nettie," May 8, 1862, in Chase, *Inside Lincoln's Cabinet*, 78; Gillis to Goldsborough, May 8, 1862, and Constable to Chase, May 9, 1862, both in *ORN*, 22:232–33.

6. Lincoln to Goldsborough, May 7, 1862, in Lincoln, *The Collected Works of Abraham Lincoln*, edited by Roy P. Basler (New Brunswick, N.J.: Rutgers University Press, 1953), 5:207; Stanton to McClellan, May 9, 1862, and Jeffers to Goldsborough, May 9, 1862, both in *ORN*, 22:338–39, 340.

7. Chase to "my darling Nettie," May 11, 1862, in Chase, *Inside Lincoln's Cabinet*, 82.

8. Egbert Viele, "A Trip with Lincoln, Chase, and Stanton," *Scribner's Monthly* (October 1878), 821; Stephen W. Sears, *To the Gates of Richmond* (New York: Ticknor and Fields, 1992), 90.

9. Stanton to Watson, May 10, 1862, *OR*, 11 (part 3): 162; Chase to "my darling Nettie," May 11, 1862, in Chase, *Inside Lincoln's Cabinet*, 85.

10. *Washington Star*, May 12, 1862.

11. Henry C. Baird, "Narrative of Rear Admiral Goldsborough, U.S. Navy," *U.S. Naval Institute Proceedings* (July 1933), 1025.

12. Ibid.; Stanton to McClellan, May 7, 1862, *OR*, 11 (part 3): 147.

13. Welles to Du Pont, October 12, 1861, *ORN*, 12:215.

14. Reed, *Combined Operations*, xviii.

1

Burnside When He Was Brilliant: Ambrose Burnside and Union Combined Operations in Pamlico Sound

David E. Long

Few names from the Civil War era inspire more loathing and contempt than that of Ambrose Everett Burnside. It is a curious legacy for a man whose prewar contemporaries found him a likeable and collegial fellow officer. Of course, their perceptions of Burnside were not yet clouded by the knowledge that on one unfortunate day at Fredericksburg in December 1862, Burnside would order what was undoubtedly the most futile charge in the history of the U.S. Army, and who a day later sought to fall on his sword by renewing the attack and personally leading it in another lethal and equally hopeless advance. And yet in 1861 when the war began, Burnside was one of the most forward-looking and innovative officers in the Union army, especially in terms of his willingness to think about, and plan for, combined operations.

It was Burnside, himself a Rhode Islander, who first proposed to George B. McClellan in October 1861 the wisdom of recruiting a few brigades from the maritime regions of New England to fight on the Southern coast and in the estuaries of Virginia and the Carolinas. In Burnside's vision, this force would be composed of men who would not only fight, but also maneuver along the coast in their own boats, giving them a mobility unavailable to shore-bound soldiers. McClellan was Burnside's close prewar friend, and though he casually dismissed Burnside's explanations regarding the disaster at Bull Run, he liked the idea of the coastal division, and Burnside soon found himself promoted to brigadier general and charged with raising and training a division whose special mission it would be to perform maritime operations. At this point, Burnside's vision did not include the navy, so it was not a truly combined operation, but it was nevertheless innovative in its concept and opened up the possibility of combined operations in the future.[1]

Burnside called on the New England governors for troops to make up his specialized division; he exercised the authority McClellan gave him to purchase or charter vessels for those troops; and he established a temporary camp for his division at Hempstead, Long Island. By late 1861, Ambrose Burnside was arguably the foremost Union officer involved with amphibious operations. At this point in the war, Burnside was on top of his game, and that game was to train troops for special operations work and to accumulate the necessary transportation conveyances to move a force approaching fifteen thousand troops and sailors through coastal waters to whatever their ultimate destination might be.

Because Burnside envisioned his marine division as operating independently of the navy, inter-service rivalry was not yet a limiting problem, but he did encounter some *intra*-service rivalry. In both raising the troops and purchasing or leasing the ships and boats, Burnside had to compete with General Thomas W. Sherman, who was raising a force for an army–navy attack on Port Royal, South Carolina. Both expeditions planned to use Annapolis, Maryland, as the staging area, and Burnside could not move his force there until Sherman's force departed on October 21. Burnside also had to purchase several score surf boats, which could be loaded quickly and could carry his soldiers to a hostile beach. Throughout this process, Burnside demonstrated his attention to detail, inspecting the small craft closely for seaworthiness and materials that would survive inclement weather. He was not about to invest in boats that would capsize in a heavy surf or come apart the first time it rained.[2]

In her pioneering study *Combined Operations in the Civil War*, Rowena Reed argues that McClellan had a clear vision of how Burnside's amphibious division was to be employed as part of a comprehensive plan "to paralyze the South's internal lines of communication." She asserts that his goal was to "gain a large and secure base for operations against the Wilmington and Weldon Railroad." If so, apparently Little Mac did not let Burnside in on these plans, for Burnside himself was unsure where his specialized division would be deployed. At one point he asked for a detailed report on affairs in Texas from a man familiar with that state; Burnside may have been sizing up the sparsely populated Gulf Coast as a tempting target. In the end, however, McClellan ordered Burnside's division to the North Carolina Sounds to occupy both New Bern and the mouth of the Neuse River. From there, he could either proceed inland to the railroad hub at Goldsboro, or south to the important seaport of Wilmington.[3]

One person who ultimately played a major role in determining the site for operations was a volunteer New York officer named Rush Hawkins, the aristocratic colonel of the dapper 9th New York Volunteer Zouave regiment. Hawkins was somewhat supercilious in his attitude toward other commanders. After participating in the capture of Forts Hatteras and Clark in August 1861, he characterized the troops of another regiment as "vandals" for pillaging Confederate camps and homes, insinuating that their colonel was a party to the looting. He threatened to turn the guns of Fort Clark on those men if they did not behave. When, instead of being promoted to brigadier general he was relieved of his command at Hatteras, Hawkins wrote an insubordinate letter to the department commander who had sent the orders. The grapes, apparently, were sour indeed: "Brigadier-generals are made of such queer stuff nowadays," Hawkins wrote, "that I should not esteem it any very great honor to be made one." Within a few weeks of the new commander's arrival, Hawkins managed to get himself arrested for another act of insubordination. But in spite of this kind of confrontational belligerence, Hawkins won a summons to the White House because of a suggestion he had made in an early dispatch that had intrigued President Lincoln.[4]

Meeting in the rarefied air of a White House conference room with the president and General McClellan as his audience, Hawkins laid out his argument that the counties surrounding Pamlico Sound in North Carolina were teeming with Union sympathizers who could easily be recruited to help in suppressing the rebellion. Lincoln still believed that there were large numbers of latent Unionists in the South who needed only direction and support to reclaim their governments from the control of the separatists. Hawkins, therefore, was speaking in terms that Lincoln desperately wanted to believe, for here was his first real opportunity to reestablish a loyal state government in a seceded state. McClellan was interested as well, not so much for the political potential as for Hawkins's strategic conceptions. Hawkins insisted that the capture of Roanoke Island would permit the occupation of both the Neuse and Pamlico Rivers in addition to the important town of Beaufort, opening several lines of advance into the rebel interior.[5]

The notion of a North Carolina campaign quickly picked up steam on both the government and civilian level. On November 7, at the Cooper Union in New York City, historian George Bancroft introduced two North Carolina ministers who had come directly from the Outer Banks, and who described the suffering of the loyal people there. The speakers who followed were Ambrose Burnside and William Cullen Bryant, famous poet and editor of the *New York Evening Post*. The meeting raised funds to pay for one of the ministers to return to Hatteras where, ten days hence, he would convene a rump convention to charter a provisional loyal state government with the Reverend Marble Nash Taylor as governor.[6]

Whatever political advantages might redound from an operation into the North Carolina Sounds, it would have clear strategic benefits. Even as Burnside was speaking at the benefit in New York, General Thomas Sherman's soldiers were occupying the works around the harbor at Port Royal, South Carolina, where the navy would establish its principal port for the support of the blockade. Having another deepwater port between Port Royal and Fort Monroe would be of tremendous service to the navy, and Beaufort, North Carolina, did have a deepwater harbor. Its capture, therefore, would fulfill Lincoln's vision of aiding North Carolina loyalists, support McClellan's strategic goal of disrupting and perhaps even permanently severing the important Wilmington and Weldon Railroad connection (often referred to as "the lifeline of the Confederacy"), and perhaps serve as another deepwater port for the blockade. When, several days later, Flag Officer Louis M. Goldsborough, commander of the North Atlantic Squadron, sent a memorial to Gideon Welles, setting out a plan for capturing the Pamlico Sound area by means of a joint army–navy action, that pretty much settled the matter.[7]

Burnside went to work at once, choosing officers, gathering equipment and supplies, and mapping out an operational strategy. Most important, he chose a team of field officers and staff officers who would be amenable to his style—hardworking, dedicated, patriotic, and highly competent. A few days before Christmas, the entire headquarters family gathered at Annapolis, wives included. Ambrose and Molly Burnside held a Christmas party on December 20, celebrating the holiday prematurely in anticipation of the early commencement of what still remained for everyone but Burnside a mysterious voyage to an unknown place. The newspapers had made much of the organization of this large military formation, and the fact that it appeared ready to depart on some major mission, but nobody could seem to find out any information as to where it would be going.

As 1861 came to a close, things began moving rather quickly. On the last Sunday of the year, Burnside met with Lincoln and McClellan to outline final details for the operation, and Burnside reported his division ready to go. He then returned to Annapolis and conferred with Flag Officer Goldsborough. Here the absence of any protocol for a combined operation became evident. On January 2, Burnside wired Goldsborough that he was ready to depart and requested that the flag officer return a big steamer the army had loaned to the navy. The telegram took a very circuitous route, going first to Baltimore and then to Fort Monroe. But because Goldsborough was at sea on blockade duty, it was not delivered for several days. As a result Burnside's departure was delayed by three crucial days, which might have been all the difference considering the weather they were about to encounter.[8]

In the early morning hours of January 2, 1862, nearly one hundred sailing vessels of virtually every description, plus steam transports, propeller gunboats, and floating batteries, awaited in the waters off Annapolis, Maryland. Most of these craft belonged to the army, including all the transports and a few of the gunboats. There were navy vessels too, under Goldsborough's direction, but there was no clear protocol concerning command relationships between the two expedition commanders. It was the largest flotilla that had dropped anchor off Annapolis, and the largest ever assembled by the U.S. armed forces, surpassing even the armada that Flag Officer Samuel F. Du Pont had taken to Port

Royal. Ashore, nearly thirteen thousand cold, wet soldiers stamped their feet and did what they could to ward off the effects of the falling snow and the near-freezing conditions. A continuous procession of small craft plied the waters from the dock to the ships, carrying the soldiers to be loaded aboard. It took two full days (January 6–7) to load the soldiers, and finally, on January 8, Burnside boarded the army transport *George Peabody*. This large vessel seemed appropriate to the dignity of the commander of the expedition, but when Burnside learned that some of the ships might be unseaworthy, and that the expedition was headed into bad weather, he concluded it was his duty to share these perils with his men; he shifted his headquarters to the *Picket*, a propeller-driven army gunboat, the smallest and most vulnerable craft in his command. Apparently it never occurred to him to take passage on a navy ship, perhaps even on Goldsborough's flagship so that he could discuss the forthcoming operation with his counterpart. The navy was there as a cooperating element, not an intrinsic part of the expedition.[9]

The next morning Burnside toured the floating division in his launch, exchanging a few words with the captain of each of the army vessels, as the soldiers leaned over the rails to get a view of him and cheer him, as he acknowledged their cheers by removing his hat even though the drizzle that continued during this entire time had drenched his bald head. On January 9, 1862, aboard the smallest boat in the largest flotilla in American history, Ambrose Burnside led his command off to war. Not until they had departed Fort Monroe two days later, striking for the foreboding Atlantic, did all the ships' captains open their sealed orders and learn that their destination was Hatteras Inlet.

Now the perils of committing soldiers to Neptune's element became evident, as the fleet began to encounter violent winds and as small vessels like the *Picket* were suddenly at serious risk of foundering. Equipment and supplies came adrift from their lashings and were lost at sea; many—perhaps most—of the embarked soldiers became horribly seasick. The next morning the seas subsided, but a thick fog enveloped the fleet, isolating each ship and rendering useless all the intricate signals that had been established. At dusk a breeze blew troublesome clouds away, but soon the breeze became a gale of greater force than that of the night before. Even the big steamers hove frightfully, while on smaller boats like the *Picket* it was all they could do just to stay afloat. That night one of the big army transports, the *Eastern Queen*, suddenly appeared just off the *Picket*'s bow, and the small headquarters boat popped off a round to warn the *Queen*, only to have her swing even closer. It was very fortunate there was no collision.

The gale scattered the fleet the length of the coast between Cape May and Hatteras Light, and only a small portion of the convoy lay within Burnside's view the morning of January 13. As the *Picket* limped the final leg of the journey to the inlet, she collected ships along the way that had been blown off course. By noon they reached Hatteras, and a guard boat fought its way out from the shore to offer greetings. That afternoon it led the *Picket* through the breakers and over the bar. One by one, the smaller ships began to work their way in as well.[10]

The intelligence Burnside had received about conditions at Hatteras Inlet was that the bar there was ten feet deep. It wasn't—the bar was only eight feet deep, and only at high tide. He had deliberately sought to acquire light-draft vessels for his fleet, the deepest of which was supposed to draw about nine feet. He quickly attempted to get his shallow-draft vessels across immediately to protect them in case the weather turned ugly again, as it soon did later that day. Then the bigger ships started across. The supply ship *City of New York* grounded on the bar to windward, and found herself in a very difficult situation as the hull was pounded on the hard bottom by an endless sequence of waves. The crewmen swarmed into the rigging and lashed themselves there until the following day when somebody could rescue them, but their ship was doomed. Many of the troops on the transports were able to land on the barrier islands near Hatteras so their ships could be lightened enough to cross the swash. The enlisted men were so happy to be on terra firma again that they scampered around in all directions like children. Indeed, the officers had difficulty getting them into formation for the six-mile march to the Union camps near Hatteras Village.

The storms that began on the thirteenth and fourteenth lasted nearly a fortnight, and some of the most far-flung of the expedition had much difficulty getting to the sound's entrance at all. The army transport *Pocahontas* never did make it, driven aground off the cape and lost along with the hundred horses onboard intended for the Hatteras expedition. The *Colonel Satterly* was among the last of the transports to arrive. She had been blown about four hundred miles off course, and didn't make it back to Hatteras until January 27, with her food and water nearly exhausted, firing off distress signals as she approached the inlet. New York newspapers had reported the ship as lost at sea; one creative journalist even reported having counted sixty of her dead washed ashore north of the inlet. Other ships at Hatteras also found themselves in a dangerous situation, anchored very close to one another in the crowded anchorage, and threatening to go aground with alarming frequency. The gunboat *Zouave* sank inside the bar, and nothing could be done to raise her because the eight tugboats that had been chartered by Burnside in Baltimore had not dared to leave the Chesapeake Bay because of the ferocious weather.[11]

Colonel Hawkins, who was familiar with the area and had been so influential in convincing Lincoln and McClellan to undertake this campaign, had told Burnside there would be local pilots who would be helpful in leading his ships over the bar, but Hawkins was wrong (and not for the last time in this campaign). Outer Banks knowledge and expertise would be in very short supply throughout the operation, but Yankee ingenuity was present in abundance. Burnside had the troops and supplies unloaded from the biggest transports, then ordered their skippers simply to steam into the inlet and ground themselves in the swash. Then boat crews would carry anchors to their farthest extension and ground them at that point, thereby anchoring the vessels to hold fast against the outgoing tide. The tide would wash the sand from beneath their hulls, allowing them to advance a little further. It was slow work but it was succeeding.

Burnside wrote to McClellan setting out his difficulties, and entrusted the letter to a civilian observer, a Mr. Sheldon. Sheldon not only delivered the letter, but in a personal conversation with the president he also described all the obstacles Burnside faced. Accustomed as he was already becoming to disappointing news, Lincoln nevertheless grew very discouraged and muttered that it was "all a failure. . . . They had better come back at once." Surprised by the president's morose response, Sheldon assured him that it was not a failure at all because Burnside was progressing remarkably well in spite of the obstacles, and that he had been able to find solutions and employ them to overcome each problem.[12]

Burnside's public display of confidence never faltered. None of the thousands of soldiers and sailors who saw him every day could recall ever seeing a gloomy or less-than-confident general. But Burnside's problems were far from over, and he grew increasingly anxious as time passed, a fact evident in the letters he sent back to "Dear Mac." The main problem was logistical support. It was one thing to move an army by transport from one harbor to another. It was quite another to keep that force supplied with food and fresh water. Already the fleet's supply of fresh water was about to run out. Although the general had arranged for a schooner each day to bring fresh water from Baltimore, none had yet arrived as of January 26. Several different vessels that would have brought supplies of fresh water had been driven out to sea by the continuing bad weather, and with nearly twenty thousand very thirsty soldiers in his command, armed guards were assigned to what little water they had. Scores of ships from his flotilla were flying the Stars and Stripes upside down signaling that they had completely run out of water. As he turned his glasses to the horizon looking in vain for relief ships carrying water, he faced the prospect of being unable to do anything for his men. There was certainly nothing that could be done for them on Hatteras, nor did he have sufficient provisions to be able to return to Fort Monroe or any other friendly port where supplies could be obtained. At one point Burnside walked to the prow of the *Picket*, convinced that all was lost and that possibly the only way to save his men was to surrender to an inferior force. For a moment, Burnside's infectious optimism and ebullient personality seemed to desert him.[13]

Burnside needed a miracle, and precisely at that moment he got one. As he peered over the prow of the *Picket*, he saw the black clouds of a squall moving toward the inlet. Signals ran up the halyards ordering the sailors to spread sails in order to collect the rainfall. The rain came in torrents, directed by sailcloth into the empty barrels, and within the hour the fleet's immediate problem had been solved. Over the next three days four of the schooners carrying water from Baltimore arrived. On January 30, five more tugs arrived and the process of pulling the biggest of the steamers over the bar and into the Carolina Sounds began in earnest. Burnside was once again his bubbly, optimistic self.

The final phase of the campaign started on February 5, 1862, and within three days Burnside had more than nine thousand men ashore on Roanoke Island. The initial landing took place on February 7. Burnside had poked around the island seeking a spot to land his troops; a young contraband named Tom had suggested Ashby's Harbor, located in the hollow of Roanoke's cupped hand. Goldsborough had already silenced the small Confederate mosquito fleet and engaged the guns of Fort Bartow, which was the only rebel fortification containing any guns that could threaten a landing at Ashby's, though a couple of companies of North Carolina soldiers were there to contest the expedition.[14]

In one of the earliest examples of interservice planning, Burnside and Goldsborough met to discuss how to conduct the landing, and they reached agreement quickly and harmoniously. General John G. Foster loaded nearly five hundred of his men aboard the army steamer *Pilot Boy*, and nearly a thousand more waited in a long queue of surfboats that would trail behind the steamer like so many ducklings behind the mother duck. The *Pilot Boy* steamed quickly toward shore, then cut loose the surfboats, which were whipsawed in toward the beach. When they touched, two dozen men leaped over the side of each boat and those aboard the *Pilot Boy* leaped into the shallow water; within twenty minutes thousands of Union soldiers had secured Ashby's Harbor. The Confederates had quickly departed.[15]

The following day these soldiers conducted a spectacular and successful assault on the primary Confederate defensive position on the middle of Roanoke Island. Before the day was out, Burnside and his forces had captured all the rebel works on the island, had more than 2,500 prisoners (including two colonels), and had effectively assured that the "back door to Richmond" would be closed to the Confederacy for the remainder of the war. It was easily the biggest Union victory of the war up to this time, and the news coverage in the North overshadowed the capture of Fort Henry and its garrison of fewer than a hundred men two days earlier.[16]

Within a month of capturing Roanoke, Burnside set his sights on New Bern, the principal city of coastal North Carolina and its first capital. Located at the

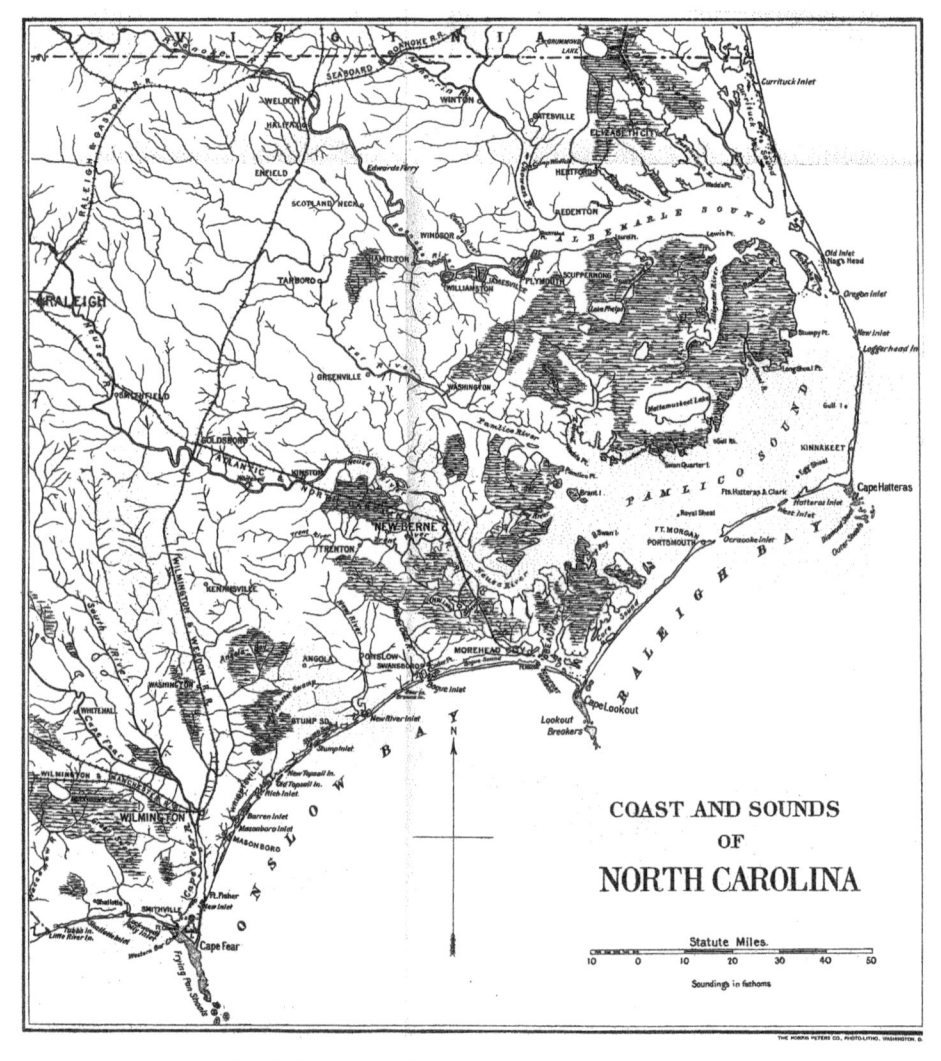

Coast and Sounds of North Carolina

confluence of the Neuse and Trent Rivers, it was the headquarters of Lawrence O'Bryan Branch, the Confederate brigadier who commanded the District of Pamlico, whose force was both larger and better led than the forces Burnside had dispatched on Roanoke Island. Branch set up his headquarters in New Bern and worked hard to improve the city's defenses. Below the town he had constructed seven forts along the river, mounting a total of thirty guns that covered the river approach. The largest of these installations was Fort Thompson, and among its armaments was a thirty-two-pounder pivot gun that could fire down the flank of any force that attempted to approach by land. Ten miles south of town, Branch created another line of strong fortifications that he referred to as the Croatan breastwork, which he calculated could be held by a small brigade.

To assault these defenses, Burnside had a new partner. In late February 1862, following the departure of Goldsborough, Commander Stephen Rowan assumed command of the naval forces in the sounds. Rowan, however, proved easily as cooperative as Goldsborough had been, and nearly as cooperative and agreeable as Burnside himself. The two men forged a close working relationship that resulted in one of the most effective interservice partnerships of the war. In this instance they planned to bypass the Neuse River forts and land the army at the mouth of Slocum's Creek, several miles downstream from the Croatan breastwork, while the navy would continue up the Neuse to a point from which they could rake the Confederate position with their huge naval ordnance. Those guns should have made the capture of the rebel works much easier, and at that point the fleet would parallel the movement of the troops toward New Bern, thus subjecting each successive fort to infantry assault from the land side while simultaneously being bombarded by naval guns from the river side. The two Union commanders even worked out a system of rocket communications by which the army would be able to signal the navy as to where they were and the accuracy of their cannonade.[17]

When the operation actually got underway on March 12, it was attended, as usual, by Burnside's ever-present nemesis, inclement weather. But Burnside had certainly learned by this time how to conduct operations in wet, rainy conditions, and in the early morning of March 13, he once again mounted an amphibious assault in the murky mist. In an ironic twist, the leadsman in the bow of the troopship *Delaware*, sounding the shallows for a place to land, was Harvey H. Helper, a native of Rowan County and the brother of Hinton Rowan Helper, whose book *The Impending Crisis of the South* had scandalized the nation a decade before.

Despite the weather, and having to negotiate some very swampy and difficult ground, the combined attack was a great success. The Confederates, taken by surprise by the proximity of the Yankees, and unnerved by the big guns of Rowan's fleet, dispersed quickly, and in the case of the infamous 35th North Carolina, even before they were attacked. There was some crisp fighting by the 26th North Carolina (a regiment that would suffer near destruction and gain immortality at Gettysburg some fifteen months later), but the Confederates who stood and fought were simply overwhelmed by a Union attack line that overlapped them on both flanks. The rebels did set fire to a bridge over the river as they retreated, thereby making possible the escape of much of Branch's force. They were also successful in getting most of the locomotives and sidecars out of town before the Federals came charging in. If there was anything about the day that was less than a total Union success, it was that so many Confederates escaped. Still, given the Northern record of success up to this point in the war, this was a bracing victory.[18]

In the weeks ahead, Burnside orchestrated the operations that led to the capture of Elizabeth City in the northeastern part of the state, and a drive to the southern terminus of the Dismal Swamp Canal, where a spirited contest took place at South Mills. He also dispatched General John G. Parke and his brigade to capture Fort Macon, the last Confederate fortification on the sounds. An old pentagonal masonry fort of the same class as Fort Sumter, Fort Macon had its guns sighted on the approach to the harbor entrance, and the base provided safe haven for blockade runners. It was far too formidable to assault directly, and when Parke's troops got there in late March, all the Confederate forces in the area retreated inside the fort with a month's worth of supplies. Parke issued the obligatory call for surrender, which was refused, and a siege ensued. By April 23 Burnside had his big guns in place to open on the fort, but he called for a personal meeting with the commander to urge his surrender. On April 25 the Federals opened with their large mortars and thirty-pounder rifles. Eleven hours later the white flag was raised. The artillery fire had been very accurate, and more than two dozen rebels lay dead or wounded. The capture of Fort Macon made the port at Beaufort available to the Federal navy for the remainder of the war, and it would become the all-important fueling station for the North Atlantic Blockading Squadron.[19]

By the summer of 1862 Ambrose Burnside's amphibious division had produced a number of important victories. Though he did not fulfill McClellan's notion of using the North Carolina Sounds to penetrate into the heart of the Confederacy and disrupt its transportation network, he had conceived, organized, and effectively executed the first important amphibious operations of the war. He had worked effectively with both Goldsborough and Rowan to accomplish the conquest of the North Carolina Sounds and gain a foothold on the rebel coast. He had been, in turn, a cheerleader, promoter, organizer, leader, and chief decision maker for a task force that included nearly twenty thousand men, a hundred ships, and millions of dollars worth of supplies, ordnance, and hardware. Though he had encountered unexpected problems, he had persevered.

Most important, he had shared command responsibility and engaged in cooperative decision making with two different naval officers—a rare characteristic in either service—in a campaign that produced important victories. Indeed, for a short period in the early months of 1862, Ambrose Burnside was the most successful general officer in the country, which explains why the White House twice seriously considered him for command of the Army of the Potomac. Had Burnside been killed in the summer of 1862, he might have been remembered as a great hero of the war whose potential had not been realized. It is difficult to reconcile the heroic and innovative Burnside of early 1862 with the Burnside who sent wave after wave of infantry against Marye's Heights at Fredericksburg in the most unimaginative battle of the war. In recalling that battle it is hard to remember that for six months in late 1861 and early 1862 Burnside had been brilliant.

Notes

1. Ambrose E. Burnside, "The Burnside Expedition," in Robert U. Johnson and C. C. Buel, eds., *Battles and Leaders of the Civil War* (New York: Century Company, 1884–87), 1:660.
2. McClellan to Burnside, January 7, 1862, OR, 9:352–53.
3. Rowena Reed, *Combined Operation in the Civil War* (Annapolis, Md.: Naval Institute Press, 1978), 38–40.
4. Hawkins to Wool, September 13, 1861, Weber to Hawkins, September 3, 1861, and Wool to Scott, October 8, 1861, all in OR, 4:608, 611–12, 623–34; Rush C. Hawkins, "Early Coast Operations, in North Carolina," in Johnson and Buel, *Battles and Leaders*, 1:639–40.
5. Hawkins, "Early Coast Operations," 639.
6. William Marvel, *Burnside* (Chapel Hill: University of North Carolina Press, 1991), 34–35.
7. Goldsborough to Welles, November 11, 1861, ORN, 6:421–22.
8. Rowan to Welles, June 2, 1861, ORN, 4:493.
9. Burnside, "Burnside Expedition," 663
10. Ibid.
11. Ibid., 665; Burnside to McClellan, January 26, 1862, OR, 9:355–57.
12. Marvel, *Burnside*, 48.
13. *New Bern Daily Progress*, January 27 and 29, 1862; Marvel, *Burnside*, 49.
14. Burnside, "Burnside Expedition," 663.
15. Ibid., 663–68.
16. Branch to Holmes, March 26, 1862, OR, 9:241–42; Abstract from Return of District of the Cape Fear, January 1862, ORN, 9:424.

17. Burnside to Thomas, March 5, 1862, *OR*, 9:369; Marvel, *Burnside*, 65.
18. Reno to Richmond, March 16, 1862, and report of Colonel H. J. B. Clark, March 17, 1862, both in *OR*, 9:221–26, 267.
19. Parke to Richmond, May 9, 1862, and White to Holmes, May 4, 1862, both in *OR*, 9:284–85, 294.

2

A Thorn, Not a Dagger: Strategic Implications of Ambrose Burnside's North Carolina Campaign

David C. Skaggs

Historians have largely overlooked the strategic significance of Burnside's campaign in the North Carolina Sounds. James M. McPherson does not discuss the New Bern expedition in his excellent and prize-winning *Battle Cry of Freedom*, nor does Vincent Esposito include a map of the campaign in his *West Point Atlas of American Wars*. One author who does discuss the campaign is Rowena Reed in her book *Combined Operations in the Civil War*. In Reed's view, Burnside's thrust into the North Carolina Sounds was part of Little Mac's "logistical strategy" to cut the supply lines to the Confederate armies in Virginia and "paralyze the South's internal lines of communication." Reed praises George B. McClellan for his strategic vision, and especially for his plan to use the army and the navy in a combined operation designed to establish Union control of critical transportation nodes. Reed argues that, if fully developed, Burnside's operation would have inserted a strategic dagger into the heart of the Confederacy. In the end, however, the thrust fell far short of having the kind of impact McClellan envisioned, and it proved to be no more than a thorn in the Confederacy's side.[1]

McClellan's emphasis on the centrality of logistical support was a product of three influences: his experience in the Mexican-American War, his study of the Crimean War, and his experience as a railroad engineer in the 1850s. He was convinced that the key to cutting off supplies to Confederate forces in Virginia was to establish Union control of the railroad junctions at Knoxville, Tennessee, and Goldsboro, North Carolina. Once these critical transportation hubs were in Union hands, McClellan believed that the Confederacy would be forced to evacuate Virginia. It might even lead to a rebel capitulation and a peace settlement. At the very least, Union control and fortification of these critical junctures would compel the rebels to mount a campaign to retake them, and if they made such an attempt, Federal forces would have the advantage of fighting on the defensive using modern rifled weaponry against attacking infantry.

This plan fit McClellan's desire to win the war while avoiding excessive bloodshed or social revolution by forcing Confederate leaders to accept national reunion without interfering with the South's "peculiar institution."

But it ran counter to the expectations of some Republican congressional leaders who saw the secessionist crisis as an opportunity to strike at the institution of slavery, and of much of the public who found voice in Horace Greeley's exhortation that Union forces should immediately proceed "on to Richmond." Of course, McClellan himself was not exempt from the Richmond disease. He envisioned these logistical thrusts in both Tennessee and North Carolina as secondary contributions to his grand campaign on the Virginia Peninsula and the capture of the rebel capital.

Historians (with the notable exception of Reed) have been generally critical of McClellan's plan, often attributing his preference for an indirect approach to an unwillingness to come to grips with the enemy. By far the least discussed aspect of McClellan's logistical strategy, however, was his quest to close the inlets through North Carolina's Outer Banks and then seize the critical railroad junction at Goldsboro, which would cut off the supplies coming from the deep-water ports of Wilmington and the newly established port of Morehead City. The Atlantic and North Carolina Railroad from Morehead City ran through New Bern before heading for its junction with the Wilmington and Weldon Railroad at Goldsboro. As Reed notes, the capture of Goldsboro would have constituted an important threat to the rebel armies in Virginia.[2]

What Reed overlooks in her assessment of this scenario is the reality of military operations. As the late Archer Jones wrote in *Civil War Command and Strategy*, McClellan's concept required a "persisting strategy" of seizing and holding critical terrain. Such a policy demanded large forces and a long-term commitment to hold the positions taken. A thrust toward Goldsboro might have interfered with Confederate logistics, but Union troops could not have stayed there without a logistical tail of their own, and Goldsboro was too far inland to be sustained by waterborne shipping. The reverse of a "persisting strategy" is a "raiding strategy," in which a force destroys critical logistical nodes and then moves on, but this option has much less of an impact, for often the destroyed property can be restored in a relatively short time.[3]

If, as McClellan believed, the war proved to be a short one, well-timed raids against critical logistical bases might inhibit Confederate ability to reinforce or supply the main rebel army in Virginia. Under these circumstances, a raid against Goldsboro could have contributed significantly to Union success in the Peninsula Campaign by either cutting off supplies to Joseph E. Johnston's main army or compelling him to send part of his army south to protect his supply lines. In either case, it would significantly assist McClellan's main thrust against Richmond. If, on the other hand, the war proved to be a long one, the Union would have to occupy Goldsboro permanently, since the Confederates could repair the short section of track and the bridge there with relative ease once the

Union raiding party withdrew. In the end, however, neither George McClellan nor Abraham Lincoln had the necessary *sangfroid* to implement this logistical strategy when push came to shove in the spring of 1862.

Without doubt the Atlantic coast of the Confederacy was vulnerable. Without a blue-water fleet, and lacking even a brown-water navy, the Confederacy in 1861 faced an extraordinary strategic dilemma of having to protect its extensive coastline while at the same time concentrating armies against Union incursions in both Virginia and Tennessee. The best indicator of the critical nature of this problem was the recommendation of Robert E. Lee—appointed commander of the Southern Department, including the offshore islands of Georgia and South Carolina—to virtually abandon the coastline to the enemy. After Flag Officer Samuel F. Du Pont's easy conquest of Port Royal Sound in November 1861, Lee saw that it was impossible for the Confederacy to defend all the offshore islands along the coast with the forces available. He therefore recommended three courses of action. First, he sought to reinforce existing major fortifications; second, he obstructed the waterways through which the Federals might approach the coast; and third, he established garrisons beyond the range of gunboats that would deploy to threatened areas as needed. In this latter point he recognized the great problem of both sides in this conflict: the force-to-space ratio. One could not deploy sufficient defensive forces to protect every location; therefore, it was necessary to establish a mobile reserve that could react with agility and power at the point of attack. Unfortunately, North Carolina received no officer of Lee's ability to conduct its defenses.[4]

The geography of coastal North Carolina presented numerous obstacles for both the defenders and for the attackers. To begin with, the Confederacy was unable or unwilling to provide sufficient manpower or artillery to defend each of the four critical inlets along the Outer Banks: Hatteras, Okracoke, Oregon, and Beaufort. This became clear on August 27–28, 1861, when the two small forts guarding Hatteras Inlet fell to a Union naval squadron under Flag Officer Silas Stringham. The log-and-sand rebel forts were soon overwhelmed by fire from the squadron, and despite some difficulty in getting ashore, 860 Union soldiers under Brigadier General Benjamin Butler occupied the forts after the defenders evacuated them. Following this, the Confederates abandoned their even-smaller forts at Okracoke and Oregon Inlets, giving the Union complete access to Albemarle and Pamlico Sounds. Only two Confederate outposts remained on the North Carolina coast: Fort Macon guarding access to Beaufort Inlet and Morehead City, and Fort Fisher at the mouth of the Cape Fear River, which guarded access to Wilmington, the state's leading port.

The Confederates now had to decide where to concentrate their limited resources. One possibility was Roanoke Island at the junction of Pamlico and

Albemarle Sounds, the locus of England's first attempt to establish a permanent colony in North America. From there, Confederates could use small vessels to deploy troops throughout the sounds, and would inhibit Union efforts to consolidate control of the waterways or move to the interior of North Carolina. The second possibility was to defend the Atlantic and North Carolina Railroad. The critical point here was the town of New Bern, where the rail line ran close to the Neuse River and from which an attack could be launched toward the even more vital railroad junction at Goldsboro or the rear of Fort Macon. As it happened, Union planners targeted both sites.

To command the army side of these combined operations, McClellan chose a West Pointer from the class one year after his own, Ambrose Burnside. Burnside had served only six years in the regular army after graduation before resigning his commission to try—and fail—in the manufacture of a breech-loading carbine. At the same time he also became a major general in the Rhode Island state militia. At the outset of the Civil War, then colonel Ambrose Burnside commanded a Rhode Island regiment, and because of his creditable conduct at the first Battle of Manassas/Bull Run he rose in a few months to be a brigadier general of volunteers. Burnside assumed command of the North Carolina Expeditionary Corps in December 1861 and began plans to expand the Union foothold in the Outer Banks.[5]

Commanding the naval element of this expedition was Flag Officer Louis M. Goldsborough, the commanding officer of the North Atlantic Blockading Squadron. He, in turn, designated Commander Stephen C. Rowan to lead the squadron of warships that would cooperate with Burnside. Besides the deep-draft warships of the North Atlantic Squadron, Rowan's "fleet" consisted of paddle-wheel steamers, tugboats, ferryboats, even a garbage scow—in other words, almost anything with a draft shallow enough to allow it to operate within the sounds.

The expedition assembled at Annapolis, where the commanding general selected three regular army officers as his brigade commanders: John G. Foster, Jesse Reno, and John G. Parke. It is important to note that all the general officers in this expedition were West Point graduates with several years of experience as company-grade officers in the regular army, which was not the case among Confederate officers. McClellan's orders to Burnside were clear: He was to capture Roanoke Island, capture New Bern and Beaufort, and either neutralize or capture Fort Macon. Further, he was to destroy as much of the Wilmington and Weldon Railroad as possible, including the vital railroad bridge near Goldsboro.[6]

Significantly, Burnside's orders did not include the occupation of Goldsboro. The reason is that with the Peninsula Campaign pending, McClellan had changed his outlook of the North Carolina operation from a persisting occupation to a raiding strategy. Burnside was therefore to destroy the railroad bridge and as much track as possible, and then withdraw. Apparently, McClellan had come to recognize that his initial advance-and-fortify policy burdened the Union with a sixty-mile logistical tail that could itself be interdicted by Confederate forces and could not be supported by naval vessels above Kinston, where the Neuse River narrowed. In addition, to occupy Goldsboro for any length of time would require more forces than McClellan was willing to commit with his own campaign just getting underway.

Meanwhile the Confederates began their preparations to defend the North Carolina coast. The man in charge of this defense was Richard C. Gatlin. An infantry major in the regular U.S. Army until he resigned his commission in May 1861, Gatlin returned to his native state of North Carolina, received a brigadier general's commission, and commanded the Department of North Carolina. Initially his command was divided into two regions, the Wilmington District commanded by Brigadier General Joseph Reid Anderson, and the Albemarle-Pamlico sector headed by Brigadier General Daniel Harvey Hill. The latter found his command sector in a deplorable military condition and the inhabitants of many of the coastal lowland towns "indifferent about efforts to fortify them."[7]

From Richmond's point of view, Hill was too capable a commander to be left on a secondary front, and he was recalled to Virginia. This decision had important consequences, for it elevated to command two men who had little experience or proven capability: Benjamin Huger assumed control of the Albemarle sector, and former Virginia governor Henry A. Wise, who was a political general with no previous military service, assumed command of Roanoke Island. Command of the Pamlico Sound sector fell to the capable but utterly inexperienced Lawrence O'Bryan Branch.

The comparative military experience of the Union and Confederate officers is in sharp contrast. Gatlin was a West Pointer and a fifty-year-old veteran of the Mexican-American War, where he received a brevet promotion to major for gallantry at the Battle of Monterey, but who fought mostly against Indians and had extensive garrison duty. With twenty-eight years of army service he was only a major when he joined the Confederate army. Generals Branch and Wise were both political generals. By contrast, Burnside, Foster, Reno, and Parke were all regular army veterans who would gain additional experience on Roanoke Island that proved useful at New Bern.

Burnside's transports met Goldsborough's squadron at Hatteras, and the shallow-draft vessels sailed into Pamlico Sound toward Roanoke Island. Opposing the Union's squadron of nineteen warships with more than fifty guns were the nine guns of the "mosquito fleet" commanded by Confederate Commodore William F. Lynch. It was no contest. Utilizing the Union's tremendous advantage in both manpower and firepower, Rowan's squadron quickly eliminated Lynch's, and Burnside's 15,000 troops swept over the defenders on the island, capturing some 2,500 of them. David Dixon Porter later recalled that "the moral effect of this affair was very great, as it gave us . . . possession of the sounds of North Carolina if we chose to occupy them. It was a deathblow to blockade running in that vicinity and ultimately proved one of the most important events of the war."[8]

Leaving behind a garrison to defend the island, the Union combined forces next prepared to attack New Bern. Goldsborough took his larger ships northward to prepare for the Peninsula Campaign, and naval command devolved on Rowan. In a genuine combined operation, his squadron escorted the army transports and provided both logistical and naval gunfire support to the army forces assailing New Bern. On land, Reno's troops found a weak link in the Confederate defensive position. Parke's men exploited this gap and rolled up the Confederate right, forcing a precipitous withdrawal. Rowan's flagship entered the abandoned harbor at New Bern, and the first civilian he encountered was an elderly black woman. When he asked her if there were rebel troops in the town, she replied, "Massa, if you believe me, they is runnin' as hard as they kin!"[9]

Running they may have been, but it was critical that that most of the 4,000-man Confederate garrison escaped to fight another day. Branch's losses were comparatively light—64 killed, 101 wounded, and 413 captured or missing. In a battle that was a complete rout, the inability of the Union army to capture more of its opponents, and specifically the failure of Rowan's forces to attack them as they fled across the railroad bridge over the Trent River into the city, constituted the Union's greatest failure in this campaign. The Confederates even took with them all the locomotives and railroad cars between New Bern and Morehead City. Lack of effective communication between Burnside and Rowan may have contributed to this breakdown. For all the subsequent criticism of General Branch, the escape of most of his troops is one of the more important tactical consequences of this battle yet is largely ignored in the historical literature. But as most students of the war know, pursuit after victory was one of the more common failures on both sides, especially early in the war.[10]

After this initial success at New Bern, Burnside confronted the same force-to-space ratio that had previously disadvantaged Confederate commanders. As he moved inland he had to leave troops behind to secure both the railroad line and small communities such as Kinston. Each place he occupied—Roanoke Island, New Bern, Fort Macon, Kinston—required a garrison that depleted his mobile troop strength. To accomplish his march to Goldsboro and fulfill the mission's objective, he really needed about ten thousand soldiers, but McClellan was unwilling to give him that many with the Peninsula Campaign finally getting under way. Just as critically, the Neuse River narrowed significantly at Kinston, which prevented navy ships from accompanying the column or providing logistical support and firepower. As a result, the operation above New Bern ceased to be a true combined operation and became simply a column of Union soldiers pushing ever deeper into enemy territory.

Burnside ordered General Foster to command at New Bern, sent General Reno to Roanoke Island, and ordered Parke's troops to attack Fort Macon. Morehead City and Beaufort fell without a fight, and the reduction of Fort Macon was accomplished with little loss of life or time. For the remainder of the war, the Union held New Bern and the Confederacy had to be constantly aware of the threat to the railroad at Goldsboro. The Beaufort Inlet anchorage proved beneficial to the Union's blockading squadrons. New Bern also became a haven for runaway slaves. Thousands joined their liberators in the town, taking with them livestock, wagons, foodstuffs, household goods, and their own labor.

The Confederate defeat at New Bern forced the rebel high command to reconsider its options. As was often the case, the first thing done was to effect a change in commanders. The South also reinforced the troops at Goldsboro until rebel forces there exceeded the number under Burnside's command. Soon afterward, however, these reinforcements were recalled to reinforce the rebel army defending Richmond. Once that happened, the road to Goldsboro, and perhaps even Raleigh, was again open to Burnside's command. Burnside prepared to advance, but halted when, as a result of McClellan's pleas for additional troops, Lincoln wired him: "I think you had better go, with any reinforcements you can spare, to General McClellan." This effectively ended the potentially critical phase of McClellan's plan to thrust a dagger into the side of the Confederacy via the North Carolina Sounds. And, as it happened, Burnside did not arrive on the peninsula in time to assist his nervous commander.[11]

In assessing this campaign, Reed is unsparing in her criticism of the Lincoln administration. "Had McClellan's brilliant strategy been fully implemented," she wrote, "it would have ended the Civil War in 1862." What she omits in her discussion is the fact that McClellan contributed the most to its failure. To exploit what Burnside had gained in North Carolina required that he have sufficient forces to allow him to advance to the interior. McClellan denied Burnside's requests for an increase in cavalry, infantry, and artillery. In December 1862 General Foster, then commanding the troops at New Bern, conducted a raid toward Goldsboro to assist Burnside's Fredericksburg campaign. His soldiers fired the railroad bridge toward Goldsboro, but the arrival of Confederate General James J. Pettigrew's brigade forced them to retire. The destruction was so insignificant that the Wilmington and Weldon Railroad was operational again within two weeks. The lesson here is that in adopting a raiding strategy to interdict enemy supply lines, it is necessary to commit enough troops to ensure both the destruction of the vital lines of supply and prevent their swift reconstruction. This is what William T. Sherman did in his campaign through Georgia and South Carolina. Sherman effectively implemented McClellan's logistical strategy by conducting operational-level raids that fulfilled McClellan's objectives without the liability of having to hold captured territory. In 1864, however, the strategic situation was far different from what it was in the spring of 1862.[12]

Largely because of McClellan's own unwillingness to endow Burnside with sufficient forces, the Union lodgment at New Bern was less a strategic complement to the Peninsula Campaign than an operational cul-de-sac, one that McClellan's successors were reluctant to exploit in part because it was so closely associated with the now-discredited general. It was another lost opportunity, and in the end this combined operation into the North Carolina Sounds was merely a thorn, not a dagger.

Notes

1. James McPherson, *Battle Cry of Freedom: The Civil War Era* (New York: Oxford University Press, 1988); Vincent J. Esposito, *The West Point Atlas of American Wars* (New York: Henry Holt, 1997); Rowena Reed, *Combined Operations in the Civil War* (Annapolis, Md.: Naval Institute Press, 1978), 38.

2. Reed, *Combined Operations*, 38–40.

3. Archer Jones, *Civil War Command and Strategy: The Process of Victory and Defeat* (New York: The Free Press, 1992), 138–41, 183–86.

4. Douglas Southall Freeman, *R. E. Lee: A Biography* (New York: Charles Scribner's Sons, 1934), 1:606–18.

5. On Burnside and his campaign, see William R. Trotter, *Ironclads and Columbiads: The Civil War in North Carolina*, vol. 3, *The Coast* (Winston-Salem, N.C.: John F. Blair, 1989); Richard A. Sauers, *"A Succession of Honorable Victories": The Burnside Expedition in North Carolina* (Dayton, Ohio: Morningside House, 1996); William Marvel, *Burnside* (Chapel Hill: University of North Carolina Press, 1991). For a more negative assessment of Burnside, see Bruce Catton, *The Army of the Potomac: Mr. Lincoln's Army* (Garden City, N.Y.: Doubleday, 1962), 256.

6. McClellan's orders to Burnside are in General Order No. 2, January 7, 1862, *OR*, 5:36. The various reports concerning the expedition to New Bern are in *OR*, 9:74–109.

7. Quoted in Trotter, *Ironclads and Columbiads*, 256.

8. Quoted in ibid., 41.

9. Quoted in ibid., 119.

10. Ambrose Burnside, "The Burnside Expedition," in Robert U. Johnson and C. C. Buel, eds., *Battles and Leaders of the Civil War* (New York: Century Company, 1884–87), 1:668–69.
11. Burnside's report, dated April 17 and 20, 1862, is in *OR*, 9:270–73.
12. Reed, *Combined Operations*, xviii.

3

"Very Crude Notions on the Subject": William B. Franklin's Amphibious Assault at Eltham's Landing

Mark A. Snell

Not every combined operation attempted by Union forces during the Peninsula Campaign foundered on the rocks of interservice rivalry. One that proved remarkably successful was the amphibious landing near the head of the York River at Eltham's Landing on May 7, 1862, during George B. McClellan's advance up the Virginia Peninsula. There, Brigadier General William B. Franklin's army division and a detachment of vessels from Commander William Smith's division of the North Atlantic Blockading Squadron successfully secured a lodgment on a hostile shore while incurring very few casualties. For this assault, the army developed tactical landing schedules, employed specialized landing barges, and used effective naval gunfire support. Indeed, this early combined operation is one that operational planners in later wars might well have studied to their benefit. In her 1978 book, *Combined Operations in the Civil War*, the late Rowena Reed claimed that "Army engineers showed more skill in the management of combined operations during the Civil War than did their naval counterparts."[1] Regardless of whether this was universally true, at Eltham's Landing it was an army engineer who orchestrated the most successful combined operation of the campaign.

That army engineer was Major Barton Stone Alexander of the Corps of Topographical Engineers. In his after-action report of the operation, Alexander noted, "When the way of effecting a landing was first discussed I found officers of great intelligence entertained very crude notions on the subject, and many of them were disposed to leave matters to the sailors on the transports." Unwilling merely to rely on the navy, Alexander took matters into his own hands. Though this amphibious operation did not fulfill its objective of preventing the Army of Northern Virginia from escaping to the defenses of Richmond, it is a rare case study of effective combined operations and a testament to the ingenuity of Major Alexander and his engineers.[2]

After bringing his huge and well-equipped army to Fort Monroe at the tip of the peninsula of land formed by the York and James Rivers, McClellan's planned advance toward Richmond was stalled by the presence of the Confederate ironclad CSS *Virginia*, which prevented U.S. naval vessels from ascending the James River, and by fortifications at Gloucester Point, which blocked the York River. Nevertheless, by April 5 McClellan began a tentative advance from Fort Monroe toward the old Revolutionary battlefield at Yorktown. There, Confederate general John Magruder had strengthened the eighty-year-old British fortifications from the Revolutionary War and incorporated them into his own defensive line, which stretched across the Peninsula from Yorktown to the Warwick River.

Unable to get around these defenses, McClellan decided to take Yorktown not by frontal assault, but by a combination of siege and a turning movement. To open the York River to the navy, on April 4 McClellan ordered Major General Irvin McDowell's corps, which was still in the Washington defenses, "to land at least one division on the Severn [River], in order to insure the fall of Gloucester." In particular, he wanted to land William B. Franklin's First Division and he telegraphed Colonel Daniel Rucker of the Quartermaster Department "to get your First Division embarked as soon as possible . . . to make this movement." Then his plans went awry. On April 5 McClellan learned that McDowell's corps was being retained in Washington to bolster the defenses of the capital, which President Lincoln believed had been left all but unprotected by McClellan's move to the Virginia Peninsula.[3]

This decision promised to wreck McClellan's plan to use McDowell's corps for an amphibious end run around the Confederate defenses, and he sent an urgent message to President Lincoln on the evening of April 5, imploring him not to detach the First Corps from the Army of the Potomac. "If you cannot leave me the whole of the First Corps," he begged, "I urgently ask that I may not lose Franklin and his division." A day later, McClellan sent another telegram: "I again repeat the urgent request that General Franklin and his division may be restored to my command." McClellan saw Franklin's division as crucial to his plans because Brigadier General Daniel Woodbury's engineer brigade was attached to it, and that unit had been specially equipped and trained to conduct an amphibious landing. Initially, McClellan had hoped to land McDowell's entire corps, but now he sought at least to keep Franklin's division.[4]

On April 11 McClellan sent a message to Edwin Stanton again requesting reinforcements. Finally the administration relented and released Franklin's division. During the time that Franklin's division was detained, however, the Confederates had reinforced their Gloucester Point defenses with additional infantry and dug more gun emplacements for its upper fortifications, making a Union assault from the rear, via the Severn River, much more hazardous. The Union naval commander, Captain John S. Missroon, suggested an alternate landing site for Franklin's division, three and a half miles south of Gloucester

Point. There, an open, wide beach would readily support a large landing operation, and the Confederates might still be taken by surprise. Once Franklin arrived on April 14, he joined McClellan in a reconnaissance of the beach. Missroon, however, promised only limited naval support for the operation, which made the two generals wary. Meanwhile, the Confederates continued to strengthen the Yorktown defenses, making it apparent that Franklin soon would have to take Gloucester with or without the support of the navy.[5]

The next day, April 15, McClellan informed the War Department that he had found a suitable landing site for Franklin's division. By now, Major Alexander had arrived at Franklin's headquarters below Yorktown to infuse new energy and direction into the effort. Alexander had vast experience with coastal terrain, beach composition, and shoreline topography, partly as a result of an antebellum assignment to oversee the construction of the Minot's Ledge Lighthouse in

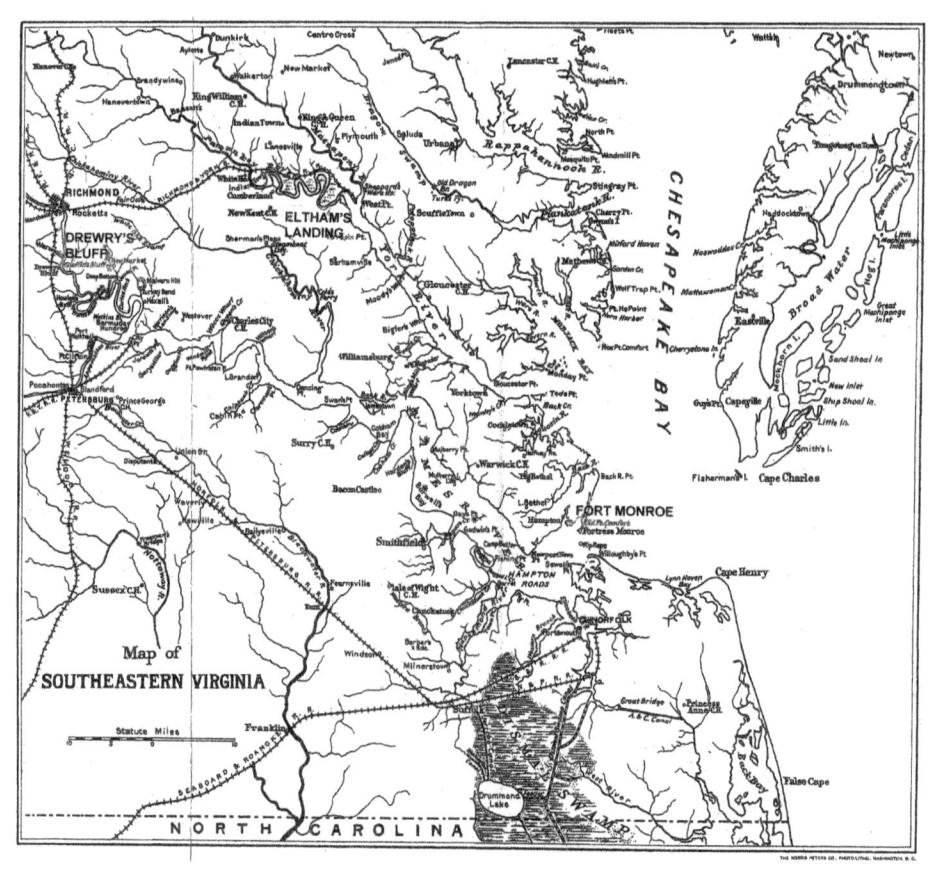

Southeastern Virginia

Massachusetts, considered at the time to be the most difficult construction project ever attempted by the U.S. government. Alexander joined Franklin, McClellan, and Commander John Rodgers of the navy in another reconnaissance of the proposed landing site, and he returned afterward to take depth soundings and determine the nature of the river bottom. He concluded that the infantry could be landed within 250 feet of the shore, but the artillery would have to be taken all the way in to dry land. Alexander wrote in his report, "As soon as this information was obtained I set about preparing the means to effect a rapid landing when it should be ordered."[6]

With 250 men of the 15th New York Engineers, Alexander built a series of landing platforms that could be used to ferry the artillery and horses as close to the shore as possible without running them aground. The engineers also built bridge sections that could be attached to the barges and connect to the shore. And he conducted practice landings. According to Alexander, "When the bridge was completed, the artillerymen were drilled in bringing on their artillery and horses and afterward taking them off." The engineer crews also trained to land the infantry in pontoon boats. Alexander observed that his troops "soon became quite expert in handling them."[7]

Despite Alexander's successful training in these new procedures, the inevitable problems arose in coordinating plans with the navy. According to Captain Missroon, Franklin and Alexander were to discuss the operation with him aboard the USS *Wachusett* on April 20, but bad weather prevented it. Ten days later Missroon reported that "I have neither heard from nor seen General Franklin since." By implication, at least, Missroon put the blame on Franklin for the lack of progress for the proposed landing, when in fact Franklin and Alexander had been making preparations all along and Missroon simply didn't know about them. Missroon now refused to attack the Confederate defenses with his naval force, and he asked to be relieved on April 23; his request was subsequently granted.[8]

Missroon's replacement, Commander William Smith, proved to be much more cooperative and immediately began planning the navy's role in the upcoming operation. Smith wanted ironclad gunboat USS *Galena* and a gunboat squadron to dash past the Yorktown defenses under cover of darkness and the protection of McClellan's siege guns, but he was overruled by Flag Officer Louis M. Goldsborough, who thought the operation too risky. He wanted the army to take the Yorktown and Gloucester defenses before the navy ran past them; McClellan, of course, wanted the navy to run past the batteries in order to take the rebel defenses in flank and rear. A meeting between McClellan, Franklin, Alexander, and Colonel John Newton on April 29 proved inconclusive. Nevertheless, on April 30 McClellan opened fire on the Confederate defenses at Yorktown with his big siege guns, and a day later Commander Smith joined in, lobbing a few shells from one of his gunboats. The Confederates were badly outgunned, and the Confederate commander, General Joseph E. Johnston, had been planning an evacuation of Yorktown for some time. He was now convinced that the time had arrived.[9]

On the evening of May 3 Confederate artillerymen randomly fired away all their ready ammunition in the general direction of the Yankees, hoping to distract and occupy the Northern soldiers while twenty-six Confederate brigades pulled out of the defenses as quietly as possible. By daylight on May 4, the Confederates were gone. Though McClellan had ordered Franklin's men to disembark from their transport ships to reinforce the Army of the Potomac's Third Corps, which had been selected to make the infantry assault on Yorktown, he now ordered them to re-embark in order to move upriver and land behind the retreating rebels near West Point, where the Mattaponi and Pamunkey Rivers joined to form the York, and which was also the terminus of the Richmond and York River Railroad. Meanwhile, the rest of the Union army would conduct an overland pursuit.[10]

Speed was crucial, for it was essential that Franklin and his troops get to West Point before the Confederates. Had McClellan not ordered Franklin's division ashore to reinforce the Third Corps in the planned attack on the Yorktown defenses, the transport vessels and gunboats could have started for West Point as soon the Confederates began their retreat. Unfortunately, precious time now was lost as Franklin's soldiers struggled to get the ships repacked, their efforts hampered even more by torrential downpours.[11]

On May 5, from aboard his vessel in the Poquosin River south of Yorktown, Franklin wrote, "As soon as the news [of the Confederate evacuation] was confirmed, I was ordered to reembark & come around to Yorktown, and after working hard all day & night we got off this morning at four." That same day, the Union force conducting the overland pursuit fought a sharp engagement with the Confederate rear guard at the old colonial town of Williamsburg. While that battle raged, Franklin's men continued loading their transports and securing the artillery on the canal barges that newly promoted Lieutenant Colonel Alexander had rigged for the Gloucester landing. One barge even included observation balloons, which had been ordered to accompany Franklin's expedition. More time was lost waiting for first light on May 6, for the navy was reluctant to navigate the York River narrows in the darkness.[12]

By the afternoon of May 6, Franklin's division sat offshore Eltham's Landing, some twenty-five miles up the York River from Yorktown and about three miles up the Pamunkey River from West Point. The voyage had not been without its problems. Alexander observed that "the fleet was much scattered, and

... some of the pontoons which were towed by the steamers broke loose, causing considerable delay." The initial contingent of vessels arrived around noon, Alexander wrote, and a quick examination of the offshore area told him that "the landing place was not unlike that for which preparations had been made below Gloucester." Consequently, the same landing techniques could be employed, and the gunboat commanders positioned their vessels so that a cross fire could be brought to bear on any Confederate force that might oppose the landing.[13]

The vessels carrying General Franklin and the bulk of his command arrived around 3:00 P.M., but the artillery barges did not show up until 5:00 P.M. Captain Richard Arnold, Franklin's chief of artillery, reported that as soon as the disembarkation point was designated, "the steamer Boardman, towing the principal part of the artillery and the pontoon train, moved successfully, without obstructions or detention, directly to the shore, where wharves of canal boats were speedily placed, and three batteries were run on shore at 10 P.M." Discharging the entire force of over eleven thousand men and their equipment took almost half a day, but it would have been much longer had it not been for the preparations taken by Alexander and his engineers. "The landing commenced as soon as a reconnaissance of the shore was finished," Franklin wrote, "and the infantry was all landed, under the brigade commanders, by 2 A.M., and the artillery . . . was ready for action on the 7th instant, the greater part of it having been landed by midnight."[14]

Colonel Henry Slocum's brigade went ashore first, followed by Colonel John Newton's brigade. Most of another brigade, under Colonel George Taylor, was held in reserve. Alexander described the area where the troops were put ashore as "a large level plateau, only a few feet above the level of the river, and cleared for about a mile from the landing place . . . [with] wooded heights beyond." The open plateau was under the cross fire of the gunboats, thus precluding Confederate opposition in force to the actual landing. "As soon as the infantry began to land I directed my attention to the construction of a wharf," Alexander reported. A line of double canal boats, bridged by heavy gangplanks, connected the shore to a light steamer that served as a pier head "some 220 feet farther into the stream . . . and at this point we had a sufficient depth of water for our light transports to come alongside and discharge." Events were unfolding smoothly, but delays experienced both at Yorktown and en route significantly weakened the tactical impact of the move. The hours lost by the need to re-embark Franklin's division, plus the hours spent waiting for daylight on May 6, made it less likely that Franklin could cut off the rebel retreat.[15]

The chief engineer of the Army of the Potomac, Brigadier General John G. Barnard, believed that had the Battle of Williamsburg not been fought on May

5, 1862, the Confederate forces would not have evacuated as quickly as they did and allowed Franklin's force to achieve its objective. Testifying before the Joint Congressional Committee on the Conduct of the War, Barnard stated that the battle at Williamsburg "was a blunder which ought not to have happened." A rush to attack without proper reconnaissance and coordination between corps and division commanders cost the Army of the Potomac "several thousand men, and we gained nothing." Continuing, Barnard testified:

> If we had not fought till next day a battle would in all probability not have been necessary, but if it had been, we could have had time to have brought up our resources, reconnoitered our position, and delivered our attack in such a way that some results might have flowed from it. We had every advantage. Franklin's division landed at West Point the next day and Sedgwick's division on the day following. These two divisions, had the enemy waited another day at Williamsburg, could have cut his communications, and in that case, we would have been superior in his front, and have had two divisions in his rear. His hasty retreat, and perhaps his capture, must inevitably have followed, and the great object of keeping Franklin so long embarked, and finally sending him to West Point, would have been accomplished.[16]

In other words, had the Confederates not been in such a hurry to evacuate Yorktown—made even more urgent by the Battle of Williamsburg—Franklin's command would have been able to disembark, advance inland unmolested, and block the retreat of the Southern forces. Instead, as Franklin's men began to push into the woods at the end of the open plateau, they ran into skirmishers of the Army of Northern Virginia's "reserve," commanded by Major General Gustavus W. Smith.

Smith's command was the advance guard of the Army of Northern Virginia as it made its way toward the Richmond defenses. Smith halted his troops at the town of Barhamsville, about seven miles inland from Eltham's Landing, in order to protect the baggage trains of the Army of Northern Virginia during the retreat to Richmond. It was while Smith was at Barhamsville that Franklin's division came ashore. "After examining their operations I selected a position for the division of General [W. H. C.] Whiting," Smith recalled, "and directed him to prevent the enemy from advancing upon Barhamsville until the trains had passed." Smith knew that the open terrain and the ordnance of the Union gunboats would render a Confederate attack useless, so he waited until Franklin's men entered the woods. Then, he ordered Whiting to drive the Yankees back to the open plateau and get his artillery in position to shell both the ground troops and the naval vessels.[17]

The fighting began around 7:00 A.M. when Brigadier General John B. Hood's brigade entered the woods to drive out the Union skirmishers. Franklin was not surprised, for he had suspected that he would be attacked even as his force was landing the day before. "The fact that the enemy's cavalry and infantry were seen in the woods surrounding the plain upon which we landed as soon as the landing began, convinced me that something was to be feared from the enemy in the morning," he later reported. During the night, two captured Confederates confirmed that an attack would begin in the morning, and at daybreak on May 7 Franklin and Colonel Newton reconnoitered their position and determined it to be secure, except for an area between the center and their left flank. Franklin then returned to the ships, "endeavoring to expedite the departure of the transports which had brought us up [so that another division could be transported from Yorktown], when the [heavy] firing commenced, and I did not hear it until signaled by General Slocum, between 10 and 11 o'clock." Franklin quickly went ashore, and was satisfied that his division "could repel any force which the enemy could bring against us."[18]

Communication, a key failure in many other combined operations, was effective in this case. The fledgling U.S. Army Signal Corps made it possible for instantaneous communication between ship and shore, giving Franklin the flexibility of being either aboard a vessel or ashore and still able to control the entire operation. First Lieutenant Frank Yates, Franklin's signal officer, reported that "while the troops were disembarking . . . I opened a station on shore to communicate with the Mystic, General Franklin's headquarters, and the gunboat if necessary." Not only could Franklin exercise effective and timely command and control of both army and navy elements, but the signal officers accompanying the expedition also could coordinate naval gunfire support for the landing forces, a tactical innovation that proved to be ahead of its time.[19]

Hood's Texas Brigade, along with Brigadier General Wade Hampton's South Carolina Legion and a few other regiments from Whiting's division, were instructed to keep the Union force at bay, not drive it back to the water's edge. Delay was all that was necessary, since the Confederate objective merely was the protection of their trains. Hood's men nevertheless aggressively pushed the Yankee skirmishers out of the woods. General Newton commanded the left wing of the Union defense while Slocum commanded the right. Most of the fighting occurred in Newton's sector. Newton thrust the full force of his brigade into the woods after his skirmishers had retreated, which, along with accurate fire from the Union field artillery, checked the Confederate advance. Whiting moved some of his own artillery forward on his right flank to shell the Union transport vessels, but the counterfire of the large-caliber naval ordnance drove the battery back. Whiting was impressed with the accuracy of the navy's guns and the rapidity with which they fired, though only two of his solders were wounded. A few days after the fight, Whiting wrote a note to the editor of the *Richmond Daily Dispatch* to downplay reports of the gunboats' effectiveness:

> The panic caused by the enemy's gunboats is not, perhaps, unreasonable, considering the manner in which their deeds have been trumpeted and exaggerated; but it is very absurd and needless. I will state a few facts: Horizontal, or rather direct shell firing, as from Dahlgren or rifled pieces, is destructive only to shipping or beddings [masonry substructures]. It has very little effect upon batteries, either with or without parapets, or upon troops deployed. This is due, I think, partly to the difficulty of causing the shell, even if well directed, to explode exactly at the object, but chiefly to the great velocity of the missile, which carries the fragments after explosion beyond the point of bursting. . . . I have never known a shell from the gunboats, exploding over an open battery or group or line of men, to do any harm. The other day, at the engagement between a part of my command and the enemy at Eltham's Landing, near West Point, one of the enemy's gunboats opened upon a position from which a few moments before Lieut. Col. [Stephen D.] Lee and Captain [James] Reilly had in vain endeavored with four pieces to reach the transports; and though the boat got the range with great accuracy, and burst her shells directly over the heads and within a few feet of the 6th North Carolina regiment, commanded by Col. [Dorsey] Pender, but one man was hurt; and although their gunboats shelled the woods in which Hood's brigade and the Legion were drawn up, after the enemy were driven out, not a man was touched by them.[20]

While Whiting tried to downplay the effectiveness of the naval gunfire, the presence of the gunboats helped to bolster the confidence of Franklin's men and intimidate the Confederates. One naval officer, Lieutenant T. H. Stevens, commented, "It is the generally received opinion, so I gather from the officers and men of Franklin's command, that the accurate and destructive fire of the gunboats was greatly instrumental in saving the army from serious reverse and disaster." That was probably not true, but the overwhelming firepower of the gunboats' heavy ordnance was certainly a psychological factor for both sides.[21]

Most of the fighting was over by 3:00 P.M. when Brigadier General John Sedgwick's division began landing. At one point in the battle, Franklin even ascended in one of the observation balloons for a bird's-eye view of the enemy. The Confederates prevented Franklin's division from pushing inland, thereby accomplishing their objective of protecting the trains. Although Franklin's generalship had little impact on the outcome of the battle, he must be given credit for overall command of a very difficult amphibious operation deep in enemy territory, and then holding on to his beachhead after the Confederates attacked. Franklin's division outnumbered the Confederate force by almost two to one, but Whiting's men repelled the Union advances from the protection of rifle pits, and the rest of the Army of Northern Virginia was not far away, making the situation very precarious. It is no wonder that in Franklin's initial report to McClellan he exclaimed, "As it is, I congratulate myself that we have maintained our position." The number of Union casualties, amounting to 48 dead, 110 wounded, and 28 captured or missing, certainly indicates either aggressiveness on the part of the Union commanders, extraordinary Confederate marksmanship, or perhaps a little of both. A company commander in the 4th Texas later reported to his hometown newspaper that as his troops advanced, "here and there one, and sometimes more [enemy dead were encountered], until at one place, seven were found weltering in blood, being struck down by the cool and unfailing aim of the men." The Southerners' casualties, however, amounted to only 8 killed and 40 wounded.[22]

And so, as the chief engineer of the Army of Potomac later testified, an operation that held so much promise ended without conclusive results. Nonetheless, the Eltham's Landing operation proved that joint operations not only were feasible but also, if properly planned and timed, could produce a decisive tactical outcome. If, as Rowena Reed contended, "the American Civil War was a great 'watershed' between the eighteenth and twentieth centuries with respect to amphibious warfare," Eltham's Landing was an excellent example of what could be accomplished if everything fell into place—though it also was proof positive of a good idea that just did not work as envisioned. Military strategists and tacticians in the twentieth century would experience similar, though much more costly, results at Gallipoli in 1915, Dieppe in 1942, and Anzio in 1944.[23]

Lieutenant Colonel Barton Alexander—who finished the war as a brevet brigadier general for his meritorious service during several campaigns—deserves the most credit for the successful amphibious operation. Like the American and British army engineers whose exploits during the Normandy invasion were a significant factor in the successful Allied landings and subsequent logistical operations, Barton's own engineers pulled off a noteworthy feat with limited resources and untested doctrine. His pontoon boats, artillery barges, and ship-to-shore bridges were the nineteenth-century equivalents of World War II Higgins boats, rhino barges, and the floating piers that connected the Mulberry harbors to the Normandy shore. The U.S. Navy, along with the communication support provided by the U.S. Army Signal Corps, also must be given their just due, for the fire support provided by Commander Smith's gunboats played an important role at Eltham's Landing, just as the U.S. Navy's destroyers did at Omaha Beach in June 1944. General Franklin even took advantage of aerial observation provided by Professor Thaddeus Lowe's balloon—a precursor to the reconnaissance aircraft of both world wars. Bad timing, not the plan itself or its execution, prevented the Eltham's Landing operation from achieving its tactical mission. The interservice cooperation witnessed on May 6–7, 1862, set a standard for other commanders and staff officers to follow, despite, as Major Alexander had observed, that "officers of great intelligence entertained very crude notions on the subject." As amphibious assaults in later wars would demonstrate, those "crude notions" were not limited to the Civil War commanders.[24]

Notes

1. Rowena Reed, *Combined Operations in the Civil War* (Annapolis, Md.: Naval Institute Press, 1978), xxv–xxvi.

2. "Report of Lieutenant Colonel Barton S. Alexander, U.S. Army, Engineer Officer, of Operations from April 20 to July 12 [1862]," *OR*, 11 (part 1): 134–39 (hereafter Alexander's Report).

3. McClellan to McDowell, April 4, 1862, *OR*, 11 (part 3): 68; Stephen Sears, *To the Gates of Richmond: The Peninsula Campaign* (New York: Ticknor and Fields, 1992), 33–39.

4. McClellan to Lincoln, April 5 and 6, 1862, both in *OR*, 11 (part 3): 71, 73–74. The order specifying an amphibious landing is Special Order No. 5, March 23, 1862, *OR*, 11 (part 3): 50. A more recent interpretation of McClellan's strategy to defend Washington while the Army of the Potomac was attacking Richmond is offered by Thomas J. Rowland, "'Heaven Save a Country Governed by Such Counsels': The Safety of Washington and the Peninsula Campaign," *Civil War History* (March 1996), 6–17. Rowland concludes that although "the stunning irony of the Peninsula campaign . . . is that it was McClellan, not Lincoln and Stanton, who was willing to take acceptable risks concerning the safely of the capital. Lincoln and Stanton are the ones who blinked" (17)

5. Stanton to McClellan, April 11, 1862, *OR* 11 (part 3): 90. Though this telegram is dated April 11, McClellan somehow found out on April 10 that Franklin was being ordered to embark for the peninsula, since he notified Goldsborough on that date that "Franklin's division is ordered to join me." McClellan to Goldsborough, April 10, 1862, *OR*, 11 (part 3): 87. See also Reed, *Combined Operations*, 145–47; Hitchcock to Stanton, April 15, 1862, *OR*, 11 (part 3): 100.

6. Information about the history of Minot's Ledge Lighthouse is available at http://lighthouse.cc/minots/history.html; Alexander's Report.

7. Alexander's Report, 134–37.

8. Missroon to Goldsborough, April 30, 1862, *ORN*, 7:290–91.

9. Reed, *Combined Operations*, 154–57; Franklin to Anna Franklin, April 30, 1862, William B. Franklin Papers, York County Heritage Trust, York, Pennsylvania.

10. Sears, *To the Gates of Richmond*, 156–57.

11. McClellan to Stanton, May 5, 1862 (9:00 A.M.), *OR*, 11 (part 3): 139. McClellan noted: "Raining hard now & most of the night—roads consequently infamous. . . . The weather has delayed Franklin."

12. Franklin to Anna Franklin, May 5, 1862, Franklin Papers, York County Heritage Trust; Lowe's report on his "aeronautic service" is in OR, series III, 3:277.
13. Alexander's Report, 137.
14. Arnold's report is dated May 13, 1862, and is in OR, 11 (part 1): 618.
15. Franklin's report, dated May 17, 1862, is in OR, 11 (part 1): 615–16. Slocum's troops were the first to land. See Robert McAllister to his wife, May 7, 1862, in McAllister, *The Civil War Letters of General Robert McAllister*, edited by James I. Robertson (New Brunswick, N.J.: Rutgers University Press, 1965), 151.
16. Appendix A to the report of John G. Barnard in the *Report of the Joint Committee of the Conduct of the War* (Wilmington, N.C.: Broadfoot Publishing, 1998), 1:417.
17. Report of Gustavus Smith, May 12, 1862, in OR, 11 (part 1): 627. After the war, Edward Porter Alexander wrote, "On the 7th [of May] the whole [Confederate] army was concentrated at Barhamsville." Most likely, the rest of the Army of Northern Virginia had moved past Barhamsville by the time Franklin's men came ashore at Eltham's Landing. It was still within striking distance, however, had Smith needed to call on it for support. E. P. Alexander, "Sketch of Longstreet's Division—Yorktown and Williamsburg," *Southern Historical Society Papers* 10 (January–December 1882): 45.
18. John Bell Hood's report, May 7, 1862, and William B. Franklin's report, May 17, 1862, both in OR, 11 (part 1): 630–31, 615. In his preliminary report of May 7, Franklin stated that the skirmishing began around 7:00 A.M., and he told his wife the same thing in a letter sent that day, but in his May 17 report he stated that the battle began at 9:00 A.M.
19. Report of Frank E. Yates, June 11, 1862, in James B. Hewitt et al., eds., *Supplement to the Official Records of the Union and Confederate Armies* (Wilmington, N.C.: Broadfoot Publishing, 1994), serial 2, part 1, 2:342–43.
20. Sears, *To the Gates of Richmond*, 85; W. H. C. Whiting letter, May 23, 1862, *Richmond Daily Dispatch*, May 27, 1862.
21. T. H. Stevens report, May 7, 1862, ORN, 7:319.
22. Franklin's division counted 11,332 men present for duty on April 30, 1862; Whiting's division totaled 6,545 men on the same date. OR, 11 (part 3): 30, 483; Franklin's report, May 7, 1862, OR, 11 (part 1): 614; Gustavus Smith's report and the quotation from the commander of the 4th Texas are found in Hewitt, *Supplement*, serial 2, part 1, 2:347–49. Writing nineteen years later in response to a question from the editor of *Century Magazine* for the *Battles and Leaders* series, Franklin denied ever having received orders to advance, even though McClellan's May 5 orders stated that he was to be "cautious yet *bold* in your advance" (emphasis added). Franklin wrote: "My instructions were to await orders after landing, and not to advance. . . . We were attacked on the 7th, the object of the enemy being to drive us into the river. We had not made any attempt to advance, as such attempt would have been in conflict with my orders." Gustavus W. Smith, "Two Days of Battle at Seven Pines (Fair Oaks)," in Robert U. Johnson and C. C. Buel, eds., *Battles and Leaders of the Civil War* (New York: Century Company, 1884–87), 2:221–22. Franklin either forgot the original content of his orders or was making an excuse for what was, in hindsight, a lost opportunity.
23. Reed, *Combined Operations*, xxx.
24. "Barton Stone Alexander," *Appleton's Cyclopedia of American Biography*, available at http://www.famousamericans.net/bartonstonealexander/. Alexander had a long and distinguished career with the U.S. Army before and after the Civil War working on a number of construction projects, including the Smithsonian and the U.S. Soldiers' Home. He died in 1978 and is buried in San Francisco National Cemetery.

4

The Union Attack at
Drewry's Bluff: An
Opportunity Lost

Robert E. Sheridan

One week after Union forces secured a beachhead at Eltham's Landing on the York River, Union gunboats assailed Drewry's Bluff on the James River in the first major confrontation between iron-armored warships and shore fortifications. After the perceived success of the USS *Monitor* against the *Merrimack/Virginia* in Hampton Roads in March, the Union secretary of the navy, Gideon Welles, and the assistant secretary, Gustavus Fox (who had witnessed the historic clash of ironclads on March 9), had great expectations that armored warships could defeat coastal forts. These expectations were diminished, but not destroyed, in mid-May 1862 when a five-ship flotilla that included three armored vessels endured a humiliating repulse at Drewry's Bluff just seven miles down the James River from Richmond. Armored warships, apparently, were not a magic bullet after all. In fact, the Union attack on Drewry's Bluff not only demonstrated the limitations of attacking forts with ships alone, it also exposed the weakness of army and navy forces acting independently rather than as part of a coordinated campaign. This essay will first summarize the battle as it was fought, and then suggest how things might have gone quite differently if instead the military and naval leaders had been more open to the notion of a combined operation. The fact that these lessons were ignored says much about the communications gulf between the army and navy in 1862 and the consequent difficulty of effecting combined operations. Despite the repulse, the flawed tactics of the Union assault on Drewry's Bluff did little to deter either Welles or Fox from their belief that armored warships could defeat rebel forts without assistance from the army.

The Battle

Events unfolded rapidly in the vicinity of Hampton Roads in the spring of 1862. On March 9, 1862, the smaller USS *Monitor* fought the Confederate *Merrimack/Virginia* to a draw, thereby ensuring that the rebel ironclad "monster" would not destroy the entire Union blockading fleet. Relieved of that concern,

General George B. McClellan's Army of the Potomac began its measured advance up the peninsula from the Union beachhead at Fort Monroe, and in early May, General John Wool's Union forces crossed the roadstead and reoccupied Norfolk. By May 10, the Gosport Naval Yard was again in Union hands, thus depriving the *Merrimac* of a home base. Unable to reduce the draft of the *Virginia* to less than nineteen feet to enable it to ascend the James River, the ship's new commander, Flag Officer Josiah Tattnall, ordered it destroyed to prevent its loss to the Yankees. It was a great blow for the Confederacy, both materially and psychologically, and Tattnall was vilified in the Richmond papers. The criticism led Tattnall to demand a court-martial, at which he was vindicated for having made the correct military decision.[1]

Nevertheless, the destruction of the *Virginia* opened the James River to operations by the Union Navy, and, prodded by President Lincoln, Flag Officer Louis M. Goldsborough, the commander of the North Atlantic Blockading Squadron at Hampton Roads, sent a flotilla of five ships under the command of Captain John Rodgers upriver to support the left wing of McClellan's army and to attack Confederate positions as far upriver as possible. These ships were the USS *Monitor*; the USS *Galena* (another ironclad, and flagship of the flotilla); the screw propeller, wooden gunship USS *Aroostook*; the wooden-sided, paddle-wheel steam gunship USS *Port Royal*; and the tiny one-gun ironclad USS *Naugatuck*. On May 8, three of these ships (the *Galena*, the *Aroostook*, and the *Port Royal*) attacked Confederate gun emplacements at Rock Wharf and Mother Tyne's Bluff, already some distance up the James. Five days later, the *Monitor* and the *Naugatuck* joined the flotilla, and on May 13 the five ships crossed the shoal at Harrison's Landing and appeared off City Point.[2]

The major obstacle in a further ascent of the James River was Drewry's Bluff. Situated about seven miles south of Richmond on the south bank of the James River, it was the first high ground close enough to the river to be of strategic importance. Situated some ninety feet above the river where Cretaceous sediments created a northeast-southwest trending tending line of hills and meander belt, the bluff was on land owned by Captain Augustus Drewry. As in many other battles of the Civil War, the geologically determined topography influenced the details of the subsequent fight, from the location of the infantry and artillery to the positioning of the flotilla—and even the eventual outcome of the struggle.[3]

Construction of the Confederate fortifications on Drewry's Bluff had begun on March 17, eight days after the battle between the ironclads, when Captain Drewry's Southside Artillery Company began digging gun pits and earthworks. The Cretaceous sands yielded easily to the spade, and the defenders quickly constructed substantial ten-foot-high ramparts protecting three artillery platforms mounting two eight-inch Columbiads and a ten-inch Columbiad. These heavy guns were state-of-the-art coastal defense guns, and the emplacements had pivot rings that allowed them to traverse an arc of fire downriver; even relatively small movements on the pivot rings gave them an overlapping field of fire that covered the entire James River. The defenders also dug a deep magazine and a bombproof, which allowed the gun crews to survive even the heaviest bombardment, ready to emerge and man the guns whenever the attack slackened. These formidable defenses, subsequently named Fort Darling, came under the direction of navy Commander Ebenezer Farrand.[4]

After the destruction of the *Virginia*, many of its gunners under the command of Lieutenant John Taylor Wood joined the defenders of Drewry's Bluff and added five more gun emplacements north of the fort. Here they placed three thirty-two-pounders and two sixty-four-pounders. The grandson of President Zachary Taylor, Wood was proficient in artillery, having taught the subject at West Point before the war. Later, one more heavy gun was mounted north of the fort, bringing the total number of heavy guns to nine.[5]

In addition to these batteries, a key element of the Drewry's Bluff defenses was the presence of obstructions in the river itself. Farrand ordered that several sloops, schooners, and river steamers loaded with stone and earth should be sunk in the river channel, held in place by rows of pilings and other structures filled with rock and earth. Two rows of these substantial obstructions were in place by May 14. These barriers would prevent Union ironclads from running past the fort, as David Glasgow Farragut's ships did on the lower Mississippi in April.[6]

Against these defenses, the Union sent five ships, three of them armored. The largest vessel in the Union flotilla was USS *Galena*. Some 210 feet long and 36 feet abeam, with a draft of 11 feet, it required a personnel complement of 164 officers and men. Built in Mystic, Connecticut, by the Bushnell brothers, it was one of the three ironclads (including the *Monitor*) that had been approved by the Navy Ironclad Board in the fall of 1861. The basic frame of the ship was that of a typical wooden sailing ship of the schooner type, though its steam engine and screw propeller were its main sources of propulsion. What made the *Galena* both unique and, ultimately, a failure was its iron armor. Strips of armor eighteen inches wide and half an inch thick were installed in a clapboard fashion atop its wooden frame, with the long axis of the strips running fore and aft. The edges of these strips had tongue-and-groove–like connections for interlocking the layers of armor one atop the other. This allowed a buildup of layers of the iron plate so that the ultimate thickness of the armor varied from two inches on the top deck to four inches at the gun deck. As events would prove, this was insufficient to repel shot from heavy guns such as the Columbiads atop Drewry's Bluff.[7]

The armament on the *Galena* consisted of four nine-inch Dahlgren smoothbore cannons and two one-hundred-pound Parrott rifles mounted three-on-a-side in fixed-gun positions, with the Parrotts forward of the Dahlgrens. The *Galena* could therefore bring to bear only a three-gun broadside. Still, of the ships in the James River flotilla, the *Galena* had the most firepower. Another important feature of her armament was the arrangement of her gun ports: the gun port doors opened outward, which, combined with the severe tumblehome of the bulwarks, allowed the guns to be elevated against forts at a higher elevation. The *Galena* had arrived in Hampton Roads too late to engage in the fight with the *Merrimack/Virginia*, so the attack on Drewry's Bluff would be its first combat test.[8]

John Rodgers and his subordinates had some knowledge of the presence of the enemy fortifications on Drewry's Bluff. Fireman George S. Geer of the USS *Monitor* noted in his account of the battle that an escaped slave had come aboard at City Point and revealed the presence of the rebel fort several miles upstream, though apparently the escaped slave did not know of the obstructions in the river. Partly as a result of this information, on May 14 the Union flotilla moved carefully to a position just downstream of Drewry's and around a bend in the river. Rodgers ordered the flotilla to anchor, planning to initiate the attack in the morning. There was some sniper fire from the shore where the Confederate infantry had dug rifle pits, and the exposed leadsman on the *Galena* was wounded and two others were killed.[9]

At 7:30 A.M. on May 15, the James River flotilla hove into view of the batteries on Drewry's Bluff. The *Galena* steamed up to within six hundred yards of the rebel batteries, but in order to present its broadside, it had to anchor across the current. Rodgers ordered a spring line on the bow anchor, and pulled the ship's stern around to port. During this maneuver, the batteries on Drewry's Bluff found the range and hit the *Galena* twice.

For its part, the *Monitor* anchored even closer to the enemy guns. Since it had already survived a severe test with the *Merrimack/Virginia*, the belief was that it could take the greater risk of engaging at a closer range. Moreover, the rotating turret on the *Monitor* meant that it could use a single-point anchor and still bring its guns to bear in all directions. Alas, those guns could not be elevated sufficiently to target the fort on its ninety-foot rise, especially from so short a range. That, and the fact that the *Monitor* was a smaller target than the *Galena*, led rebel gunners almost to ignore the *Monitor* and concentrate their fire on the larger and more powerfully armed *Galena*. The other ships of the

James River flotilla, two of them wooden, remained at a distance of as much as 1,300 yards.

In terms of available ordnance, the two sides were evenly matched. While the flotilla had a total of about twenty guns, some of them were deck howitzers and twenty-four-pounders, which were unlikely to do any serious damage to the fort. A few of the larger naval guns, including the eleven-inch Dahlgren on the *Aroostook* and the one-hundred-pounder on the *Naugatuck*, fired from very long range and were equally ineffective. Moreover, the *Naugatuck*'s one-hundred-pound gun exploded early in the fight. As a result, the flotilla could bring only nine heavy guns to bear. Given that the defenders on Drewry's Bluff also had nine heavy guns, the flotilla had no significant advantage of firepower.[10]

The intense firing went on for four hours. While the *Galena* fired about two hundred forty shots, the other Union ships fired far less often and with less effect. Altogether, the flotilla fired perhaps five hundred shots at the fort. Meanwhile, the return fire from the Confederate defenders was at least as heavy and far more effective. The Confederates concentrated their fire on the *Galena*, since it was recognized as the flagship and was anchored across the channel in broadside position, presenting the largest target. As a result, the *Galena* was hit about forty times, holed thirteen times, and was badly battered. The *Monitor* was struck only once on the turret and twice on its side armor; the damage was minor and amounted to no more than a few dented plates.[11]

As in all naval battles, the real work was done by the sailors in the gun crews and, in the case of the *Monitor*, in the turret. While John Ericsson's armored turret proved as invulnerable to enemy fire here as it had in Hampton Roads, other factors disabled a number of the *Monitor*'s gunners. The interior of the turret was notoriously hot in the best of circumstances, and adding the acrid fumes from the gunpowder and the engine exhaust, plus the physical exertion of manning the large Dahlgren guns and the port stoppers, some crewmen became exhausted and had to be removed into the lower hull. The *Monitor*'s commanding officer, Lieutenant William N. Jeffers, determined that his men suffered so severely that he broke off contact so the men could recover.[12]

On the *Galena*, the casualties were much greater and more serious. The system of interlocking armor plates did not hold up to the heavy solid shot from the fort, which easily penetrated the bulwarks and the *Galena*'s gun deck. Masters Mate Sam Washburn was in charge of the forward gun division when a solid, eight-inch shot tore through the forward port-bow armor. The shot cut the man next to him in half and knocked Washburn fifteen feet across the deck, injuring his hip and tearing off his pants. Washburn reported that the gun division was decimated.[13]

Subsequent witnesses declared that the *Galena*'s deck looked like the floor of a slaughterhouse. The hull and smokestack had so many holes that it looked like the ship had a case of smallpox. In total, the casualties on the *Galena* amounted to thirteen dead and eleven wounded. Marine Corporal John Mackie exposed himself in order to engage the rebels in the rifle pits along the shoreline. When casualties among the gun crews threatened to make it impossible to return fire, Mackie put down his rifle and joined a gun crew to keep the gun firing. For these actions Mackie became the first U.S. Marine to be awarded the Medal of Honor. Though there were no casualties on the *Monitor*, one man was killed and another wounded when the one-hundred-pound gun on the *Naugatuck* exploded.[14]

Atop Drewry's Bluff, the Union bombardment was also having some effect. The solid shot from the flotilla threw up showers of earth and debris, and portions of the Confederate earthworks were badly damaged. Some of the rebel damage was self-inflicted. The big ten-inch Columbiad had such violent recoil that it dismounted itself and was out of action for the rest of the fight. Still, the damage and losses on the rebel side were significantly less than damage to the flotilla; the Confederates reported casualties of seven dead and eight wounded.[15]

After four hours of fighting, at about eleven thirty, the *Galena* was running out of ammunition and Rodgers signaled the flotilla to withdraw. Rodgers was concerned that the rebels might sink more obstructions downriver from his position and trap him in the river. The flotilla proceeded to City Point to recover and effect repairs; the *Naugatuck* continued on to Hampton Roads for repairs and to report the situation to Goldsborough. Three days later, on May 18, Goldsborough sent reinforcements up to City Point in the form of the ten-gun steam sloop USS *Wachusett* and three other gunboats. Because the *Wachusett*'s commanding officer, Commander William Smith, outranked John Rodgers, he took command of the Union naval forces on this part of the James River.[16]

The Battle of Drewry's Bluff exposed several deficiencies in the Union ironclads, some of which had already been demonstrated. The *Monitor*'s relative lack of seaworthiness had been evident during its trip down to Hampton Roads from New York, and the awkward positioning of its pilothouse had been proved in its fight with the *Merrimack/Virginia*. Now, more deficiencies in the *Monitor* emerged as a direct result of the action at Drewry's Bluff. Lieutenant Jeffers noted that because the *Monitor*'s rate of fire was so slow, the rebel gunners could clamber into their bombproofs when the *Monitor* fired, then climb out to man their guns between shots. Only if the rate of fire from the ships could be continuously sustained, he argued, could a naval bombardment destroy the guns and break down the earthworks. Another problem was that although the

Monitor's turret was composed of eight inches of armor, her deck armor was only two inches thick backed by pine deck planking on ten- by ten-inch oak beams spaced several feet apart. This armor scheme was fine for grazing shots from other ships at gun deck level, but for plunging shots from forts at higher elevations the deck armor was vulnerable. This became more evident later in the spring of 1863 when the *Monitor* squadron attacked the forts at Charleston Harbor and was badly battered (see Chapter 6).[17]

The most serious defect in the *Monitor* exposed in the fight at Drewry's Bluff was that the guns could not be elevated sufficiently to bear on the fort on the higher bluff. This required the *Monitor* to drop back to a greater range in order to bring its guns to bear, and this extension of its range lessened the impact of the shots on the earthworks. John Ericsson had intentionally designed the *Monitor*'s gun ports to be narrow so that shot and shell could not enter the turret; his goal was to make the turret invulnerable and protect the gun crews at all costs. For this goal the *Monitor* also had gun port door stoppers on the inside of the turret wall, where the crew could manipulate them without exposure. These stoppers and the brackets for their movement further prevented the guns from being run far enough outside the turret to be elevated. While the gun port designs were commendable in protecting the crew, and quite adequate for action against other ships at gun deck level, they severely limited the *Monitor*'s effectiveness against forts.[18]

Even greater deficiencies were exhibited in the *Galena*. The clapboard style of armor was repeatedly shattered and penetrated. The interlocking and interlayering of so many individual sheets of iron plate weakened the overall iron cladding. In any case, the armor failed and heavy casualties resulted. As on the *Monitor*, the *Galena*'s armor was thickest where it was likely to be targeted by other ships firing on a level trajectory, but like the *Monitor*, it vulnerable to plunging shot fired from above.[19]

The *Galena* was temporarily repaired in the City Point area, where the ship played a role later in supporting General McClellan's aborted Peninsula Campaign. McClellan himself came aboard the *Galena* on July 1 during the Battle of Malvern Hill, where the Union infantry was assisted by the cannon fire from the James River fleet to hold off the attacking rebels. For the rest of the summer, the *Galena* continued to protect the Army of the Potomac as it was transported down the James River from the base at Harrison's Landing. Later, from September 1862 to May 1863, the *Galena* was detached from the James River fleet and returned to blockade duty at Newport News and Hampton Roads. After that, the *Galena*'s ineffective iron cladding was removed in Philadelphia in 1863. Now merely a wooden steam sloop, the *Galena* joined the blockading fleet.[20]

The Alternative

The Battle of Drewry's Bluff was a mere footnote in the Peninsula Campaign of 1862. With only forty-one killed or wounded on both sides, it fades in apparent importance to the slaughter ashore. Moreover, the battle did not change the strategic status quo as it existed before May 15, 1862. The participation of the USS *Monitor*, the most famous Union ironclad, lent some notoriety to the event, but other than that, it might be considered unworthy of historical notice. Admiral David Dixon Porter insisted that the naval attack was under-resourced and should not have been attempted by only five vessels. He argued that more ships should have been taken from the blockade force at Hampton Roads. Goldsborough did send reinforcements to the flotilla by May 18, including the additional firepower of the ten-gun USS *Wachusett*, but by then the battle was over.[21]

Even more important than adding additional ships, however, was the need for cooperation from the army. When he heard about the operation, Rear Admiral Samuel F. Du Pont offered his view that "it was a very ill-advised and incorrect operation to expose those gunboats before the Army could take the fort in the rear." Jeffers agreed and later argued that one lesson of the engagement was that it proved that naval attacks on earthwork forts were doomed to failure, and he was emphatic that such enterprises could be successful only if the naval attack was combined with a coordinated attack by land forces. Similarly, in his report on the battle, Rodgers suggested to McClellan that troops could have been landed above City Point on the south side of the James. There they would have been within ten miles of Richmond and able to cooperate with the attacking flotilla. And indeed, the Confederates' greatest fear was that the Federals would do exactly that. John Taylor Wood later stated that had the Federals landed a few brigades beyond City Point on the south side of the James, the fort at Drewry's Bluff could have been taken easily and "Richmond would have been evacuated."[22]

Why, then, was this not attempted? The short answer is that the decision makers in both the Union army and navy were unaccustomed to the notion of interservice cooperation and were determined to act independently. To be sure, General Ulysses S. Grant and Flag Officer Andrew H. Foote had successfully cooperated in their capture of Forts Henry and Donelson on the western rivers in February, but because there was no protocol for combined operations, such enterprises required voluntary cooperation. It is tempting to speculate what might have happened had that kind of cooperation been present in May 1862 during the attack on Drewry's Bluff.

Constraints on the speculation include: the location of combat assets, including both land and naval forces, in mid-May of 1862; the logistics possible for both forces, including the distances involved in force movements, times required, road conditions, and to what extent the river could be forded; the communications available between the ground commanders on the general and flag officer level, and between the ground commanders and Washington; and finally, but most important, the unity of command needed to make rapid and timely decisions based on the changing situation on the ground. In the end, the missing ingredient was the willingness of the commanders to cooperate.

First, rather than attack Drewry's Bluff on May 15, Commander Rodgers might instead have conducted a reconnaissance in force to learn the number of guns on the bluff and the nature of the obstructions in the river. To be sure, this would surrender the element of surprise, but since the Confederates were expecting a river assault and fully prepared for it, this would have made little difference. Once having assessed the rebel defenses, Rodgers might then have sent the *Naugatuck* down the James to Hampton Roads to deliver the intelligence about the location and character of the fortifications on Drewry's Bluff, and to request reinforcements and resupply. This could have been achieved by May 18.[23]

Meanwhile, on May 16–18, the land forces of McClellan's Army of the Potomac were being concentrated in a major supply and communication base at White House plantation on the Pamunkey River. Part of the army was delivered by navy transports up the Pamunkey (see Chapter 3), and part of the army arrived after following the Confederate army up the peninsula from Yorktown and Williamsburg. The Confederate army under General Joseph Johnston was concentrated in defensive positions east of Richmond on the south bank of the Chickahominy River between the Mechanicsville crossing and the crossroads at Seven Pines.[24]

In receipt of Rodgers's intelligence report on May 18, Flag Officer Goldsborough could have telegraphed General McClellan the news that a reinforced naval flotilla was on the James River within striking distance of Drewry's Bluff. These forces could have transported a few brigades—perhaps a full division—from the vicinity of Harrison's Landing to the south side of the James River. This force could then have moved up the south side of the James to be in position to attack the fort on Drewry's Bluff on May 24. The artillery cover from the James River flotilla would allow the infantry to travel more rapidly on existing roads and along railroad beds.

In order to prevent Confederate interference with this movement or the attack on Drewry's Bluff, McClellan would have had to pose a credible threat to the rebel army at Seven Pines and north of the Chickahominy at Mechanicsville by conducting coordinated attacks at these locations between May 20 and

May 24. That is certainly a major variable in this alternate scenario, for McClellan would not only have had to overcome his inherent sluggishness and caution, but he also would have had to be willing to pin his hopes on the success of the campaign on this single division south of the James and the cooperation of the navy. Still, such coordinated attacks were entirely feasible since McClellan's forces first crossed the Chickahominy on May 20 and captured Mechanicsville on May 24.

With the reinforced and resupplied James River flotilla attacking simultaneously with the transported army division on May 24, the greater firepower of the fleet would have kept the rebel troops in their bombproofs while the Union infantry breached the weak defenses from the landward side. Once the fort was taken, the navy could then have easily removed the river obstructions and made a rapid advance to Richmond itself.

This scenario for a combined operation is feasible, but only assuming that the officers in charge—McClellan and Goldsborough—had been willing to cooperate. Much of the blame for the failure of the Peninsula Campaign has been placed on General McClellan, the "Virginia Creeper." His conservative mind-set favored a slow and methodical approach with secure lines of supply and communication. He also believed in overwhelmingly superior mass, with set-piece battles that led to a siege of Richmond and bombardment by heavy artillery. Such a frame of mind was simply not adaptable to changes of situations on the ground, such as the opening of the James River and the possibility of a left-flank water attack on Richmond. McClellan's obsession with mass made him reluctant to weaken the main body of the Army of the Potomac even by a single division.

To be sure, McClellan was also a victim of poor intelligence and evaluation of information. He continually overestimated the number of Confederate forces facing him. Although the Army of the Potomac had numerous cavalry regiments, their scouting and intelligence gathering were thwarted by the Confederate cavalry of General J. E. B. ("Jeb") Stuart. As a result of this poor intelligence, McClellan was constantly telegraphing Washington for reinforcements.[25]

One of the results of McClellan's many pleas to Washington was President Lincoln's growing lack of confidence in the general. This increased the president's frustration with the lack of speedy progress on McClellan's part, and he began to insert himself in the management of the Peninsula Campaign via telegraph. From May 18 to May 24, Washington urged McClellan to extend his right flank to join with General Irvin McDowell's army coming south from Fredericksburg in order to mount a strong land attack on Richmond from the north. McClellan later complained that these telegraphed orders from Washington compelled him to remain north of the Chickahominy, tied to the base at White House on the Pamunkey River, and prevented him from exploiting any move up the James River. He insisted that had it not been for this interference from Washington, he would have preferred to abandon the Pamunkey and move across to the James where he would have better and more direct logistical support for an attack up the south side of the river. Of course, all this second-guessing was after the fact and therefore of uncertain reliability.[26]

Still, had McClellan been the kind of commander who was willing to tie the outcome of his campaign to a partnership with the navy, a combined movement up the James River might well have accomplished all that he failed to achieve during the tedious move up the peninsula and the bloody Seven Days Battle. It was a measure of both McClellan's megalomania and the lack of any existing tradition or protocol for combined operations that this alternate scenario never had a chance to play out. The lack of unity of command, where McClellan would have been free to make such quick changes in plans and give direct orders to naval forces, prevented this potentially significant combined operation from ever getting under way.

Notes

1. A. A. Hoehling, *Thunder at Hampton Roads* (Englewood Cliffs, N.J.: Prentice Hall, 1976), 183, 199.
2. Bern Anderson, *By Sea and By River: The Naval History of the Civil War* (New York: Knopf, 1962), 81–83.
3. *Great Battles of the Civil War* (New York: Gallery Books, 1984), 156.
4. Richmond National Battlefield Web site at http://www.nps.gov/rich/; Civil War Richmond Web site at http://www.mdgorman.com/.
5. John Taylor Wood, "The First Fight of Ironclads," in Robert U. Johnson and C. C. Buel, eds., *Battles and Leaders of the Civil War* (New York: Century Company, 1884–87), 1:692–711.
6. William F. Keeler letter dated May 16, 1862, in Keeler, *Aboard the USS Monitor: 1862*, edited by Robert W. Daly (Annapolis, Md.: Naval Institute Press, 1964).
7. Naval Historical Center Web site at http://www.history.navy.mil/.
8. Ibid.
9. Kerck Kelsey, *Remarkable Americans: The Washburn Family* (Gardiner, Maine: Tilburg House Publishers, 2008), 155–61.
10. John Ericsson, "The Building of the Monitor," in Johnson and Buel, *Battles and Leaders*, 1:743.
11. George Geer, William Manvel, and William C. Davis, *The Monitor Chronicles: One Sailor's Account* (New York: Simon and Schuster, 2000), 71; A. H. Guernsey and H. M. Alden, *Harper's Pictorial History of the Civil War* (New York: Fairfax Press, 1866), 257.
12. Geer, Marvel, and Davis, *The Monitor Chronicles*, 71.
13. Kelsey, *Remarkable Americans*, 155–61.
14. Guernsey and Alden, *Harper's Pictorial History*, 257.
15. Richmond National Battlefield Web site at http://www.nps.gov/rich/.
16. Geer, Marvel, and Davis, *The Monitor Chronicles*, 76.

17. Robert E. Sheridan, *Iron from the Deep: The Discovery and Recovery of the USS Monitor* (Annapolis, Md.: Naval Institute Press, 2004), 20, 25; Guernsey and Alden, *Harper's Pictorial History*, 257.

18. Guernsey and Alden, *Harper's Pictorial History*, 257; David A. Mindell, *War, Technology, and Experience Aboard the USS Monitor* (Baltimore: Johns Hopkins University Press, 2000), 42.

19. Kelsey, *Remarkable Americans*, 155–61.

20. Ibid.

21. David Dixon Porter, *The Naval History of the Civil War* (New York: Sherman Publishing, 1886), 406; Geer, Marvel, and Davis, *The Monitor Chronicles*, 76.

22. Du Pont to Sophie Du Pont, May 29, 1862, in Du Pont, *Samuel Francis Du Pont, A Selection from His Civil War Letters*, edited by John D. Hayes (Ithaca, N.Y.: Cornell University Press, 1969), 2:79; Guernsey and Alden, *Harper's Pictorial History*, 257; Porter, *Naval History*, 405; John Taylor Wood, "First Fight of Ironclads," in Johnson and Buel, *Battles and Leaders*, 1:711.

23. Geer, Marvel, and Davis, *The Monitor Chronicles*, 76.

24. George B. McClellan, "The Peninsular Campaign," in Johnson and Buel, *Battles and Leaders*, 2:160.

25. Tom Wheeler, *Mr. Lincoln's T-Mails: The Untold Story of How Abraham Lincoln Used the Telegraph to Win the Civil War* (New York: HarperCollins, 2006), 52.

26. Ibid., 54; McClellan, "Peninsular Campaign," 164.

5

Union Combined Operations on the Texas Coast, 1863–64

John P. Fisher

Abraham Lincoln's announcement of a blockade of the Southern coast on April 19, 1861, inaugurated the strategy, derisively labeled the "Anaconda Plan" by its critics, to seal off the rebels from the outside world while a Union naval flotilla and land force engaged in a combined movement down the Mississippi to cut the Confederacy in two. While the blockade remained its primary focus, the numerous duties of the navy included raiding the Confederate seacoast, transporting military forces, providing gunfire support, cooperating in the capture of port cities, and participating in riverine warfare. All these features were evident along the coast of Texas, where the West Gulf Blockading Squadron operated against places like Galveston and Sabine Pass. But naval leaders soon discovered that without army support, the navy alone could not hold positions on the coast against Confederate counterattacks, and as a result the naval victories of 1862 were both incomplete and temporary.[1]

The Strategy Board or Blockade Board—created by Gideon Welles in June 1861—consisted of both navy and army representatives and suggested a high-level commitment to interservice cooperation. Captain Samuel F. Du Pont, former commandant of the Philadelphia Navy Yard; A. D. Bache, superintendent of the Coast Survey; and Major John G. Barnard of the army engineers served on the board. When considering the approach to be taken in the Gulf of Mexico, the board decided to partition the region into six divisions based on geographic features and different degrees of settlement. The sixth division consisted of part of the Louisiana coast and the entire shoreline of Texas from Grand Pass, Vermilion Bay, to the Rio Grande. Like other Southern coastal states, Texas possessed an extensive shoreline with numerous rivers, inlets, and small port towns. The shallow waters along the bars of these inlets prohibited the entry of large vessels, but a significant overseas and coastal trade did exist. Large barrier islands and peninsulas protected the inner shoreline, which extended almost the entire length of the Texas coast. Though the coast of Texas never ranked high on the list of Union naval and military priorities, its significance increased throughout the war for diplomatic and economic reasons.[2]

With the onset of active operations, an ambitious squadron commander, Flag Officer William Mervine, planned to bring an end to blockade-running through Sabine Pass and Galveston, interdict coastal shipping through the interior bays, establish control of the mouth of the Rio Grande, and make Texans feel the war's pressure. Mervine dispatched naval forces to the western Gulf with orders to capture blockade-runners, attack coastal shipping, occupy strategic shore positions, and shell Confederate defenses. In the summer of 1862, Union naval raids along the poorly defended South Texas coast, including the bombardment of Corpus Christi in August, demoralized that region's residents and military forces.[3]

The next month the new commander of the West Gulf Squadron, Rear Admiral David G. Farragut, assembled a fleet of five vessels for a direct assault on Galveston. Farragut ordered Commander William Renshaw to fill up with coal at Ship Island and proceed to the coast of Texas to capture blockade-runners, attack coastal defenses, and gain "command of the inland navigation." Farragut also suggested that Renshaw should capture Galveston itself if the city were not too heavily defended.[4] In October, Renshaw's ships bombarded the forts defending Galveston and compelled the defenders to flee the city. A truce gave the Confederates time to abandon Galveston, and by October 8, when the island fell to the Union fleet, a large majority of the population had left their homes. The Confederates thus lost the most important city on the Texas coast and suffered a considerable psychological blow, and the Union navy occupied a significant strategic position in the western Gulf. If properly developed and garrisoned, Galveston could serve as a valuable base to enforce the blockade, supply and maintain the fleet, and carry out assaults against the eastern and western Texas coasts.[5]

Sabine Pass emerged as another early target of opportunity for the Union blockading fleet. At the northeastern extremity of the Texas coast, Sabine Pass played an important role in the trade of East Texas because the town of Orange, thirty-five miles to the north, connected Texas and Louisiana via the Opelousas Railroad. During the first year of the war, much of the local economy's limited prosperity depended on successful blockade-running. Schooners left Sabine Pass bound for the Gulf of Mexico carrying lumber and cotton to exchange for coffee, sugar, medical supplies, and other goods. A successful Union landing at Sabine Pass would disrupt the land route between Texas and Louisiana and present a direct threat to Houston and Galveston. Finally, troops landed at the pass could be transported up the Sabine and Neches Rivers to destroy or capture the steamers laid up along those rivers.[6]

The Union Navy first directed its attention to Sabine Pass in late 1862. On the morning of September 23, the screw steamer *Kensington*, schooner *Rachel*

Seaman, and the mortar schooner *Henry Janes* arrived off Sabine Pass. At daylight the *Henry Janes* opened up from about three miles with her mortar on the Confederate battery, hoping to see the defenders "skedaddle." One shell fell twenty feet from the center of the battery, exploded, and covered one of the surprised defenders with mud from head to toe. The *Rachel Seaman* then joined the action, firing her twenty-pounder rifle and two thirty-two-pound broadsides. When the fort returned fire, the Union vessels ceased shelling, made sail, and took up a position in line one and a half miles from the fort. At about 5:00 P.M. the ship batteries once again opened fire, bursting one heavy shell over the defenders and forcing them to abandon the fort. Union sailors then went ashore and occupied Sabine City. This gave Union forces effective control of shipping through the pass and interdicted Confederate communications. It also provided Union naval forces with the opportunity to operate eastward in the waters of Louisiana.[7]

By early October, a pleased Farragut informed Secretary Welles that Galveston, Sabine City, and Corpus Christi were all in the possession of the Federal fleet. Success had crowned Union efforts along the coast and as Farragut reported to Welles, "I have the coast of Texas lined with vessels, all trying to do something. If I had a military [army] force I would go down and take every place from the Mississippi River to the Rio Grande." Union naval forces had destroyed the shipping and occupied the most significant strategic and economic positions along the Texas Gulf coast. All that was needed now was an army force to occupy these places.[8]

Haphazard Confederate defenses reeled under these swift blows, and the Union occupation of key strategic areas boded well for the prosecution of the blockade. Confederate abandonment of Galveston offered the Union navy both the use of a deepwater port and a more effective way to halt blockade-running. As Farragut noted in his letter to Welles, however, a landing party of sailors could not hold these places permanently; if adequate U.S. Army forces could not be found to hold them, the Confederates could mount successful counterattacks against the navy. And that is exactly what happened.

Following the city's capture, Commander Renshaw requested that military forces be dispatched from New Orleans to take over occupation duties at Galveston, relieving the navy for operations on the lower coast. He wanted the army to hold Galveston, and had no desire to administer the town's occupation while commanding the blockading fleet. He passed a request up the chain of command to Farragut, who appealed to Major General Benjamin F. Butler, commander of the Department of the Gulf. Of course, without a unified command Farragut could express his need for soldiers only as a request. Butler informed Farragut that he might "spare a regiment" and a few pieces of artillery

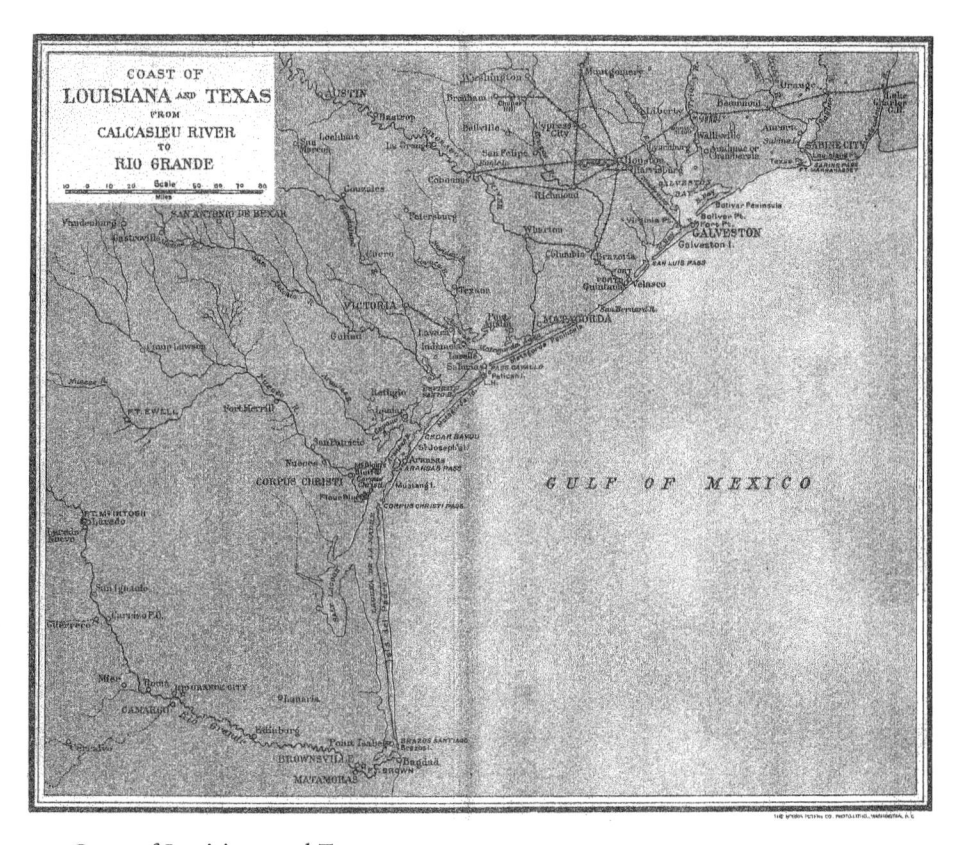

Coast of Louisiana and Texas

to hold the city, and Farragut, eager to facilitate this cooperation, offered to send ships to transport and provide gunfire support for the troops. But Butler stalled, and in the end he sent no soldiers and the navy remained responsible for holding Galveston. Farragut would not be the last naval officer to experience frustration in trying to coordinate a combined operation with Ben Butler.[9]

The lack of occupation forces also stalled the naval offensive in the western Gulf. Farragut again reminded Welles that he was "ready for anything, but desire [army] troops to hold what we get." According to his estimate, Butler needed twenty thousand more troops to occupy Galveston and the other places along the coast while campaigning in the Mississippi Valley. Farragut tried to reassure the skittish Renshaw with news that Butler would soon send a regiment, that Colonel Edmund J. Davis was recruiting loyal Texas refugees, and that the navy hoped to move pro-Unionist Texans stranded in Matamoros to

Galveston. Nevertheless, the following month Renshaw sent Farragut several gloomy reports in which he indicated that Union forces might have to abandon Galveston or be driven out. Farragut censured Renshaw for defeatism and insisted that "the gunboats must hold Galveston until the Army arrives" or until "driven out by actual force."[10]

Meanwhile, Confederate general John Bankhead Magruder assumed command of the Confederate Military District of Texas, Arizona, and New Mexico and brought with him a more aggressive attitude regarding coastal defense. Magruder planned to launch an offensive, regain possession of the state's coastline, and drive the Union blockaders away. He appointed Leon Smith to his staff, placed all steam vessels on the Sabine River and in Galveston Bay under Smith's command, and ordered him to arm the *Bayou City* and *Neptune* for an attack on the fleet in Galveston Bay. Smith, a seasoned mariner, had captained the mail steamer *Pacific* on the San Francisco to Panama route and during the 1850s plied the waters of the Gulf for Charles Morgan's Southern Mail Steamship Company.[11]

In mid-December General Nathaniel P. Banks, the "fighting politician," replaced Butler as commander of the Department of the Gulf and immediately promised to send one or two thousand men to garrison Galveston. On December 24, some 260 men of the 42nd Massachusetts landed at Galveston and occupied Kuhn's Wharf. When this small Union occupation force reached Galveston, Magruder realized that more troops might soon arrive and he accelerated his plans to attack the city. Worse, the drunken coxswain of the U.S. Navy gunboat *Owasco* deserted and informed the Confederate general that the Union fleet could be easily driven out of the area.[22]

On New Year's Day, 1863, Confederate troops rushed across the railroad bridge from the mainland to Galveston Island and began their assault. With the assistance of Union naval gunfire support, it appeared at first that the small number of Union troops would successfully defend their precarious hold on the island, but then the Confederate gunboats *Bayou City* and *Neptune* steamed down the harbor and attacked the *Harriet Lane*, which was soon captured and towed to the wharf to remove her wounded. Commodore Smith sent a flag of truce to Renshaw demanding the surrender of the entire Union squadron. Renshaw refused to surrender and instead ordered all civilian and navy vessels to leave the harbor while he attempted to blow up the grounded *Westfield*. Tragically, the powder exploded prematurely, killing him and several crewmembers on the *Westfield*.[13]

After this disaster, the defeated and demoralized Union ships and crews, now under the command of Lieutenant Commander P. L. Law, left the harbor, abandoned the blockade, and sailed for New Orleans. The loss of Galveston had immediate and long-term strategic repercussions for the Union. It was the most important port city in Texas and its occupation would have made blockading the Texas coast much easier. Moreover, with Texas so remote from the nearest naval bases at Ship Island and Pensacola, Galveston might have been developed as a base for the Texas blockade division and further operations along the coast. Now those hopes were dashed. Deeply disturbed, Farragut at first thought about steaming down the Mississippi to look in on the Texas coast himself. As it happened, however, he and Commodore Henry H. Bell were dining on board the *Hartford* the afternoon of January 3 when news of the disaster arrived. Bell casually remarked that he was "ready for any service" so Farragut told him to "go down as soon as you can."[14]

Soon afterward, the blockading fleet at Sabine Pass also suffered a serious defeat. Quincy Hooper, commander of U.S. naval forces there, received reports in early December indicating that his fleet might be attacked by a combined Confederate naval-land force. Because he had sent off a large number of his sailors as prize crews, Hooper worried that he was shorthanded to handle a full-scale assault. On the evening of January 20, the Confederate fleet assembled in the bay and made preparations to attack. At dark the two Union blockading ships made sail hoping to gain sea room to maneuver in case of Confederate aggression.[15]

The next morning the Confederate fleet cleared for action, headed for the Union vessels, and after a two-hour pursuit the Confederate steamers closed range and opened fire from two and a half miles. The *Morning Light* replied, working her guns as rapidly as possible. For two hours the combatants exchanged long-range fire, but eventually the Confederate steamers moved in closer and opened with small arms. At that point a rifle shell exploded on the *Morning Light*'s forward port gun, dismounting it, killing one man, and wounding the entire gun crew. Withering fire from Confederate sharpshooters swept the decks, drove the men from the other guns below, and convinced the captain to surrender. Meanwhile the *Uncle Ben* bore down on the *Velocity* and after a short exchange of fire forced her to strike her flag. Now the blockade of Sabine Pass had been lifted. A promising beginning by the navy at Galveston and Sabine Pass had been sacrificed, not only to more important Union priorities along the Mississippi River, but also to a lack of interservice cooperation.[16]

During the course of 1862, trade across the Rio Grande boundary also drew the attention of Union officials in Washington and naval officers of the West Gulf Blockading Squadron. Robert W. Shufeldt, the U.S. consul at Havana, emphasized the importance of Mexico, and in particular Matamoros, "as the key to western Texas" and the only point through which unrestricted commerce might be carried on with the Confederacy. In January 1862, William Seward, George B. McClellan, and Gideon Welles all believed that occupation of some point on the Rio Grande close to Matamoros was essential to halt the trade through Mexico. By March 1862 Leonard Pierce Jr., the U.S. consul at Matamoros, identified that city as "the great thoroughfare to the Southern states," with fourteen vessels standing outside the port passing "coffee, flour, and in fact all the supplies they receive through here," while "a large pile of cotton" lay on the east bank of the Rio Grande ready for overseas shipment.[17]

At this time, the beleaguered Union could not support such an ambitious proposal, but later in 1862 and 1863 a number of factors contributed to a renewed Union interest in occupying the Texas coast. Confederate blockade-running into Texas ports, the illicit trade across the Rio Grande River, plus concern about the French intervention of Mexico all convinced Union officials that Federal influence had to be reasserted in Texas. Most important, French intervention in the Mexican Civil War had convinced Lincoln that "early action in Texas [was] more important than ever." In consequence of that, he urged Ulysses S. Grant to reestablish "the national authority in Western Texas as soon as possible." Therefore, on August 6 General-in-Chief Henry Halleck telegraphed Nathaniel P. Banks an order to invade the Texas coast. Halleck originally suggested that Galveston, Indianola, or any other point would satisfy political demands, but later suggested an attack by a joint army–navy expedition up the Red River to Alexandria, Natchitoches, or Shreveport to occupy northern Texas and separate northern Louisiana and southern Arkansas from supplies and reinforcements in Texas.[18]

Banks initially opposed Halleck's plan to focus on the Red River and North Texas. He believed instead that a combined attack up the Sabine would ease logistical problems, could be achieved with a smaller force, provide a base for a movement on Galveston, and accomplish the administration's political goals. Following a successful assault at Sabine Pass, Banks could then occupy Beaumont, capture Galveston, and then attack the Rio Grande or return to New Orleans. With Farragut away in Washington, Banks received the cooperation of Commodore Henry Bell, Farragut's temporary replacement. Bell had seen long service in the navy and played an instrumental role in the attack on the Barrier Forts in the Canton River in 1855, where he displayed the aggressive side of his nature. Although a Southerner (like Farragut), Bell remained loyal to the Union. When Farragut received appointment as commander of the West Gulf Squadron, Bell came along as fleet captain and played a significant role in the capture of New Orleans, cutting the cable across the river and leading the 2nd Division past the forts on board the *Sciota*. He also participated in running the

Vicksburg batteries. Further, Farragut had implicit trust in Bell's judgment and believed at that moment he could be employed best on the Texas coast.[19]

But when Farragut received a dispatch from Bell at the Navy Department stating that he had agreed to support Banks's campaign, Farragut laid down the paper and predicted to Gideon Welles that "the expedition will be a failure." He explained why:

> The Army officers have an impression that naval vessels can do anything, this call is made for boats to accompany an army expedition, it is expected the Navy will capture the batteries, and the army being there in force with a general in command, they can take the credit. But there will be no credit in the case, and you may expect to hear of disaster. These boats which Bell has given them cannot encounter batteries, they might cooperate with and assist the army, but that is evidently not the object. The soldiers should land and attack in the rear, and the vessels aid them in front. But that is not the army plan. The soldiers are not to land until the Navy had done an impossibility, with such boats. Therefore there will be disaster.[20]

Nevertheless, on August 31 Banks ordered Major General William B. Franklin, commander of the 19th Army Corps, to embark the 1st Brigade, 1st Division, and 3rd Division of his 19th Army Corps, the Reserve Brigade, the Texas Cavalry, and a battalion of the 1st Engineer Regiment at New Orleans. He also ordered Franklin to consult with Bell and Acting Volunteer Lieutenant Frederick Crocker, commander of the cooperating naval force, to facilitate coordination of the roles assigned to both army and navy forces. Banks envisioned that the gunboats would precede and cover the landing of troops, and specifically ordered Franklin that if a landing was "found impracticable at the point now contemplated [it] should be attempted at any place in the vicinity where it may be found practicable to attain the desired result." After landing, Franklin's instructions suggested that he occupy and fortify a strong position and then seize some point on the railroad that ran between Houston and Beaumont. But Franklin's heart was not in it. When he had been sent to the Department of the Gulf, Franklin had written his wife, "I am convinced now, that I was only sent here to get rid of me." Additionally, Franklin showed little respect for or confidence in Banks, admitting to one friend that he found Banks ignorant.[21]

Bell assigned Crocker the side-wheel steamer *Clifton* as flagship, plus the screw steamer *Sachem*, under the command of Acting Volunteer Lieutenant Amos Johnson; the side-wheel steamers *Arizona*, commanded by Acting Master Howard Tibbits; and *Granite City*, commanded by Acting Master C. W. Lamson. These vessels were old, mechanically unreliable, and not heavily armored, but they were the only ships available with a shallow enough draft to pass over the bar at Sabine Pass. Bell ordered the *Granite City* directly to Sabine Pass and the *Arizona*, *Clifton*, and *Sachem* to convoy the army transports bound from Southwest Pass. Bell wanted Crocker to approach Sabine Bar at night on the sixth and be in the river by dawn the next day to attack or pass the fort with his ships. Poor intelligence led Bell to underestimate the strength of Confederate fortifications and believe that Crocker could easily pass or destroy the forts. But during the summer of 1863 the Confederates had strengthened their fortifications at Sabine Pass considerably. Fort Griffin was now armed with two thirty-two-pound and two twenty-four-pound smoothbores plus two thirty-two-pound howitzers, and the fort's company was well trained with extensive practice ranging and firing their guns.[22]

The planning and execution of the invasion of Texas at Sabine Pass offers a good example of how *not* to carry out combined operations. The *Granite City* arrived off Sabine Pass on schedule and anchored at the mouth of the channel. Unfortunately, soon after anchoring Lamson sighted a large ship, which he assumed was the dreaded *Alabama*, and he consequently headed for the Calcasieu River, abandoning the assembly point. At 7:00 A.M. on September 6, the army transports and *Arizona* arrived at Berwick Bay, Louisiana, where they rendezvoused with the *Clifton* and *Sachem*. They sailed for Sabine Pass, but missed their destination twice and hove to Calcasieu Bar. After consultation, Crocker and Brigadier General Godfrey Weitzel decided to shelve the landing that day, collect all the transports, and attempt to land the next day. But the division under General Franklin passed the remainder of the fleet unseen and anchored off Sabine Pass, alerting the Confederates of the coming attack. With surprise now lost, on the evening of September 7 the entire force anchored off the bar.[23]

At eight o'clock the next morning Crocker crossed over Sabine Bar in the *Clifton* and he and Franklin decided on a plan of attack. Their plan called for the *Clifton* to take up a position in the Texas channel and bombard the Confederate battery, while the *Sachem* and *Arizona* passed the forts on the Louisiana side of the channel. After the *Clifton*'s sharpshooters drove the Confederate gunners from their pieces, the *Granite City* would cover the landing of the troops above the fort, which would then drive the enemy out of its works. According to Crocker, both Franklin and Weitzel understood the plan, and Crocker's last words when leaving them were that if he grounded under the battery he "should be entirely destroyed should he [Franklin] fail in landing the troops as he proposed."[24]

The assault began at four o'clock that afternoon. The *Clifton* steamed up the Texas channel, firing shells from her nine-inch forward gun. The *Sachem* steamed up the Louisiana side and joined the action, followed by the floundering *Arizona*. When the *Sachem* reached the upper end of the middle shoal lying between the two channels, a Confederate shell struck her steam drum, killing and wounding thirty-two men and causing most of the rest of the gun crew to jump overboard. The *Sachem* anchored and desperately signaled the *Arizona* to come up and take her in tow, but the *Arizona* instead backed down the channel and abandoned the beleaguered *Sachem*.

To the west, the *Clifton* continued upstream under a full head of steam battered by Confederate shot. Crocker continued valiantly fighting his ship when a shot passed through her steam drum, completely disabling the vessel. Gunfire from the fort continued pounding the ship, setting fire to her twice and wounding a large number of the crew. Confederate fire killed the executive officer and wounded two other officers. With a demoralized crew and disabled ship, Crocker continued firing for another half hour hoping that help might arrive, but after another shell struck the *Clifton*, Crocker admitted defeat and surrendered.[25]

General Franklin watched this disaster inside the mouth of Sabine Pass from his seven transports containing 1,200 infantry, 12 guns, and 50 wagons. Despite his previous success at Eltham's Landing (see Chapter 4), Franklin showed no interest in finding some place "practicable" to disembark. He claimed later that his guns and wagons could not be landed in the face of the Confederate guns at Fort Griffin. Further, he claimed that Confederate cavalry might attack his troops, though there was no enemy cavalry nearby. Citing a lack of fresh water and rations, Franklin decided to put about and steam for New Orleans. Ironically, on the return trip the defeated and demoralized invasion force threw 100,000 rations overboard from the grounded transport *Crescent* and 200 mules from the steamer *Laurel Hill*.[26]

This ignominious retreat provided a fitting end to a poorly planned and executed combined operation. Welles castigated the army as "spectators" and the entire expedition as "badly conceived, planned, and executed." Clearly Bell should not have sent four small vessels to challenge Confederate forts in such narrow and shallow channels, and Crocker proved a poor choice for command since he had little experience in combined operations. For his part, Franklin's timidity at Sabine Pass contributed to the downward spiral of his military career. He should not have abandoned the expedition once the gunboats surrendered, when he could have landed ten or twelve miles below the pass along the Gulf coast. The poor organization of the landing and the lack of surprise gave the Confederates time to prepare their defenses, which proved extraordinary under the leadership of Lieutenant Richard ("Dick") Dowling. The main problem, once again, was that cooperation between the army and navy was minimal, causing Halleck to conclude that "the failure of the attempt to land at Sabine is only another of the numerous examples of the uncertain and unreliable character of maritime descents."[27]

The spectacular Union failure at Sabine Pass strengthened Confederate morale in Texas even though state military leaders believed Union forces would soon attempt another landing on the coast. The U.S. Navy's control of the Gulf still gave the Union the flexibility to threaten the entire Texas coast, and unless they advertised their intentions as they did at Sabine Pass, it was difficult for the Confederates to pinpoint the exact location of a landing beforehand. Further, a shortage of troops and weapons made it impossible for Confederate commanders to defend the entire Texas coast. Magruder understood this weakness. During the summer and fall of 1863 he focused his attention on Galveston and Sabine Pass, but he also made an attempt to strengthen Confederate defenses along the southern Texas coast. In early September he ordered positions at Saluria and Aransas Bay strengthened and sent troops to Corpus Christi. Unable to reinforce Brownsville, he ordered Hamilton P. Bee, commander of the Western Sub-district of Texas, that if attacked he should evacuate the city and take his supplies and retire up the Rio Grande to Roma or some place near there. Bee agreed that the Confederates could not contest the initial landing on the coast, but should retreat inland, marshal their forces, and then counterattack.[28]

Edmund Kirby Smith, commander of the Trans-Mississippi Department, placed a higher priority on the mouth of the Rio Grande than did Magruder. Smith believed that Union forces would initially occupy Point Isabel or Lavaca, and then march against either the Rio Grande or San Antonio. He also believed that the Texas-Mexico boundary must be held, yet, like Magruder, he knew of no way to defend the region against a large expedition. After the abortive Union assault on Sabine Pass, Magruder concentrated 2,500 troops there and strengthened the fortifications. He ordered field fortifications erected on the western side of Sabine town and Fort Griffin to prevent a turning movement from the beaches, and on the east Confederates blocked the Texas channel by sinking several old vessels below the fort. Magruder realized he could not defend all points on the coast, but continued to believe Galveston and Houston would be the primary Union objectives.[29]

By late September, Magruder had deployed about seven thousand men along the Texas shoreline for coastal defense. To strengthen these forces, he also deployed vessels of the Texas Marine Department along the coast. The *Diana* and the unfinished gunboat *Bayou City* remained at Harrisburg. The *Uncle Ben* and *J. H. Bell* waited in the Sabine and the steamboats *John F. Carr* and *Mary*

Hill fitted out at Lynchburg for service in Matagorda Bay. Unfortunately, these boats lacked heavy armament and well-trained or seasoned sailors. Charles M. Mason, chief of marine artillery, requested that all ships be furnished with heavier long-range guns to increase their firepower, but Magruder had none to spare. Additionally, Magruder complained to General Smith that he needed crews for the Union steamers captured at Galveston, which were useless because he lacked experienced engineers and steamboat men.[30]

During the summer Leon Smith, commander of the Texas Marine Department, tried to assemble adequate naval forces for Matagorda Bay's defense. In early August he put out from Galveston with the *John F. Carr, Mary Hill*, and *Alamo* and ran down the coast to Velasco. Weather-bound there for several days, Smith established a line of signal scouts along the coast and left the *Mary Hill* armed with a twenty-four-pounder at Velasco. On August 16 he arrived at Decrow's Point on the southern tip of Matagorda Peninsula, and placed the *Carr* with an eighteen-pounder at Saluria under the command of Captain S. K. Brown to protect the inland ports along that section of the coast. Smith then placed the *Alamo* in Matagorda Bay. These vessels were intended for use inside the bays and ordered not to venture into the Gulf to contend with the Union blockaders. Without adequate guns, Smith realized his vessels were "comparatively useless," but hoped they might raise the morale of local residents and discourage Union attacks along the Gulf harbors.[31]

Meanwhile, neither the debacle at Sabine Pass nor Confederate preparations for defense deterred General Nathaniel Banks from planning another attempt to plant the Union flag somewhere in Texas. On September 13 he moved his army up Bayou Teche in western Louisiana hoping that an overland movement toward Opelousas, Alexandria, and Shreveport would lead to the occupation of East Texas. Like his earlier Sabine Pass design, this scheme failed. When he found the water level in the bayous too low for effective naval support and his forces bogged down for lack of secure supply lines, Banks ordered a retreat.[32]

The "fighting politician" next planned to move an army across the Gulf to occupy the lower Rio Grande Valley. This operation meant the further separation of Union forces operating from Arkansas and the Indian Territory, but Banks felt more comfortable with the secure supply lines provided by the Union fleet. To carry out this plan, Banks relied on the cooperation of the West Gulf Blockading Squadron for reconnaissance, troop convoys, and gunfire support in combined operations.[33]

To halt trade between Texas and Mexico, the Union high command had discussed occupation of the Rio Grande's northern bank since 1862. In September 1863 John P. Gillis, commander of the Texas Blockade Division, reminded his superiors that possession of the river would stifle trade through Texas. He also believed that pro-Union settlers in southern and western Texas might provide a core of political support to occupation troops. After the failures at Sabine Pass and Bayou Teche, South Texas presented the most attractive opportunity for the Union to reestablish its military and political presence in Texas. Following a coastal reconnaissance by the side-wheel steamer *Tennessee*, Union naval officers decided that Brazos, Santiago, and the Rio Grande were the most weakly held positions on the coast. Mindful of the geographic and logistical problems accompanying an attack on the Rio Grande, Banks still believed it would be easier and more productive than an overland march through Louisiana to East Texas.[34]

Bell ordered the screw steamers *Monongahela* and *Virginia*, along with the *Owasco*, to convey the invasion force. The expedition, consisting of the 2nd Division of the 13th Army Corps, 13th and 15th Regiments of the Maine Volunteers, 1st Texas Cavalry, and the 1st and 16th Corps d'Afrique under the command of the spectacularly named Major General Napoleon Jackson Tecumseh Dana, finally got under way at noon on Monday, October 26, and reached open sea three days later. Unfortunately, poor planning, rough weather, signaling problems, and the great distance involved in transporting troops from the Mississippi to the southern tip of Texas heightened the difficulties of the Rio Grande campaign. The vessels were overburdened with troops, animals, and equipment. The fleet tried to maintain some semblance of formation, and this along with heavy swells hampered progress the first day. A severe norther struck the fleet off Aransas Pass on Friday, October 30, causing the ships to scatter. Over the course of three days, from October 29 to October 31, the transports straggled into the rendezvous at Brazos Santiago.[35]

The expedition against Brownsville did not surprise local Confederate defenders. On October 26 the headquarters of the District of Texas issued a confidential circular indicating that it expected an imminent invasion under General Banks somewhere on the Texas coast and called for heightened alert. On November 2, Bee set in motion the plan to evacuate Brownsville. After the Confederates evacuated the town, fires burned out of control, destroying buildings and igniting eight thousand pounds of powder.[36]

Following the capture of Brownsville, Banks intended to employ a series of combined army and navy operations to turn Confederate defenses and secure all the important inlets and passes along the Texas coast. In a number of instances, valuable army–navy cooperation resulted in local Union success. For example, on November 15, 1,900 troops boarded transports and sailed north for Corpus Christi Pass in company with the *Monongahela*. About 1,200 of these soldiers landed on the southern end of Mustang Island. Once ashore, they drove the Confederates into their camp at Aransas Pass. In the meantime, the

Monongahela convoyed the remaining transports up the Gulf side of the island and covered the landing of troops four miles below the Confederate batteries at Aransas Pass. The Union warship then bombarded the fort while Federal troops marched up both sides of the island, forcing the Confederates to surrender. Altogether, the expedition captured nine officers and eighty-nine men, three heavy guns, one schooner, and ten small boats. Banks praised the cooperation and assistance of the navy in landing the troops on the island and furnishing gunfire support against the fortifications.[37]

Union forces then marched north to seize control of Pass Cavallo on Matagorda Island. Banks feared much stiffer resistance might be encountered at Fort Esperanza on the tip of the island, but knew the fort's surrender would permit Union vessels to enter the pass and strengthen the blockade inside the islands. This move threatened to drive the Confederates off the barrier islands and onto the mainland, severing all seaborne trade on the South Texas coast. Magruder could abandon the barrier islands, reinforce his troops, or organize a naval force and attack the Union fleet. Only by defeating the Union Navy could Confederate control of the interior bays be assured, so Magruder ordered the assembly of all available light draft steamers and placed them under the command of Leon Smith with orders to attack the enemy fleet. The Confederates also placed torpedoes in the channel between Fort Esperanza and the bar at Pass Cavallo, but the wide channel, deep water, and strong current limited their effectiveness. They also placed torpedoes in the trenches around Fort Esperanza with plans to explode them as land mines when Union troops assaulted the fort.[38]

Stronger Union vessels provided Federal forces with the opportunity to enter Matagorda Bay, gain control of Pass Cavallo, outflank Fort Esperanza, and force its surrender. On November 23 Major General Cadwallader Colden Washburn led Union forces up Matagorda Island while the *Granite City* steamed ahead, reconnoitering and covering the advance. On the twenty-ninth, Union field artillery and naval guns bombarded the fort and forced the Confederates to abandon their defenses. The successful combined advance gave the Union control of the coast from the Rio Grande to Pass Cavallo. Confederates fell back on the mainland toward Lavaca, Victoria, and Matagorda while Federal naval and ground forces established control of the barrier islands.[39]

The loss of the South Texas coast, the effectiveness of the blockade, and the gathering of Union shipping in the western Gulf led Magruder to revive a fantastic plan he had first developed in October. He wanted Raphael Semmes and John Maffitt to steam for the Texas coast, link up with the French blockading squadron off Mexico, and join the vessels of the Texas Marine Department to launch a joint attack on the Union blockading fleet. Confederate soldiers and sailors would then man any ships captured from the Yankees, and the combined fleet would end the Union blockade of the Gulf ports by capturing or destroying "those at Mobile, and so along the entire coast, commencing properly at this end."[40]

In December, Magruder suggested to William R. Boggs, chief of staff to Kirby Smith, that the large number of transports, steamers, and sailing vessels off the Texas coast should be attacked by Confederate commerce raiders. Captured Union ships could then be loaded with cotton and sent out to the West Indies to exchange their cargoes for arms. On December 27, Magruder sent a letter intended for Semmes and Maffitt to the Confederate agent in Havana, Charles Helm, suggesting that the two raiders sail to the Gulf of Mexico and attack ships on the Union blockade. Unfortunately for Magruder, nothing ever came of this plan.[41]

Throughout December the Union fleet harassed the Texas coastline by shelling and dispersing mounted Confederate pickets and cooperating with the army in reconnaissance missions. Moreover, the successful operations of the preceding two months permitted the navy to place its gunboats inside the bars along the southern coast. On December 23, Bell dispatched the light-draft sidewheel steamer *Estrella*, under Lieutenant Commander Augustus P. Cooke, to cooperate with the army on a reconnaissance mission in Matagorda Bay. Almost captured in the operation, the men of the 13th Maine discovered the value of naval support when the *Granite City* and *Sciota* also appeared in support and kept Confederate troops from overrunning the Union soldiers. The *Sciota* shelled rebel cavalry and steamers to protect the ground troops and finally embarked the soldiers before they were captured. What began as a simple reconnaissance turned into a harrowing experience for the Union troops. But the gunboats proved their worth protecting an outnumbered body of troops from being overrun by the Confederates.[42]

Then in February the Union mounted a four-day joint army–navy expedition against Lavaca. Operating in Matagorda Bay, the *Estrella* shelled Confederate merchant vessels and gunboats. Union vessels also headed for Indianola and Tres Palacios Bay, where they captured one sloop, burned another, and captured two more small boats.[43]

By late April an apprehensive John B. Magruder feared that Admiral Farragut might lead an expedition against the coast at either Caney Creek or the San Bernard River. Unknown to the Confederate general, Farragut's Mobile campaign meant U.S. forces would instead evacuate the Texas coast. On May 17, Banks received the order to abandon non-vital areas along the Texas coast and concentrate the forces in the Department of the Gulf at some point on the Mississippi River. Although the government still planned to maintain a force in Texas, U.S. leaders considered a single fortified and garrisoned position adequate. As a result, by June the only Federal forces in Texas were at Brazos Santiago to maintain control of Boca Chica and Point Isabel. Union withdrawal from South Texas in the spring of 1864, in preparation for the Red River and Mobile campaigns—not Confederate resistance—is what led to the discontinuance of operations on the South Texas coast.[44]

In conclusion, Union military operations on the Texas coast highlight some of the classic elements of tactical failure and success in combined operations. The Sabine Pass expedition failed because Union leaders chose to assault a well-defended position with inadequately trained troops, showed little initiative, and mounted an operation that lacked surprise. Moreover, the Union force did not possess adequate ships for shore bombardment, and, most important, poor command coordination led to incompetent execution. Unlike Admiral David G. Farragut, Commodore Henry Bell, commander of the West Gulf Blockading Squadron, did not understand the need for more powerful warships and closer command coordination between the army and navy. The Union army and navy commanders at Sabine Pass, General William B. Franklin and Volunteer Lieutenant Frederick Crocker, failed to establish concerted leadership for the landing. As a result, naval vessels failed to cooperate with one another, and army and naval forces acted independently. While Crocker fought his ships bravely, Franklin made no effort to overcome unexpected difficulties and chose instead to abandon an alternative landing site and sail back to New Orleans. Of course, some credit must go to the Confederate defenders of Sabine Pass, and especially to Lieutenant Dick Dowling and his defenders at Fort Griffin. Their victory, one of the most lopsided of the Civil War, boosted Confederate morale at a critical time.

The Union expedition to the Rio Grande proved more successful. Though poorly executed from an operational perspective, Union forces achieved surprise by confusing the Confederate high command, landed unopposed at Brazos Santiago, and captured Brownsville. Moreover, the weakness of Confederate defenses along the South Texas coast permitted Union forces to move northward in a series of combined operations as far as Caney Creek. Union control of the waters in the region permitted the navy and army to turn the most formidable Confederate defenses at Aransas Pass and Fort Esperanza, giving the Union complete control of the barrier islands and forcing the Confederates back to the mainland. As a result, Union warships operated more freely along the barrier islands, were not hemmed in as they were at Sabine Pass, and were able to provide effective gunfire support to the ground troops.

Notes

1. Herman Hattaway and Archer Jones, *How the North Won: A Military History of the Civil War* (Urbana: University of Illinois Press, 1983), 25, 135; James M. McPherson, *Ordeal by Fire: The Civil War and Reconstruction* (New York: Knopf, 1982), 206; navy report, August 9, 1861, ORN, 16:618–30.
2. Eugenia R. Briscoe, *City by the Sea: A History of Corpus Christi, Texas, 1519–1875* (New York: Vantage Press, 1985), 210–11; H. P. Bee to C. M. Mason, August 26, 1862, OR, 9:620–21.
3. Hobby to Gray, August 16 and 18, 1862, both in OR, 9:621–23.
4. Farragut to Renshaw, September 19, 1862, ORN, 19:213.
5. Renshaw to Farragut, October 8, 1862, and Cook to Franklin, October 9, 1862, both in ORN, 19:255–60, 262–63.
6. Hunter to Rousseau, July 8, 1861, ORN, 16:831–32.
7. Crocker to Farragut, October 2, 1862, Hooper to Farragut, October 5, 1862, and Pennington to Renshaw, September 29, 1862, all in ORN, 16:217–19, 219–21, 221–24.
8. *Houston Triweekly Telegraph*, October 17, 1862; Farragut to Welles, October 9, 1862, ORN, 19:289.
9. Renshaw to Farragut, October 8, 1862, Farragut to Renshaw, October 14, 1862, Butler to Farragut, October 25, 1862, and Farragut to Butler, October 28, 1862, all in ORN, 19:255–60, 260–61, 315–16, 317–18.
10. Farragut to Welles, November 14, 1862, quoted in Loyall Farragut, *The Life of David Glasgow Farragut, First Admiral of the United States Navy* (New York: Appleton, 1882), 297–98; Farragut to Renshaw, November 14, December 12, and December 15, 1862, all in ORN, 19:344, 404, 409–10.
11. Magruder to Cooper, February 26, 1863, ORN, 19:470–77; James M. Day, "Leon Smith: Confederate Mariner," 3 *East Texas Historical Journal* (March 1965): 34.
12. Forshey to Debray, December 25, 1862, OR, 15:908–9.
13. Magruder to Cooper, February 26, 1863, OR, 15:470–77.
14. Ibid.; Farragut, *Life of Farragut*, 304; diary of Commodore Bell, ORN, 19:735.
15. Sheify to Welles, April 12, 1864, ORN, 19:558–62.
16. Ibid.; Watkins to Turner, January 23, 1863, ORN, 19:564–66.
17. Shufeldt to F. Seward, January 16, 1862, W. Seward to Stanton, January 29, 1862, and Welles to W. Seward, January 27, 1862, all in OR, series III, 1:870–72; Price to W. Seward, March 1, 1862, OR, 9:674; Pierce to Swartwout, March 7, 1862, OR, 18:54–55.
18. Lincoln to Banks, August 15, 1863, and Lincoln to Grant, August 9, 1863, both in Lincoln, *The Collected Works of Abraham Lincoln*, edited by Roy P. Basler (Brunswick, N.J.: Rutgers University Press, 1953), 6:364–65, 374; Halleck to Banks, August 6 and 10, 1863, *Report of the Joint Committee on the Conduct of the War*, 38th Congress, 2nd session: *Red River Expedition* (Washington, D.C.: Government Printing Office, 1865), iv–v.
19. Banks to Halleck, August 26, 1863, *Report of the Joint Committee*, 107–9; J. T. Headley, *Farragut and Our Naval Commanders* (New York: E. B. Treat, 1867), 523–30; diary of Commodore Bell, ORN, 19:735.
20. Welles, *Diary of Gideon Welles*, edited by Howard K. Beale (New York: Norton, 1960), 1:441–42.
21. Banks to Franklin, August 31, 1863, *Report of the Joint Committee*, 112–13; Banks to Franklin, August 31, 1863, OR, 25 (part 1): 287–88; Mark A. Snell, *From First to Last:*

The Life of Major General William B. Franklin (New York: Fordham University Press, 2002), 278.

22. Bell to Welles, September 4, 1863, *ORN*, 20:516–17; Banks to Halleck, September 13, 1863, *OR*, 26 (part 1): 288–90; memorandum order of Commodore Bell, *ORN*, 20:517.

23. Crocker to Welles, April 21, 1865, Madigan to Bell, September 13, 1863, and Weitzel to Hoffman, September 23, 1863, all in *ORN*, 20:544–48, 524–25, 531–32.

24. Crocker to Bell, September 12, 1863, and Crocker to Welles, April 21, 1865, both in *ORN*, 20:544–48.

25. Crocker to Bell, September 12, 1863, and Crocker to Welles, April 21, 1865; Johnson to Thatcher, March 5, 1865, *ORN*, 20:552–53.

26. Franklin to Banks, September 11, 1863, *OR*, 26 (part 1): 294–97.

27. Welles to Bell, October 9, 1863, *ORN*, 20:538; Halleck to Banks, September 20, 1863, *Report of the Joint Committee*, 117.

28. Turner to Bee, August 13, 1863, Bee to Turner, August 14, 1865, and Special Order No. 245, September 9, 1863, all in *OR*, 26 (part 2): 164–65, 166–67, 216.

29. Kirby Smith to Magruder, September 7, 1863, Magruder to Boggs, September 13, 1863, Yancey to Kirby Smith, September 22, 1863, and Magruder to McCulloch, September 28, 1863, all in *OR*, 26 (part 2): 214–15, 223–24, 247–48, 265–67.

30. Magruder to Kirby Smith, September 26, 1863, and Mason to Turner, June 24, 1863, both in *OR*, 26 (part 2): 260–62, 281.

31. Leon Smith to Turner, August 9 and 20, 1863, and Leon Smith to Commanding Officer, *Indianola*, August 16, 1863, all in *OR*, 26 (part 2): 155–56, 174–75, 171.

32. Testimony of Nathanial Banks, *Report of the Joint Committee*, 4.

33. Ibid.

34. Gillis to Bell, September 18 and October 12, 1863, both in *ORN*, 20:593–94, 622–23.

35. Alden to Banks, June 20, 1863, *ORN*, 20:241; Nannie Tilley, ed., *Federals on the Frontier: The Diary of Benjamin F. McIntyre* (Austin: University of Texas Press, 1963), 243; Strong to Bell, November 3, 1863, *ORN*, 20:645–46.

36. Bee to Dye, October 24, 1863, and "Strictly Confidential Circular," October 26, 1863, both in *ORN*, 20:350, 357–8; Duff to Tarver, November 11, 1863, *OR*, 6 (part 1): 439–43.

37. Banks to Halleck, November 4, 1863, *Report of the Joint Committee*, 121; Ransom to Sexton, November 18, 1863, Strong to Bell, November 17, 1863, and Banks to Bell, November 17, 1863, all in *ORN*, 20:681–82, 679–80, 680–81.

38. Turner to Bradfute, November 16, 1863, *OR*, 26 (part 2): 446–47; Bradbury to Duff, January 1, 1864, *OR*, 34 (part 2): 854.

39. Murray to Turner, November 26, 1863, and Bradfute to Turner, November 26, 1863, both in *OR*, 34 (part 2): 447–48; Strong to Bell, November 21, 26, and 30, 1863, *ORN*, 20:694–95, 698, 702–3.

40. Magruder to Slidell, October 14, 1863, *OR*, 34 (part 2): 313–15.

41. Magruder to Boggs, December 25, 1863, and Magruder to Helm, December 27, 1863, both in *OR*, 34 (part 2): 532, 545–46.

42. Strong to Bell, December 21, 1863, Bell to Gillis, December 23, 1863, and the abstract logs of the *Monongahela* and *Sciota*, all in *ORN*, 20:736, 733, 745–46.

43. Special Order No. 77, April 11, 1864, and Caldwell to Irwin, April 15, 1864, both in *ORN*, 21:189, 190.

44. Magruder to Bates, April 22, 1864, and Christensen to Banks, May 17, 1864, both in *OR*, 34 (part 3): 784–85, 631–32.

6

Assailing Satan's Kingdom: Union Combined Operations at Charleston

Francis J. DuCoin

With the exception of Richmond, no city in the Confederacy was the object of more Federal interest and effort than Charleston, South Carolina, where the first shots of the war had been fired, and which was in the minds of many Northerners the very heart and soul of the rebellion. As Gustavus Fox wrote in 1863, "The fall of Charleston is the fall of Satan's kingdom." And yet the Union campaign against Charleston, like the thrust up the James River to Drewry's Bluff, foundered on the shoals of poor interservice relations. Despite opportunities, the failure of Union army and navy leaders to cooperate in a genuine combined campaign resulted in frustration, disappointment, and failure.[1]

It started out well enough. On June 2, 1862, the army transport *Flora* and the navy steamer *Bienville* transported Brigadier-General Isaac Stevens's Second Brigade, Northern Division of Department of the South, to a landing site on James Island just south of Charleston. These Union troops advanced cautiously toward Fort Johnson, the capture of which was believed to be the key to opening the harbor. Then on June 16, this Union probe met a sharp reversal near the little town of Secessionville. That, and bickering among the Union commanders afterward, led to a decision in Washington to withdraw Union army forces from James Island. Despite that reversal, inside the Navy Department both Gideon Welles and Gustavus Fox remained optimistic. They hoped that with the withdrawal of the army, the navy was in position to win both official credit and public acclaim for the capture of the city by executing a bold dash into the harbor itself. Fox wrote to Rear Admiral Samuel F. Du Pont that "we have added a story [floor] to our Navy Department building and erected a fine flag staff thereon and shall not raise the American flag upon it until Charleston falls." He would wait a long time. Not until February 1865 did Charleston finally fall, and when it did it was not to a navy squadron, or to any army force working with it, but because it was cut off by William T. Sherman's army advancing northward from Savannah.[2]

Active Union operations against Charleston actually began as a result of a relatively insignificant event, when the small Confederate steamer *Planter* appeared off Fort Sumter on the night of May 12–13, 1862. It was flying a white flag and soon enough the blockaders discovered that it was under the control of its black pilot, Robert Smalls, who, with the rebel officers ashore, had taken control of the vessel and steamed out of Charleston at 3:00 A.M. with a dozen family members and friends on board. He was immediately taken to Flag Officer Du Pont and informed the Federal commander that rebel defenses at Cole's Island and along the Stono River were being abandoned. This provoked Du Pont to order an immediate reconnaissance of the Stono River, and led eventually to Stevens's ill-fated probe to Secessionville.[3]

Coincidentally, that same week in Norfolk, Virginia, Confederate authorities destroyed the CSS *Virginia* to prevent its capture by approaching Union land forces. That not only changed the strategic balance in Hampton Roads, it made the ironclad *Monitor* available for other service. Fox was already thinking about how once things were settled in Hampton Roads, it would be possible to reinforce Du Pont with ironclads for an attack on Charleston. "Now things are breaking up entirely in Virginia," he wrote Du Pont on May 12, "we are ready to give you a force for Charleston. . . . If we give you the *Galena* and *Monitor*, don't you think we can go squarely at it by the Channel, so as to make it *purely navy*?"[4] The very next day, Welles, who by now knew about the destruction of the *Virginia*, wrote to Du Pont that "this Department has determined to capture Charleston as soon as Richmond falls, which will relieve the iron boats *Galena* and *Monitor* . . . . The glorious achievements of our Navy, inaugurated by yourself, give every reason to hope for a successful issue at this point, where rebellion first lighted the flames of civil war. . . . The War Department sends instructions today to General [David A.] Hunter, with whom you will consult and with whom you will cooperate fully, unless the move should be purely naval."[5]

Du Pont received both of these letters on May 18, but he had already ordered commander and senior officer at Charleston John B. Marchand on a reconnaissance up the Stono River, because of the news brought to him by Smalls. Marchand returned from his reconnaissance to confirm not only that the river was open, but also that once past the bar, it had sufficient depth of water for Union gunboats. He also presented Du Pont with a plan to transport troops up the Stono River, land on James Island, and take Fort Johnson from the rear.[6]

It was evident to Du Pont from the beginning that this would have to be a combined operation. That very month, he reacted to the news of the repulse of the ironclads at Drewry's Bluff by writing his wife that "it was a very ill-advised and incorrect operation to expose those gunboats before the Army could take the fort in the rear." Moreover, not only was the navy dependent on the army, the army was dependent on the navy. Two days later he wrote to Fox that the army was helpless without transportation. "They have to throw themselves on me," he wrote, "but they give me no notice until they are in a state of despondency or despair." Brigadier General Henry Benham had proposed to Du Pont on May 1 a plan "to make a dash on Charleston" by way of James Island. Hunter had vetoed the idea, but the news from Smalls led him to reconsider. Navy Commander C. R. P. Rodgers was at the meeting when Hunter agreed to Benham's plan, and he suggested that Benham confer with Du Pont about the transportation that would be required for his troops. Rodgers reported this to Du Pont, who was about to leave on an inspection of the blockade. After waiting two days for Benham, who never came nor sent any communications, Du Pont surmised that the attack had been canceled, and on May 18 he sailed away.[7]

One problem was that Du Pont neither liked nor respected Benham, describing him privately to his wife as "the most restless of men, full of mind which he applied to every detail, of physical activity and energy, rough to his officers, coarse, pertinacious, heels over head." Even Benham's own officers said that he had an "unfortunate talent for blundering." On May 3, Benham had insisted that steamers going to New York must return immediately to Port Royal, to which Quartermaster General M. C. Meigs replied caustically that "the authority of the military commander at Port Royal does not extend to the steamers in New York Harbor." None of this affected Benham's confidence and he responded to Meigs by declaring that he proposed to take Charleston "with such troops as could be spared from my division alone (as it appeared that we had no hope of reenforcements [sic])." His plan was "to take over one-half of the disposable force to Edisto . . . and then to start with the balance all afloat at once, and in one day, with a bound as it were, join the others and spring upon the island adjacent to and this side of Charleston Harbor." But he complained that he was prevented from accomplishing all this because he lacked sufficient transportation. "I cannot now take 2,000 men with our two or three small steamers here, instead of the 5,000 or more, as I need for safety . . . and all because our means of movements are to be decided upon and taken away from us by the quartermaster's department in New York."[8]

Without the necessary transports, and with Du Pont away, Benham went directly to Rodgers for assistance, blaming the navy for delaying the assault. On May 22, Benham sent Rodgers a letter, which, after Rodgers reread it, made the navy commander "a little savage in my feelings" because of its tone. Du Pont returned to Port Royal late on the twenty-fourth, and that evening he wrote what he called "a pretty stiff letter to General Hunter" about Benham's attitude toward the navy. During a conference at General Hunter's quarters on May 30 between Hunter, Du Pont, and Benham, the issue of transporting the troops for the assault on James Island was finally resolved. More than half the troops would travel overland, and the rest would be transported on board the army transport *Flora* and the navy steamer *Bienville* for an amphibious landing. Because the USS *Henry Andrew* could cross the Stono bar, it would be used to ferry the troops from the *Bienville* to the James Island landing site in two trips. This landing would be under the covering fire of six ships in the Stono River in addition to the *Andrew*. All this constituted a genuine combined operation, but there was still no one officer in overall command. Instead it depended, as all such operations did, on mutual cooperation between army and navy leaders. So long as that cooperation lasted, the operation could proceed. But any bump in the planning meant that the officers had to meet again to discuss alternatives.[9]

The movement got underway on June 2. Naval gunfire, directed by army signal officers, provided excellent cover and drove the rebel forces back behind their defensive lines. Brigadier General Horatio G. Wright commanded the division on Edisto Island, about twenty-five miles from the proposed landing site. His troops were to cross over to Seabrook Island, then to Johns Island, and then march to Legareville, directly opposite the landing site, where the navy would ferry them across to join the already-landed amphibious troops. Wright was delayed, however, and his command did not arrive at Legareville until the fifth. Thus the coordinated landing Benham had envisioned was delayed, losing any element of surprise and the possibility to take the island by a coup de main. By June 9, however, some 9,472 soldiers had been landed near Grimball's plantation on the north bank of the Stono. General Hunter entrenched his camp and, as Du Pont predicted, awaited reinforcements. Although the generals believed that 30,000 rebels opposed them, rebel forces actually numbered only about 4,000 men deployed behind approximately five miles of earthworks.[10]

This combined operation demonstrated what could be accomplished when the services cooperated. Edwin M. Stanton told Hunter, "You are authorized, at your discretion, to operate with the Navy in the operations against Charleston as far as the forces now under your command will permit." Similarly, Du Pont told Commander Percival Drayton, the senior naval officer in the Stono River, that his desire was "that your cooperation with the army be harmonious, rendering their forces all of the assistance in your power, but will you please keep yourself in communication with Major-General Hunter, except when he may not be present." Hunter made a special effort to be courteous with his naval partner. Prior to the landing, he asked Du Pont, "If you can spare any force from your command to act on the land, it will give me great pleasure to assign it to an honorable position." Earlier Hunter had extended a similar courtesy when, on April 9, he invited Du Pont to send naval gunners to work two

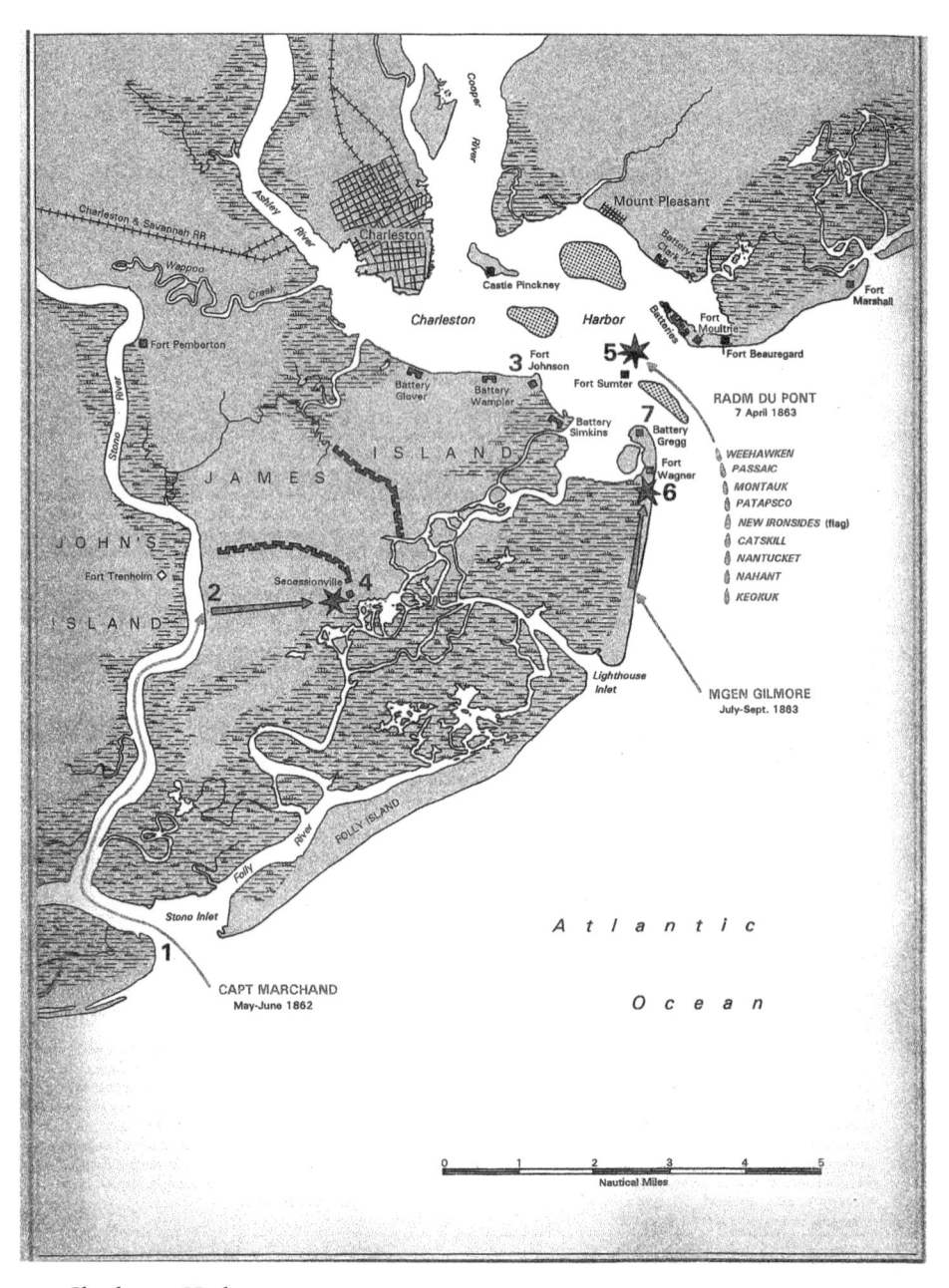

Charleston Harbor, 1862–63

of the breaching batteries in the reduction of Fort Pulaski. Du Pont informed Welles that Hunter had a "generous spirit, long to be remembered, [by] permitting the Navy to be represented" in the action. But as always, such cooperation and courtesy would last only so long as the officers in both services agreed to subordinate their own prerogatives to the larger goal.[11]

The navy continued to support the army's actions on the island. On June 10, Confederate forces attacked the Union soldiers at Grimball's plantation. General Wright reported that the navy provided close fire support and "the naval vessels in the river kept up a continual fire over the heads of our men, and as their practice was excellent it must have occasioned much loss to the enemy's reserves." On the fifteenth Drayton wrote to Du Pont that his squadron on the Stono River had "done whatever was possible, and so far no proposal has been made on the part of the generals that I have not at once acceded to, with the single exception of wasting ammunition." The navy was firing hundreds of shells at enormous ranges and, by using compass bearings, at times firing at objects they could not see. To achieve these ranges, it was necessary to elevate the guns to severe angles, and their being fired caused excessive back pressure that damaged the firing vents and ruined the guns.[12]

Hunter believed that the Union position was defendable, especially with the fire support of the naval squadron, but he also concluded that without more men no offensive actions could, nor should be undertaken. He went back to Port Royal, leaving Benham in charge, and on the tenth gave him strict orders not to take any offensive actions and to send reports back to Port Royal by every boat that was returning. Rebel batteries continued to shell the Union entrenchment, which was frustrating because the range was too great for the guns on board the navy ships in the Stono River. Unwilling to merely accept this punishment without responding, Benham, without informing Hunter, ordered a "reconnaissance in force" for June 16 with about half his men against the Confederate line at Secessionville. As much as possible, the gunboats provided covering fire at ranges of more than two miles, guided by army signal officers, both ashore and afloat. The result, however, was a complete repulse, with loses of 683 casualties out of the 4,500 engaged. Benham was relieved of his command and arrested for disobeying a direct order. His defense was that this "reconnaissance in force" was not meant to be an actual "offensive action."[13]

Benham's replacement was Brigadier General Horatio G. Wright, whom Hunter also told not to advance from the protection of the gunboats, though Hunter did tell him that if he thought his position was untenable he should abandon James Island. Wright repeatedly asked Hunter to come back to James Island and inspect the current position just "for a few hours" to help determine what should be done. Instead, on June 27 Hunter issued orders to abandon the island altogether. Drayton was disgusted and disappointed by the army's lack of initiative, and on July 2 he wrote to Du Pont, "To think of the work, transportation, loss of life, and worry of the last month being all wasted for no earthly reason. . . . It seems almost like a joke." Thus, ended this expedition against Charleston.[14]

One valuable lesson learned in this otherwise-disappointing campaign was how effective naval covering fire was because of the experience gained during earlier operations on the South Atlantic coast, and because a few months earlier the army had introduced a new system of signaling. This new system allowed the officers on land to communicate directly in real time with their counterparts on board the ships. The first use of this system in battle was during a combined operation at the small Battle of Port Royal Ferry on the Coosaw River. Early on January 1, 1862, Union gunboats advanced and fired at Confederate earthworks at the ferry. The army crossed the river and, with the gunboats shelling in advance of them, seized the fortifications. This covering fire protected the Union forces and scattered the three thousand rebels, making victory possible. Even though this visual signaling system would not be officially adopted by the army for another six months, for the first time army signal officers were placed on the navy's gunboats and used the new army code, which had been invented by Major Albert J. Myer, a physician and former assistant surgeon in the army. After the battle, Du Pont wrote that with this "code of signals for the Army they communicate any conversation, without books and by waving a flag at the end of a stick, and this without any multiplicity of gestures or rather motions of the flag." The army signal officer on the ship during the battle reported back to Myer that "by means of your signals Captain Rodgers was kept constantly informed of the position of the enemy and the disposition of our troops, and was thus enabled to direct his fire with precision and without fear of injuring our own men." Brigadier General Isaac I. Stevens, who commanded the land forces, said, "I have stated that the signaling was a perfect success. It was indeed an extraordinary success. So far as I am advised, this is the first time it has been tested in actual battle." Rodgers himself reported to Du Pont that the signals "furnished me with the means of constantly communicating with General Stevens with a facility and rapidity unknown to the naval service. I take this opportunity of recommending that the code of signals invented by Major Myer be at once introduced into the Navy." With this new method of signals, instead of the forces acting in concert in a prearranged plan, they were able to work in unison, dynamically, as the engagement evolved. Rodgers was able to provide fire support to a degree that had never been attainable before, because the forces on the ground were able to direct his firing.[15]

Despite the collapse of the combined operation, Welles and Fox continued to hope that a navy-only attack might succeed. For the naval attack on the Charleston forts, Du Pont had the largest ironclad fleet ever assembled, including seven *Passaic*-class monitors, the USS *Keokuk*, and the giant USS *New Ironsides*. Du Pont had declared to his superiors that this action—between the two hundred guns in forts against the twenty-three guns he could bring to bear at one time—was to be nothing more than an "experiment." Though Welles hoped that Du Pont would capture the city unaided, Hunter reported himself "in a state of complete readiness for the forces under my command to take the part assigned to them in the joint attack against Charleston." For this purpose, he embarked 12,250 men out of a total 16,748 he had under his command. On the morning of the battle, Hunter's troops, who were trained in "surf-boat exercises" and ready for an amphibious assault, were positioned on Folly Island. The plan was to cross Lighthouse Inlet and attack the southern part of Morris Island, which would put them just three miles from Fort Sumter.[16]

The long-awaited ironclad attack on the forts at Charleston finally took place on April 7, 1863. The engagement started around 3:00 P.M. and lasted for only about two hours. The rebels fired more than 2,200 shots and struck the ironclads 520 times, causing considerable damage, though only one man was killed and twenty-one wounded. One ship, the *Keokuk*, sank the next day. The ironclads only managed to fire 154 shots, causing little damage to the forts, killing five and wounding eight. After retiring from the engagement, Du Pont consulted with his captains and decided not to renew the fight then nor the next day. Hunter watched the battle from the beach, but would not cross the inlet to Morris Island because he "thought the attempt too hazardous."[17]

Eventually Welles relieved Admiral Du Pont of the command of the South Atlantic Blockading Squadron. Not only was he disappointed in Du Pont's perceived lethargy, he was angered at Du Pont's reaction to published criticism of him in the papers. His replacement was the ordnance specialist Rear Admiral John A. Dahlgren. One element in Du Pont's dismissal may have been Hunter's criticism. Though Hunter had praised Du Pont earlier, by May 22 he was laying all the blame for the lack of progress on Du Pont, writing directly to President Lincoln to claim that "from the nature of the plans of Admiral Du Pont, the Army had no active part" in the battle, and he asked Lincoln to "liberate" him from orders to "cooperate with the navy." Alas for Hunter, he was soon replaced as well, by Major General Quincy Adams Gillmore.[18]

Gillmore had proposed a joint operation to take Charleston by way of Morris Island in 1861. Now with Du Pont gone, he found Dahlgren ready and willing to execute that plan. Gillmore had accepted command on the understanding that he "could be allowed untrammeled execution of my plans, except so far as they involve co-operation from the navy." Dahlgren had been briefed by Gillmore in Washington and felt his primary mission was to support the army's operations. Combined operations at Charleston reached their peak of cooperation and success during this period.[19]

Gillmore's plan was to land on unfortified Folly Island south of Morris Island, build batteries on the north end of Folly Island, which would then support a movement across Lighthouse Inlet to Morris Island, where they would take Battery Wagner. After that, they could advance and take the fort at Cummings Point on the north end of the island. These troop movements would all be supported by flanking fire from the ironclads. Once Morris Island was secure, breaching batteries would be built to reduce Fort Sumter so that Dahlgren's warships could enter the harbor.

Dahlgren arrived in Port Royal on July 4, 1863, and met with Gillmore that same day. By the fifth they had worked out a plan for the combined operation. At 5:08 A.M. on July 10, the masked batteries at the north end of Folly Island opened on Morris Island to begin this critical engagement to seize it, then Fort Sumter, and then Charleston. Four monitors, led by Dahlgren in the *Catskill*, advanced up the channel and opened fire at 6:15 A.M. The Union soldiers landed at about 8:00 A.M. and, after a brief but hard-fought battle, seized the batteries on the southern end of Morris Island. As the troops advanced toward Battery Wagner, the ironclads also moved up the coast and began to shell the fort's sea face. By the end of the day Gillmore's men had captured about 80 percent of Morris Island and were in position to attack Wagner the next day. Union casualties were only 15 killed and 91 wounded while the Confederates suffered 17 killed, 112 wounded, 67 missing, and also lost 11 guns. The four monitors fired 534 shots and the *Catskill*, which was flying the admiral's flag, was hit 68 times while the other three monitors combined were only hit eight times. One shot that struck the *Catskill*'s pilothouse dislodged a bolt that just missed hitting Admiral Dahlgren in the head.[20]

The landing was an exceptional success. The implementation was flawless, and the cooperation and performance between the army and navy was brilliant. Unlike many other combined operations where the army would wait for the navy to silence the rebel forces and then advance, this battle was similar to the landing on James Island in 1862 where the army landed while the naval bombardment was still in progress. The coordinated fire from the navy moved up the beach as the troops did. This engagement clearly demonstrated what could be achieved in a combined operation with proper cooperation.

Early the next morning, however, without informing Dahlgren or asking for the same fire support that had been so successful the day before, Gillmore ordered a direct attack on Wagner. This movement was not successful, and the

Union troops suffered 339 causalities while the Confederates lost only 6 dead and 6 wounded. Dahlgren's ironclads continued to shell Battery Wagner at long range while Gillmore made plans for another assault on the eighteenth. This time there were five monitors, with Dahlgren taking the lead on the *Montauk*, and for the first time the *New Ironsides* joined the action. The Confederates found the broadside from this vessel "exceedingly demoralizing." The bombardment silenced Wagner's guns as the defenders took shelter in the bombproofs. Gillmore believed that the fort had been reduced, and at sunset sent a note to Dahlgren that he would order an attack. As darkness fell, the gunners on the naval vessels could not see well enough to support the troops effectively, so the army made its second direct assault without naval support.[21]

Gillmore either did not learn from his first assault on the fort or he overestimated the damage done to Wagner by the bombardment. Or perhaps, aware that the navy could not participate in the darkness, he sought to ensure that when Wagner surrendered, it would be to the army alone. Still, the naval vessels had fired more than 1,900 rounds of shot and shell into Battery Wagner that day, the *New Ironsides* firing about half that. This was more than three hundred shots per hour, or five every minute. The recent experience under Dahlgren's command, and using the army's new signal system, had demonstrated that the navy could provide close fire support for the army in combined operations. On July 18, without this naval covering fire, Gillmore's soldiers suffered one of the greatest losses of the war, suffering a terrible 1,515 casualties out of 5,000 men, compared to a Confederate loss of 222.[22]

This loss made Gillmore reconsider the wisdom of a direct attack on Battery Wagner, and he initiated a siege. Supported by the ironclads he moved his entrenchments continually closer to Wagner, eventually reaching within forty yards. The main objective of this operation was not Wagner but the reduction of Fort Sumter, and by August 14 he had moved close enough to establish breaching batteries that could fire over Wagner directly into Sumter. The navy supported this bombardment by keeping Wagner quiet with constant naval shelling. The ironclads also attacked Sumter directly on August 23 around 3 A.M. By August 24, Fort Sumter had been so demolished that General P. G. T. Beauregard, after a personal inspection, determined that while it was still defendable, its days as an artillery platform were over, and ordered its guns removed to the inner defenses of the harbor.[23]

Gillmore had accomplished his objective and expected Dahlgren would now force his way into Charleston Harbor. Dahlgren believed that to move into the harbor and seize Charleston, he needed to remove the many obstructions and torpedoes that had been placed in the main ship channel. He reported to Gillmore that Sumter still had one gun and it would interfere with this operation.

Gillmore disagreed and, like Hunter in his relationship with Du Pont, was beginning to have second thoughts about Dahlgren; and just as in 1862, the exceptional cooperation between the army and the navy began to break down. As the relationship between Gillmore and Dahlgren soured, their combined actions ceased, causing a quarrel as to who or what was responsible for the failure to capture Charleston in 1863. This quarrel evolved into a feud, which continued until Dahlgren's death in 1870.[24]

By the beginning of September, the constant pounding of Battery Wagner by both land and sea forces convinced the Confederates that their position was no longer tenable and the last men evacuated the fort just minutes before Gillmore launched another attack. With the fall of Wagner and the capture of all of Morris Island and the fort at Cumming's Point, Dahlgren sent a flag of truce to Fort Sumter to demand its surrender. Beauregard replied by telling Dahlgren to "come and take it." For two days the navy engaged Fort Moultrie and probed the obstructions in the channel. Fort Sumter, without guns, did not participate in the action.[25]

Dahlgren still believed he needed Sumter secure in order to remove the obstructions and enter the harbor. The clearest example of how cooperation and communication between Dahlgren and Gillmore had deteriorated by this point is the naval boat attack on Fort Sumter just after midnight on September 9. Dahlgren planned to send volunteer sailors and marines to the fort by small boats to capture it. Just hours before the attack, on the evening of the eighth, he asked Gillmore to return some launches the navy had lent to the army, only to learn that the army had planned to make a similar assault by boat on the same night at about the same time, and neither service knew about the other's plans. When they did learn, they refused to cooperate in a combined assault. Dahlgren said that he would only put his men under command of a naval officer and would send the highest-ranking officer necessary for the navy to control the attack. Gillmore replied that he did not see why the navy needed to lead an attack on a fort, and that he would recall his own assault if it was not already too late. They did agree to the password "Detroit" should the two expeditions become entangled. The sailors and marines arrived at Sumter first and were beaten back with severe losses. Of the 400 men who made the assault, 3 were killed and 106 men and 11 officers were captured. The soldiers also rowed toward Sumter but arrived after the naval attack had begun. Gillmore had given strict orders to abandon the operation if the navy landed first; so, within sight of the fighting between the rebels and the sailors, the army's expedition turned back.[26]

The boat attack was the last attempt at offensive operations against Charleston. On September 22, as a reward for his successes at Battery Wagner and the reduction of Fort Sumter, Gillmore was promoted to major general; and with Morris Island secure, he moved most of his forces to Hilton Head Island and Florida. Dahlgren proposed new combined operations to Gillmore, who was not interested, and Dahlgren's squadron spent the remainder of 1863 and all of 1864 blockading Charleston and Savannah.

There had been opportunities to capture Charleston by combined operations via James Island in 1861 and 1862 and on Morris Island in 1863. Despite moments of hope when it looked like Hunter and Du Pont, and later Gillmore and Dahlgren, might be able to work together enough to topple "Satan's kingdom," the barriers to effective interservice cooperation overwhelmed the best intentions of all four officers, and in the end Charleston did not fall until it was threatened by Sherman's March to the Sea in February 1864. There is no record of when the American flag was finally raised on the flagpole of the new second floor of the Navy Department building.

Notes

1. Fox to Du Pont, June 3, 1863, in Gustavus V. Fox, *Confidential Correspondence of Gustavus Vasa Fox: A Selection from His War Letters*, edited by Robert Means Thompson and Richard Wainwright (New York: De Vinne Press, 1918–19), 1:128.

2. Samuel Jones, *The Siege of Charleston* (New York: Neale Publishing, 1911), 97; Howard to Cushing, June 23, 1862, OR, 14:28; Samuel Francis Du Pont to Sophie Du Pont, June 3, 1862, in Du Pont, *Samuel Francis Du Pont: A Selection from His Civil War Letters*, edited by John D. Hayes (Ithaca, N.Y.: Cornell University Press, 1969), 2:98 (hereafter cited as Du Pont, *Letters*); Fox to Du Pont, January 23, 1863, in Du Pont, *Letters*, 1:177.

3. E. Milby Burton, *The Siege of Charleston* (Columbia: University of South Carolina Press, 1970), 92, 94–95.

4. Fox to Du Pont, May 12, 1862, in Fox, *Correspondence*, 1:119.

5. Welles to Du Pont, May 13, 1862, OR, 12:820.

6. Du Pont, *Letters*, 2:55; Du Pont to Marchand, May 15, 1862, and Marchand to Du Pont, May 19, 1862, both in ORN, 13:5, 13.

7. Du Pont to Sophie, May 29, 1862, Du Pont to Fox, May 31, 1862, and Du Pont to Sophie, May 1, 1862, all in Du Pont, *Letters*, 2:79, 92, 26; Rodgers to Benham, May 22, 1862, ORN, 13:25–26; Du Pont to Sophie, May 19, 1862, in Du Pont, *Letters*, 2:58.

8. Du Pont to Sophie, May 29, 1862, in Du Pont, *Letters*, 2:81; Robert M. Browning, *Success Is All That Was Expected: The South Atlantic Blockading Squadron During the Civil War* (Washington, D.C.: Potomac Books, 2002), 99; Meigs to Fuller, May 10, 1862, and Benham to Meigs, May 23, 1862, both in OR, 14:341, 344–46.

9. Rodgers to Du Pont, May 22, 1862, and Du Pont to Hunter, May 24, 1862, both in ORN, 13:24, 27; Du Pont to Sophie, May 25, May 30, and June 3, 1862, all in Du Pont, *Letters*, 2:71, 81, 98.

10. Jones, *Siege of Charleston*, 97–98; Drayton to Du Pont, June 13, 1862, ORN, 13:98; Browning, *Success*, 102.

11. Stanton to Hunter, June 9 and 19, 1862, both in OR, 14:350, 355; Du Pont to Drayton, June 4, 1862, Hunter to Du Pont, June 1, 1862, both in ORN, 13:76, 67; Rodgers to Du Pont, April 9, 1862, and Du Pont to Welles, April 13, 1862, both in ORN, 12:725, 730.

12. Wright to Ely, June 12, 1862, *OR*, 14:35; Drayton to Du Pont, June 15, 1862, *ORN*, 13:103; Du Pont to Sophie, June 13, 1862, in Du Pont, *Letters*, 2:113.

13. Hunter to Benham, June 10, 1862, *OR*, 14:46; Browning, *Success*, 103; Jones, *Siege of Charleston*, 111.

14. Burton, *Siege of Charleston*, 111; Wright to Hunter, June 20, 1862, and Wright to Halpine, June 29, 1862, both in *OR*, 14:358, 361; Drayton to Du Pont, July 2, 1862, *ORN*, 13:165.

15. Browning, *Success*, 56–58; Du Pont to Sophie, October 29, 1861, in Du Pont, *Letters*, 1:101; Cogswell to Myer, January 4, 1862, and Stevens to Myer, January 3, 1862, both in *ORN*, 6:62, 65; Rodgers to Du Pont, January 3, 1862, *ORN*, 12:450. See also Willard J. Brown, *The Signal Corps, USA, in the War of the Rebellion* (New York: Arno Press, 1974), 20–21.

16. Du Pont to Fox, February 25, 1863, in Fox, *Correspondence*, 1:182; Hunter to Halleck, March 7, 1863, *OR*, 14:424; Burton, *Siege of Charleston*, 144.

17. Burton, *Siege of Charleston*, 136–44; Hunter to Lincoln, May 22, 1863, *ORN*, 14:32–35.

18. Special Order No. 249, June 3, 1863, *OR*, 14:464.

19. Gillmore to Sherman, December 25, 1861, *OR*, 6:212; Stephen R. Wise, *Gate of Hell* (Columbia: University of South Carolina Press, 1994), 34.

20. Browning, *Success*, 220; Madeleine Dahlgren, *Memoir of John A. Dahlgren* (Boston: J. R. Osgood, 1882), 396, 398–99; Wise, *Gate of Hell*, 67; Dahlgren to Welles, July 12, 1863, *ORN*, 14:319–21.

21. Browning, *Success*, 227; Dahlgren, *Memoir*, 402–3; Wise, *Gate of Hell*, 76–77.

22. Wise, *Gate of Hell*, 92–118; Browning, *Success*, 227–28; Dahlgren to Welles, July 19, 1863, *ORN*, 14:359–60.

23. Jones, *Siege of Charleston*, 247–57; Wise, *Gate of Hell*, 154, 161; Dahlgren, *Memoir*, 409–10; Dahlgren to Welles, August 23, 1863, *ORN*, 14:501; Alfred Roman, *Military Operations of General Beauregard* (New York: Harper and Brothers, 1884), 2:147–50.

24. Jones, *Siege of Charleston*, 259; Dahlgren to Gillmore, August 29, 1863, *ORN*, 14:524; Wise, *Gate of Hell*, 189.

25. Wise, *Gate of Hell*, 202; Jones, *Siege of Charleston*, 275; Roman, *Beauregard*, 155.

26. Wise, *Gate of Hell*, 206–7; Browning, *Success*, 255; Dahlgren, *Memoir*, 413–14; Dahlgren to Welles, September 11, 1863, *ORN*, 14:611. See also *ORN*, 14:608–10, and *OR*, 28 (part 2): 88.

7

Grant Moves South: Combined Operations on the James River, 1864

Craig L. Symonds

By the spring of 1864, the Union had experienced so much disappointment with combined operations that instead of allaying suspicion between the services, the overriding sense of distrust was at least as prominent as it had been in 1862. Yet that same spring, circumstances conspired to overcome those suspicions during Lieutenant General Ulysses S. Grant's move to the James River. Even with Grant's prestige as the nation's first three-star general since George Washington (Winfield Scott had been a brevet three-star), it took a perceived crisis in command on the James River to overcome the traditional barriers to unified authority.

In April 1864, Grant was preparing to embark on what subsequently came to be known as the Overland Campaign. In conformance with President Lincoln's long-held strategic vision, Grant's plan called for the simultaneous advance of three Union armies against the Confederates in Virginia. Meade's Army of the Potomac, with Grant in company, would advance southward across the Rapidan-Rappahannock line into the Virginia wilderness; the German-born Major General Franz Sigel would lead a smaller Union army southward through the breadbasket of the Shenandoah Valley; and Major General Benjamin Butler would lead the Army of the James up its namesake river toward Petersburg and Richmond's back door. The idea was that the rebels would be overmatched in attempting to deal simultaneously with Grant's advance from the north and Butler's from the south. As Lincoln explained it to John Hay: "Those not skinning can hold a leg." Since Grant planned to initiate this campaign on May 4, he wanted Butler to begin his move that same night and "be as far up the James River as you can get by daylight" on May 5. Butler's move, of course, would have to be made in conjunction with the navy, and in particular with Acting Rear Admiral Samuel Phillips Lee (a third cousin of the rebel army commander), who commanded the Union's North Atlantic Blockading Squadron. Though their partnership began well enough, the absence of a unified command led once again to misunderstanding, confusion, and disappointment.[1]

This was neither the first nor the last time Butler would be involved with a combined operation. Soldiers under his command had occupied New Orleans after it surrendered to David Glasgow Farragut in April 1862, and he would command the landing force during the first assault on Fort Fisher, North Carolina, that coming winter (see Chapter 8). In none of these adventures did Butler emerge victorious, and it seemed curious to some that he kept getting important assignments. But Butler was an important Democrat in what the administration wanted to avoid being portrayed as a Republican war. Moreover, Butler's political savvy was useful in circumstances where strict adherence to protocol might have caused problems. It was Butler who had conceived of the notion that refugee slaves could be labeled "contraband of war" and therefore not returned to their rebel masters. Finally, Butler's seniority as a major general made it essential to give him independent commands, for if attached to the Army of the Potomac he would outrank every general except Grant.

As for Samuel Phillips Lee, he came with a certain amount of political baggage of his own. Unlike Butler, he was a career officer, but he was also well connected. He was married to Elizabeth Blair Lee, whose two brothers each held important posts: Major General Frank Blair Jr. was a corps commander under William T. Sherman, and Montgomery Blair was Lincoln's postmaster general. Moreover, their father (and Admiral Lee's father-in-law), Francis P. Blair Sr., was a confidante of the president and influential in Republican Party circles. Finally, while Lee commanded the nation's largest squadron—the North Atlantic Blockading Squadron—he remained an *acting* rear admiral, and was eager for promotion. Throughout the James River campaign, therefore, Acting Rear Admiral Lee sought to achieve some signal victory that would gain him the promotion he sought.

Butler had "positive orders" from Grant to start on schedule, and Lee told his captains, "No excuse will be received for not being ready to move at the appointed time." On May 5, 1864, therefore, Lee's five ironclads led the advance upriver. They were followed by nearly two hundred other vessels of every size and shape: tugs, double-enders, fat supply ships, packed army transports, squat river steamers, and tall oceangoing ships. The armada virtually filled the river. In the end, the movement took place without incident, and Lee was pleased to report to Welles "the successful landing of the army at City Point and Bermuda Hundred."[2]

That, however, was nearly the last piece of good news to come from Butler's theater of operations. After a few tentative probes to the west, the south, and even north toward Richmond, Butler soon retreated to his beachhead, an area known as Bermuda Hundred within a broad curve of the James River, where he fortified. It became clear almost at once that Butler was more concerned with maintaining the security of his campsite than he was in assaulting the enemy. By landing in Bermuda Hundred, Butler had thrust his army into a cul-de-sac where he was pinned down as effectively as if his men had been interned in a POW camp, or as Grant put it, "in a bottle strongly corked."[3]

Just as bad, the essential cooperation between army and navy began to break down almost at once. Each service commander wanted support from the other. Butler wanted Lee to use his gunboats to cover his flanks; Lee wanted Butler to clear the riverbank of enemy artillery so he could sweep for torpedoes. But lacking a unified command, by force of circumstances they couched their requests deferentially. On May 13 Butler asked Lee: "Would it not be possible for you to bring up the gunboats, monitors, opposite Dr. Howlett's so as to cover my flank?" Not really, Lee replied. The rebel position at Howlett's home was "over high hills and woods," and Lee's gunboats could reach them only if they could advance further upriver; this was impossible unless they could somehow clear the torpedoes, and that could not be done so long as the rebel army could ambush them from the riverbank. Acting Rear Admiral Lee put his "Torpedo Division" to work clearing the mines, but it was tedious work and required "dragging the river with grapnels & searching the banks for torpedo lines and wires." Moreover, it was likely to be interrupted at any time when rebel masked batteries opened fire from the riverbank. Lee's concerns were punctuated by the loss of the *Commodore Jones*, "torn into splinters" by a two-thousand-pound torpedo on May 6, and the *Shawsheen*, which was ambushed from shore and captured the next day. Eager as he was to move upriver, Lee insisted that he could not help Butler with the rebel batteries at Howlett's unless Butler helped clear the riverbank of enemy batteries. "In this way the two services will support each other," Lee wrote.[4]

It didn't happen. Instead, interservice relations worsened. Lee suggested to Butler that "it will promote the public service if you can conveniently keep up communication with me and apprise me of your movements." But when Butler decided to make a concerted thrust northward toward Fort Darling, he did not bother to ask Lee for his cooperation or even to inform him of the move. After Butler's northward thrust was badly mauled and he returned to his entrenchments at Bermuda Hundred, Lee asked him about it and Butler declared that his move had been only "a feint." Meanwhile the rebels continued to improve their entrenchments at Howlett's, and Lee's queries to Butler about cooperation took on a sharper edge. All through the afternoon of May 18, while Robert E. Lee fended off Grant's furious attacks at Spotsylvania Court House, his third cousin Samuel Phillips Lee bombarded Butler with a series of telegrams urging him to do something about those rebel guns at Howlett's. At three thirty he wired: "Enemy vigorously entrenching. . . . Only a land attack can dislodge

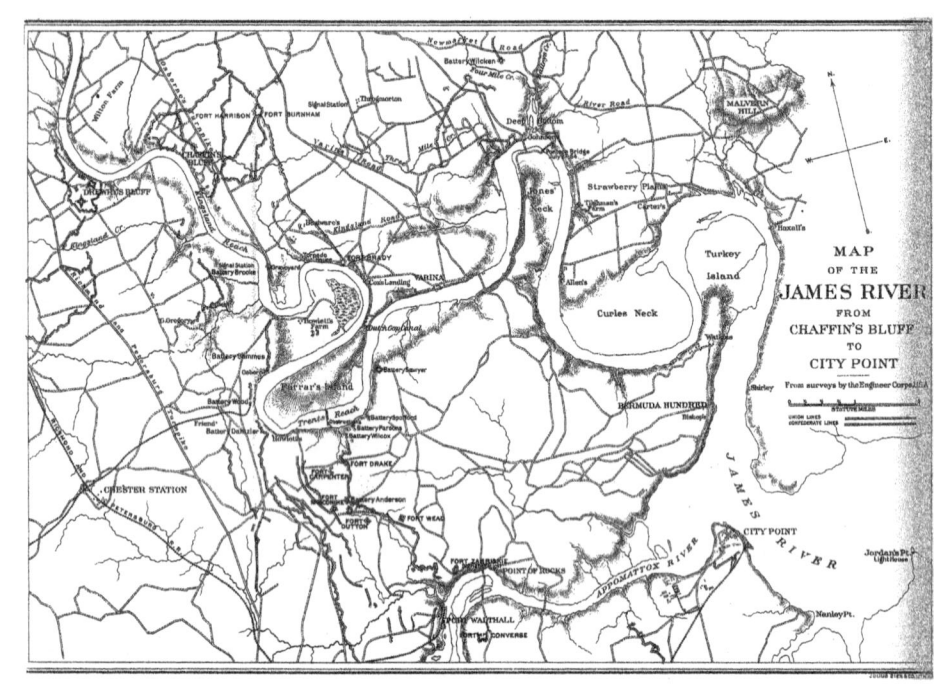

Road Between Bermuda Hundred and Enemy's Line of Intrenchments

them." A half hour later, he reminded Butler: "The enemy are working on entrenchments near Howlett's house. . . . They will mount guns to-night." An hour later he wrote: "The rebel artillery is getting in position there." And a half hour after that: "Can not the enemy be prevented from mounting guns at Howlett's to-night by a land attack?" Butler was immune to such prodding, however, and it was soon evident that for all the hopes associated with this assault on Richmond's back door, Butler had simply moved his command from Fort Monroe to Bermuda Hundred.[5]

Admiral Lee still hoped that he might achieve something worthy of notice during the campaign if the rebel ironclad squadron came downriver from Richmond to challenge him. On May 28 he learned that the rebel warships—three ironclads and six more lightly armored gunboats—had dropped down the river to Drewry's Bluff. A rebel deserter informed him that the enemy planned to send down fireships followed by an attack with their armored vessels. Butler urged Lee to protect himself from such an attack by sinking obstructions in the river in much the same way that Butler had protected himself by building entrenchments across the neck of Bermuda Hundred. Lee was dismissive of such timidity. "The Navy is not accustomed to putting down obstructions before it," he declared haughtily.[6]

But the rebel ironclads did not come downriver. Instead, a few days later, a staff officer from Grant's headquarters came on board the *Malvern* to tell him that Grant was seeking "a good location for a pontoon bridge." Having fought his way from the wilderness to Spotsylvania to Cold Harbor, Grant was now planning another flanking movement southward and eastward, across the Appomattox and James Rivers to Petersburg. It was evident that if Grant bridged the James, or the Appomattox, or both, it would be prudent to ensure the security of those bridges by blocking the river channel to prevent the small rebel ironclad flotilla from attempting to interfere. Both Butler and Major General Quincy A. Gillmore urged Admiral Lee to sink ships in the river channel, but Lee feared that if he did so, others would assume he was afraid of a contest with the rebel squadron. Anxious about what to do, he decided to "lay the subject before the Department." He asked Gideon Welles: Was it more important to block the river to ensure its security or keep it open to invite an engagement with the rebel ironclads?[7]

Welles was growing weary of Lee's constant queries. He endorsed Lee's letter, "Left to discretion of admiral in command, in whom the Department has confidence," though, in fact, that confidence was beginning to wane. When Lee got that response, he next sought to place the onus of the decision on Butler. Obstructing the river, he wrote to Butler, "must be your operation, not mine." Not surprisingly, Butler refused to take responsibility. "The vessels are wholly at your service," the general replied, "upon your good judgment, and not mine, must rest their use." Admiral Lee's penchant for careful record keeping compelled him to insist that Butler assure him, in writing, that the navy would not incur any "pecuniary liability" for the ships if he did use them to block the river. Butler did so, but Lee still did not act. He held the schooners in readiness in case of need, but he left the channel open.[8]

In the end, Lee did not have to make the decision after all. When Grant decided to move once again around the right flank of the rebel army, bypassing the old battlefields of the Seven Days, to land behind Butler at City Point, he ordered Butler to block the river to protect the pontoon bridges. Lee may have felt some relief in not having to make the decision himself, but he was also a little defensive about it, assuring himself in his private journal that "the sinking of obstructions is an army measure from first to last." In the hope of protecting himself from public criticism, he made sure to notify Welles that the sinking of the block ships to obstruct the river had been done by the army, under the orders of the army commander, and not by him.[9]

Public criticism fell on him nonetheless. The *New York Herald* announced that "Admiral Lee has just performed an act that, we doubt not, has called an honorable blush to the cheek of every officer in his fleet. He has sunk boats in the river—obstructed the channel—to prevent the rebel fleet from getting out at his ships. He has iron-clad vessels enough to blow every ram in the confederacy to atoms; but he is afraid of the trial." The *Herald* subsequently admitted that the obstructions had been sunk by Grant's order, but it also insisted that Grant had ordered it because he doubted the ability of the navy to make his communications "absolutely safe." That order, the *Herald* concluded, was a "distinct declaration on the part of General Grant that he has no confidence in Admiral Lee." Gustavus Fox told Lee to ignore the sniping from the press about the river obstructions; that he, for one, had been "in favor of obstructions from the beginning"; and that he planned to send a dozen more canal boats to make the obstruction complete.[10]

At first it looked as though Grant's swing to the south and east might lead to the swift seizure of Petersburg, which would cut Richmond's rail lines to the south. Instead, Robert E. Lee, with important help from Pierre G. T. Beauregard, countered the move, and the campaign lapsed into another siege.

In December, attention shifted to Fort Fisher, which guarded the entrance to the Cape Fear River and Wilmington, North Carolina. A much-disappointed Admiral Lee gave way to David Dixon Porter, who went off to join first Butler, and then Godfrey Weitzel, in the conquest of that citadel (see Chapter 8). Meanwhile, Porter left naval matters on the James River in the hands of Commander William A. Parker, whom Porter had selected for the job because he believed he was an old-fashioned, hard-nosed officer of the "old navy." Porter described Parker as "a sturdy old chap who looked as if he had been cut out of a big timber-head." But Porter should have known by now that looks could be misleading. Despite his thirty-three years of active service, Parker remained a commander in part because he was more comfortable following orders than exercising initiative. Given that, it was perhaps unfortunate that when Porter left with the bulk of the squadron to subdue Fort Fisher, he told Parker to "run no risks at present or while I am away." Parker apparently took those orders quite seriously.[11]

Parker had only one ironclad in his diminished command, though that ironclad was the powerful, double-turreted *Onondaga*, which boasted two 15-inch Dahlgren guns and two 150-pound Parrott rifles. These ships should have been more than adequate to maintain Union control of the upper reaches of the James River against the rebel ironclads. When heavy rains that winter washed away some of the obstructions in the river, it allowed the rebel ironclad squadron to drop downriver to Trent's Reach within a few hours steaming of Grant's supply depot at City Point. Six months earlier, Phillips Lee had hoped that the rebel ironclad squadron would sortie downriver so that he could defeat it in battle. But Lee was gone now, and instead of challenging the rebel thrust, Commander Parker took Porter's cautionary words to heart and retired downriver, claiming later that his purpose was to gain "more room to maneuver."[12]

From the start, Grant had feared that the navy would be unable or unwilling to protect his pontoon bridges or his supply depot. That was one of the reasons he had supported replacing Lee with Porter. Now he was disgusted that at the first appearance of the rebel squadron, the Union navy had apparently turned tail and run. Grant wanted Parker to send everything he had to reestablish control of the river. "It would be better to obstruct the channel of the river with sunken gunboats than that a rebel ram should reach City Point," he wired Parker. And he followed this up with an even more urgent telegram: "It is your duty, in view of the large amount of stores here, to attack with all the vessels you have." Just as Admiral Lee's frequent telegrams to Butler about the batteries at Howlett's had no apparent effect on him, Grant's urgent messages to Parker had no perceptible effect on that officer. Grant reported to Fox that he "expected little from the navy under Captain Parker," who seemed "helpless."[13]

In Washington, Grant's complaints about Parker provoked Lincoln to send for Welles who, after discussing the situation with Lincoln and Stanton, agreed that Parker had to go. Welles ordered Commodore William Radford to relieve Parker of his command, but he also mentioned to Lincoln that Admiral Farragut was in the city staying at the Willard Hotel after bringing the *Hartford* back from the Gulf. At once, Lincoln decided to send for him too. Farragut hastened over from the Willard, and once he was apprised of the command problem on the James, he agreed to go there himself. Welles notified Grant that Farragut was on his way, but neither he nor Radford could arrive in less than twenty-four hours, and until then there seemed to be no choice but to leave Parker in command, though Welles told Grant that "Captain Parker will be removed tonight if you desire it."[14]

Unwilling to wait for Radford or Farragut, Grant took matters into his own hands. Despite the long tradition that officers of one service could not give orders to officers of another service, Grant acted very much like a joint commander by issuing orders directly to the gunboat captains: "All gunboats now in the James River," he ordered, "will immediately proceed to the front above the pontoon bridge. . . . This order is imperative, *the orders of any naval commanders to the contrary notwithstanding.*" And perhaps because of the seriousness of the moment, or simply because the momentum of war had at last begun to break down the traditional barrier between the services, the naval officers obeyed. When one of Grant's aides, a mere lieutenant, came on board the USS

Minnesota to inform Commodore Joseph Lanman that "General Grant desired the *Atlanta* to proceed to Dutch Gap," Lanman immediately ordered that ship "to report to Lieutenant-General Grant."[15]

In the end, the rebel threat sputtered out when two of their three ironclads ran aground. The next morning, Parker returned upriver and opened fire on the grounded rebel ships. The *Onondaga*'s fifteen-inch bolts easily punched through their armor, and once the Confederates managed to refloat their grounded vessels, the whole rebel squadron retired upriver. By the time Farragut arrived, he was able to report to Washington: "All appears to be right. Radford is at his post with ample force." But he also added: "Things do not look well for Parker."[16]

He was right. Parker's belated return to action with the *Onondaga* was not enough to save either his reputation or his career. He seemed to be genuinely perplexed that Grant wanted him to be relieved. "I was not aware that General Grant was dissatisfied with me," he wrote plaintively to Welles, and to Porter he begged for "one more chance to retrieve my reputation and your good opinion." Porter was unforgiving. He had been furious when he had first heard of Parker's timidity ("I don't care if they hang him," he wrote to Fox). He was less draconian in his personal response to Parker's plea for another chance, writing that he regretted Parker's circumstances, but he regretted even more the fact that Parker had fumbled his opportunity. "No man ever had a better chance than you had," he wrote, adding that it was painful "to see such an opportunity lost." Eventually, Parker was found guilty by a court-martial for failing to do his utmost, though the court urged clemency in consideration of Parker's three decades of active service. In the end, Welles simply placed him on the retired list.[17]

The most important consequence of this mini-crisis, however, was not Parker's dismissal, or even the threat to Grant's supply depot—it was the extent to which navy officers proved willing to subordinate themselves to Grant's command direction. Gone was the haughty insistence by naval officers that all orders must come through the Navy Department. Gone too was resentment in the Navy Department about the army's "meddling" in its affairs. Instead of taking exception to Grant's assertion of authority, Welles, Fox, and particularly Lincoln sustained him. It was a far cry from the instructions that Welles and Fox had issued throughout the war to Du Pont, Dahlgren, Lee, Porter, and others to avoid involvement with the army whenever possible. One difference was that on those other occasions, Welles had been worried that the army might horn in on what he considered a navy operation; this time it was an army operation that was at risk. Indeed, it was the first time since the *Merrimack* had jeopardized McClellan's Peninsula Campaign in the spring of 1862 that a Confederate naval force seriously imperiled a major army campaign. With the war now coming to an end, the petty squabbling and lack of cooperation that had characterized combined operations throughout the conflict were at last beginning to give way before practical necessity.

Notes

Much of this chapter is adapted from Craig L. Symonds, *Lincoln and His Admirals: Abraham Lincoln, the U.S. Navy, and the Civil War* (New York: Oxford University Press, 2008), 316–21, 355–59.

1. John Hay, *Lincoln and the Civil War in the Diaries and Letters of John Hay*, edited by Tyler Dennett (New York: Dodd, Mead, 1939), entries of April 28 and April 30, 1864, 175, 179; Grant to Butler, April 29, 1864, and Butler to S. P. Lee, May 1, 1864, both in *ORN*, 9:713.

2. Lee's instructions are dated May 4, 1864, and are in *ORN*, 9:725; his letter to Welles, dated May 6, 1864, is in *ORN*, 10:3.

3. Grant's comment is in *OR*, 36 (part 2): 840.

4. Butler to S. P. Lee, May 13, 1864, *ORN*, 10:51; Lamson to "Kate," May 14, 1864, in James M. McPherson and Patricia R. McPherson, eds., *Lamson of the Gettysburg: The Civil War Letters of Lieutenant Roswell H. Lamson, U.S. Navy* (New York: Oxford University Press, 1997), 162; S. P. Lee to Butler, May 17, 1864, *ORN*, 10:65.

5. Butler to S. P. Lee, May 13, 1864, and Lee to Welles, May 21, 1864, both in *ORN*, 10:65, 76; The several telegrams from Lee to Butler are in *ORN*, 10:68–69.

6. S. P. Lee to Welles, May 28, 30, and June 7, all in *ORN*, 10:101, 105, 129.

7. S. P. Lee journal, May 26 and June 6, 1864, Blair-Lee Family Papers, Princeton University, box 52, folder 4; Butler to S. P. Lee, May 30, 1864, and S. P. Lee to Welles, June 7, 1864, both in *ORN*, 10:106, 129.

8. Welles endorsement is in *ORN*, 10:130. The notes between S. P. Lee and Butler are dated June 2 and 3, 1864, and are in *ORN*, 10:131–33.

9. S. P. Lee journal, June 15, 1864, Blair-Lee Family Papers, box 52, folder 4; S. P. Lee to Welles, June 15, 1864, *ORN*, 10:149.

10. *New York Herald*, June 23, 25, and 29, 1864; S. P. Lee journal, June 24, 1864, Blair-Lee Family Papers, box 52, folder 4.

11. Porter to Fox, October 11, 1864, Fox Papers, New-York Historical Society, New York; Porter to Parker, December 8, 1864, *ORN*, 11:155–56.

12. Parker to Porter, January 31, 1865, *ORN*, 11:656.

13. Grant to Parker, January 24, 1865, and Grant to Fox, several telegrams all dated January 24, 1865, all in *ORN*, 11:636, 635–36.

14. Grant to Fox, January 24, 1865 (two telegrams), *ORN*, 11:635; Welles, *Diary of Gideon Welles*, edited by Howard K. Beale (New York: Norton, 1960), 2:230.

15. Fox to Grant, January 24, 1865, Grant to Gunboat Commanders, January 24, 1865, and Lanman to Porter, January 25, 1865, all in *ORN*, 11:637, 635 (italics added), 643.

16. Farragut to Welles, January 26, 1865, *ORN*, 11:646.

17. Parker to Welles, January 26, 1865, Parker to Porter, January 31, 1865, and Porter to Parker, February 14, 1865, all in *ORN*, 11:644–45, 656, 658.

8

Closing Down the Kingdom: Union Combined Operations Against Wilmington

Chris E. Fonvielle Jr.

Long before Ulysses S. Grant made his move to the James River, the North Carolina seaport of Wilmington on the Cape Fear River had become the principal port of entry for ships carrying essential supplies to Robert E. Lee's Army of Northern Virginia. One Confederate officer observed that "after the capital of the Confederacy there was not a more important place than the little town of Wilmington, North Carolina." By the summer of 1864, as Grant fought his way through the wilderness, and Butler moved up the James River to Bermuda Hundred, the survival of Lee's army depended heavily on the flow of European arms, equipment, and provisions being imported into the Confederacy by way of Wilmington. Union military authorities did not initiate a serious campaign against this key city until late 1864. By then, however, Wilmington was the most heavily defended city on the Atlantic seaboard, with the exception of Charleston. Nevertheless, with important lessons learned in previous combined operations, the U.S. Army and Navy made plans to capture Wilmington with a large-scale combined operation.[1]

Wilmington is a beautiful old city nestled on a high, sloping sand ridge on the east bank of the Cape Fear River, at its confluence with the Northeast Cape Fear River. Founded in 1732 and incorporated seven years later, it is one of the state's oldest communities and, for most of the nineteenth century, its largest. In 1860, Wilmington boasted a population of almost ten thousand people, one-third of whom were African Americans. It had grown from a small colonial trading post into a bustling seaport with an active mercantile trade, two commercial shipbuilding yards, two iron and copper works, a military arms factory, turpentine distilleries, cotton presses, sawmills, and three railroads.[2]

The Cape Fear River is the only major waterway in the Old North State that flows directly into the sea, and it offered great advantages for blockade-runners because it could be accessed by one of two inlets: Old Inlet, the main bar at the mouth of the river, and New Inlet, a shallow passageway five miles to the northeast. Bald Head Island and Frying Pan Shoals separated the two inlets. The dual inlets provided blockade-runners with a choice of entry and exit points, and made it extremely difficult for the U.S. Navy to halt the waterborne trade.

Moreover, Wilmington itself, located twenty-eight miles upriver, was well beyond the range of naval bombardment.

Wilmington also enjoyed good port facilities and good lines of communication. The Cape Fear River was navigable all the way to Fayetteville, ninety miles upriver from Wilmington, and three railroads led from the seaport into the interior. The most important of these was the Wilmington and Weldon Railroad, which ran northward to Weldon, North Carolina, where it connected with the Weldon and Petersburg Railroad into southeastern Virginia. By 1864, the Wilmington and Weldon Railroad had become one of the major arteries of supply for the Army of Northern Virginia.[3]

Numerous sailing vessels and about seventy different blockade-running steamships operated in and out of Wilmington, and more times than not they eluded even the most vigilant blockaders. More blockade-running vessels entered Wilmington than all other Southern seaports combined. About 40 percent of the equipment, supplies, and provisions consumed by the Confederacy entered through the blockade, much of it coming into the Carolina seaport. By 1864, Southerners considered Wilmington to be the lifeline of the Confederacy.[4]

Wilmington's growing importance as the South's main seaport prompted the Confederate government to do all it could to defend it. Engineers designed and supervised the construction of a vast network of forts, batteries, and fieldworks. Artillery batteries ringed the city, while a series of outer defenses guarded it from an overland attack or amphibious landing. The strongest and best-armed forts protected the river inlets. Fort Caswell, Fort Campbell, and Battery Shaw on Oak Island, and Fort Holmes on adjacent Bald Head Island guarded Old Inlet. To safeguard New Inlet, engineers built the largest and strongest seacoast fortification in the Confederacy—Fort Fisher.

Fort Fisher was located near the end of Federal Point (renamed Confederate Point by Southerners), a narrow peninsula flanked by the Cape Fear River on the west and the Atlantic Ocean on the east. Here Confederate engineers began erecting sand batteries as early as April 1861. In September of that year, the defenses were named Fort Fisher in honor of Colonel Charles F. Fisher, commander of the 6th Regiment North Carolina Troops, killed at the Battle of Manassas (Bull Run) on July 21, 1861. Colonel William Lamb of the 36th Regiment North Carolina Troops assumed command of the military construction project on July 4, 1862. After touring works that in his view "amounted to nothing," Lamb determined to expand and strengthen Fort Fisher to withstand the heaviest cannon fire of the U.S. Navy.

Lamb's superior officer, Cape Fear District commander Major General W. H. C. Whiting, arguably the Confederacy's best military engineer, recognized the young man's talents. Under Whiting's tutelage and supervision, Lamb designed and built Fort Fisher from a patchwork of sand batteries into the mightiest fortress in America. Lamb worked his laborers six days a week—seven days a week when rumors of attack reached him. Construction of the fort took place under the watchful eye of Union blockaders off New Inlet, and they often lobbed shells onshore in an effort to disrupt the Confederate work parties. Undeterred, Lamb pressed on with the construction.

By 1864, Fort Fisher was a massive two-sided sand fortification that looked like a giant number 7 from a birds-eye view. A broad sand rampart that rose upward to twenty-four feet above ground, and stretched for more than a mile, connected a series of elevated artillery batteries mounting forty-four big seacoast cannon, while three mortars were mounted on the parade ground below.

Approaches to Wilmington, North Carolina

The fort's land face—the short shank of the 7—stretched for five hundred yards from the river's edge toward the sea, and guarded the northern land approaches. Large mounds of sand called traverses, towering nine to twelve feet higher than the parapet, were erected intermittently atop the land face to separate and protect the gun chambers and artillerists. Underneath the traverses were interconnected bunkers or bombproofs where soldiers could seek refuge during a bombardment. A palisade of heavy timbers and a web of mines buried outside the fort's northern wall supplemented the earthen defenses.

The land- and sea-face batteries intersected at the fort's northeastern corner, a massive thirty-two-foot-high battery referred to as the Northeast Bastion, about 100 yards from the ocean's high-water mark. Here the fort's walls turned southward, running parallel to the shoreline for 1,300 yards. At the south end of the sea face (the bottom of the 7) towered a forty-three-foot-high conical-shaped gun emplacement named Battery Lamb, but nicknamed the "Mound Battery." Its immense profile could be seen for miles at sea, and blockade-runners used it as a mark for both navigation and protection as they approached New Inlet. Confederate and Union military engineers alike considered Fort Fisher impregnable. Dubbed the Gibraltar of the South, the massive fort was key to Wilmington's defense.

Supplementing the forts at Old and New Inlets were fortifications built along the banks of the Cape Fear River to guard the water approaches to Wilmington. Foremost among them was Fort Anderson, a large earthen fort located in Brunswick County on the west side of the Cape Fear River, twelve miles above Old Inlet.[5]

A determined Union effort to close Wilmington to blockade-running was a long time coming, despite the fact that the U.S. Navy had targeted the city as early as the summer of 1861. In September of that year, the Blockade Strategy Board suggested attacking the Confederacy's major ports by naval bombardments and amphibious landings. After securing the seaports, U.S. troops could then move inland to attack industrial centers, railroads, and supply depots and occupy strategic cities. Wilmington was high on the board's hit list. The Cape Fear's shoal waters, however, made a purely naval attack impractical, as warships could not get close enough to shore to destroy the Confederate forts and batteries then under construction. The navy recognized the importance of Wilmington and its forts, but during 1862 and 1863 Gideon Welles was sending most of the navy's available warships to Charleston, which was a higher-priority target.[6]

While operations against Charleston took precedence in the Navy Department, Welles did not ignore Wilmington's significance. In early May 1862, he instructed Flag Officer Louis M. Goldsborough, commander of the North

Atlantic Blockading Squadron, to prepare an attack on the forts at the mouth of the Cape Fear River with "all the force [he] could spare." Among his warships would be the famed *Monitor*, fresh from her duel with the Confederate ironclad *Virginia* at Hampton Roads. But Goldsborough's mission was postponed when President Lincoln requested that his gunboats be sent instead to the James River to assist General George B. McClellan's advance on Richmond. Interest in Wilmington abated when McClellan's Peninsula Campaign ended in failure in early July 1862 and Robert E. Lee's Army of Northern Virginia invaded Maryland to threaten Washington. When Lee was pushed back across the Potomac River following the Battle of Antietam in late September 1862, Union strategists plotted a counterpunch against the Confederate capital rather than a jab at Wilmington.[7]

Nevertheless, Acting Rear Admiral S. Phillips Lee, who succeeded Goldsborough as commander of the North Atlantic Blockading Squadron in September 1862, urged the capture of Wilmington, considering it vital to the "public interest." After General Ambrose Burnside's disastrous defeat at the Battle of Fredericksburg in mid-December 1862, Admiral Lee proposed a bold plan. As he explained it to Welles, the ironclad vessels *Monitor*, *Passaic*, and *Montauk* would blast their way past Fort Fisher at New Inlet, while conventional warships pounded Fort Caswell at Old Inlet. As the navy shelled the Confederate forts at the mouth of the river, Major General John G. Foster would march his troops overland from Union-occupied New Bern to hit Wilmington on the north side, where its defenses were weakest. This strategy appeared practical, but soundings taken by the navy at New Inlet revealed that the weighty monitors had too deep a draft to cross the bar into Cape Fear River. More bad news followed. On New Year's Eve 1862, the *Monitor* sank in a gale off Cape Hatteras while being towed to Beaufort, North Carolina. After receiving the unfavorable reports, both General Foster's and Admiral Lee's confidence in capturing Wilmington was shaken.[8]

To the admiral's delight, however, Foster was not ready to give up on Wilmington just yet. He recommended a "perfect joint operation," with the navy transporting his troops down the coast from New Bern to make an amphibious landing at either Topsail Beach or Masonboro Island near Wilmington. He would then advance against the city. Despite their enthusiasm, however, Lee and Foster failed to generate much interest among the policy makers in Washington for a combined operation in early 1863. U.S. General-in-Chief Henry Halleck in particular was uninterested in Foster's proposed expedition, and decided to send Foster's troops to Charleston instead. "You are probably aware that the expedition was intended to go to Wilmington," wrote one of Foster's subordinates, "and after it was prepared to move the *Monitor* sank, and it was found the other iron-clad vessels could not cross the bar, and that the Government, in order not to lose the preparations made, ordered General Foster to co-operate in the contemplated attack on Charleston." Even the Navy Department, which for so long had advocated an attack on Wilmington, threw its support behind the change in strategy. If the only way the navy could get strong War Department and administrative assistance in the coastal war was to shift operations to South Carolina, so be it. "It is best, therefore, to push on to Charleston," Welles conceded. That the change in policy would also satisfy a psychological need in the North for a victory at Charleston was best expressed by Gustavus Fox, who wrote, "We should be inclined to skip [Wilmington] . . . for the fall of Charleston is the fall of Satan's kingdom."[9]

Disappointed by the turn of events, Admiral Lee nevertheless remained hopeful that the Navy Department would eventually empower him to strike Wilmington. Throughout 1863–64, he continued to stress the necessity of closing the seaport to overseas trade. Blockade-runners operated in and out of Wilmington on a regular basis, and the U.S. Navy proved ineffective in halting them. Some ships were caught trying to run the gauntlet, but the vast majority got through; according to one study, their success rate was an astounding 85 percent. Because of that, Lee argued that "Wilmington is of much more importance in a military and naval point of view than Charleston." Welles believed that Wilmington ranked almost as highly as the Confederate capital. "Could we seize the forts at the entrance of Cape Fear and close the illicit traffic," he wrote, "it would be almost as important as the capture of Richmond on the fate of the Rebels, and an important step in that direction." Despite the navy's persistent efforts, however, the War Department and the executive office remained largely apathetic toward the Cape Fear seaport for most of the war. Meanwhile, Confederate shore defenses to protect Wilmington were daily being strengthened and expanded, making the prospect of a later successful operation there more problematic.[10]

The government's attitude toward Wilmington finally changed in the late summer of 1864. In early August, Rear Admiral David G. Farragut sealed Mobile Bay, Alabama, to blockade-running, which left Wilmington as the only major seaport of consequence still open to trade with the outside world. Welles used Farragut's victory to convince President Lincoln of the necessity of closing the Tar Heel seaport to blockade-running. The war was going badly enough for the Union that summer that Lincoln had privately expressed his doubts that he would be returned to the White House after the presidential election in early November. A quick victory at Wilmington might reap political benefits for the incumbent chief executive, bolstering his sputtering reelection campaign.

Though Lincoln now endorsed Welles's proposal, he deferred final approval to the army's new commander, General Ulysses S. Grant.[11]

Grant expressed no enthusiasm for supplying an expeditionary force to attack Wilmington. In his opinion, he needed more soldiers, not fewer. Since the late spring of 1864, Grant's operational forces—the Army of the Potomac and the Army of the James—had been slugging it out with the Confederates between Petersburg and Richmond. He was not inclined to detach the estimated ten thousand troops from the ongoing campaign in Virginia for an amphibious operation along the North Carolina coast. Welles argued that severing the Confederacy's last lifeline and denying Lee's beleaguered forces much-needed food, clothing, and weapons could break the deadlock in Virginia. Indeed, it could well bring the South to its knees and help end the prolonged, bloody war.[12]

As political pressure built, Grant finally consented to provide troops to assist the navy in the Wilmington Campaign, although he set no timetable for the operation. He promised only to release them when the time was right. Welles understood Grant to say that they might be ready to go by the first of October. Eventually, that timing was affected by political as well as military factors. Major General William T. Sherman's capture of Atlanta in early September, and Brigadier General Philip Sheridan's triumphant "scorched earth" campaign in the Shenandoah Valley in the autumn of 1864, convinced a war-weary populace that the tide of battle had finally turned in the Union's favor. Exhibiting renewed confidence in President Lincoln, Northerners voted heavily in favor of the incumbent, giving him a mandate to finish the war militarily, and not by a negotiated peace settlement.[13]

Though Phillips Lee had long pushed for an attack on the Cape Fear River forts, he would not have the opportunity to lead it. Considered by Welles to be too timid for the aggressive campaigning necessary to close Wilmington to blockade-running, Lee was sent out west to take command of the Mississippi Squadron, and Rear Admiral David D. Porter came east to prepare the largest naval task force of the war. Sixty-four warships, including the navy's largest frigates—*Minnesota, Colorado, Wabash, Susquehanna,* and *Powhatan*—and an array of steam sloops and screw steamers gathered at squadron headquarters in Hampton Roads, Virginia. The fifty-five-gun *Colorado* alone mounted more ordnance than all of Fort Fisher. Complementing these well-armed ships were four monitors and the most powerful ship in the U.S. Navy, the *New Ironsides*.[14]

Porter figured it would take all the heavy firepower he could muster to demolish Fort Fisher, his principal target. Although the Navy Department had considered an alternative plan of attacking the Confederate forts at Old Inlet and then moving up the Cape Fear River to hit the defenses at New Inlet from the rear, Porter argued that capturing Fort Fisher would prevent blockade-runners from getting to Wilmington's docks through either passageway. Blockade-runners entering through Old Inlet could not ascend the Cape Fear River above Fort Fisher at New Inlet once it was in Federal hands.

In late October 1864, military authorities at Wilmington received good intelligence that Federal forces were preparing to attack. To lead the defense, Confederate President Jefferson Davis sent General Braxton Bragg to the Cape Fear port. Bragg was by then the most vilified officer in the Confederate army, but he remained a favorite of the president. Just as Admiral Lee was replaced on the eve of battle by David D. Porter, W. H. C. Whiting, who had supervised Wilmington's defense for two years, was superseded by Braxton Bragg. Davis's critics claimed that sending Bragg to take over command at Wilmington was a big mistake. "General Bragg is going to Wilmington," the *Richmond Enquirer* announced. "Goodbye Wilmington."[15]

Ironically, Bragg's controversial appointment to command at Wilmington coincided with General Lee's dire warning that "if Wilmington fell, he could not maintain his army." The message was clear. The survival of the Army of Northern Virginia depended on the survival of Wilmington as a blockade-running seaport. Ever the dutiful subordinate to the president, however, Lee declined to challenge Davis's questionable decision to send Bragg southward. To help defend the seaport, Lee dispatched one of his finest divisions, commanded by Major General Robert F. Hoke, from the lines around Petersburg on December 21, 1864. As Hoke's 6,400 reinforcements traveled by rail toward Wilmington, Union forces made final preparations for their attack at the Cape Fear.[16]

The politics of command also haunted Federal forces. General Grant had handpicked Major General Godfrey Weitzel to lead a 6,500-man expeditionary force—comprising Brigadier General Adelbert Ames's Second Division of white troops from the 24th Army Corps, and two brigades of U.S. Colored Troops, commanded by Brigadier General Charles J. Paine of the Third Division, 25th Army Corps, Army of the James—for the Fort Fisher expedition. But Weitzel's superior officer, Major General Benjamin F. Butler, commander of the U.S. Department of Southeastern Virginia and North Carolina, finagled his way into taking over effective command. Much to Admiral Porter's chagrin, Grant did not intervene on Weitzel's behalf. There was bad blood between Porter and Butler going back to the combined operations against New Orleans in the spring of 1862, in which Butler had been openly critical of Porter's role in the campaign. The history of combined operations in the war to date had shown that success depended greatly on the ability and willingness of the army and navy commanders to work together. The fact that Butler and Porter disliked each other did not bode well for the mission.

Porter was anxious to proceed, but Butler proposed that instead of launching a conventional attack, Fort Fisher could be destroyed with a giant floating bomb. His idea was to pack a ship to the gills with three hundred tons of gunpowder, run it ashore near the fort, and detonate it. Butler believed that the simultaneous explosion of such an immense quantity of gunpowder would create tornado force winds that would blow down the sand walls of the mighty fortress, stun its defenders, and allow his troops to march in and sweep up the Confederate garrison's survivors. Such a naval experiment had not been tried before, but Butler believed that if successful, it would revolutionize warfare against harbor defenses. As far-fetched as it seemed to naval ordnance experts and to both Grant and Lincoln, Butler and his supporters insisted that it was worth trying, especially if it might save the lives of good Union men. For his part, Porter was cautiously optimistic and willing to try it if it got the campaign underway. The navy selected the USS *Louisiana*, a patrol ship in Pamlico Sound, North Carolina, for the mission, and Butler spent much of the autumn preparing his pet project.[17]

Porter's grand armada and Butler's army transports finally sailed from Hampton Roads on December 13, with plans to rendezvous off the Cape Fear a few days later. The navy's arrival, however, was delayed by a stopover at Beaufort, North Carolina, to take on more supplies and ammunition, as well as by bad weather. Butler's ships tried to ride out a heavy gale off the Cape Fear coast as they waited for the navy, but soon had to put into Beaufort to replenish their stocks of coal and water and allow seasick soldiers to recover.

As Butler's ships refitted, Porter proceeded toward Fort Fisher. When Butler did not reappear within a short time, Porter decided to launch the attack without him. Though the whole idea was for the powder vessel to open the way for the Union army, Porter deployed the *Louisiana* before the army arrived. He may have calculated that if it succeeded, the navy was on hand to reap the laurels of success, and if it failed, Porter could blame Butler for wasting valuable time, money, and resources on the absurd project.

As it turned out, the *Louisiana*, which was loaded with only 215 tons of gunpowder, much less than Butler had planned, did little more than make enough noise to awaken Fort Fisher's slumbering garrison when it was detonated after midnight on Christmas Eve. "There's a fizzle!" remarked Commander Alexander C. Rhind of the USS *Agawam*. "The powder boat proved an ignominious failure," added Lieutenant Commander Thomas H. Selfridge of the USS *Huron*. Goaded by Porter, critics dubbed the failed experiment "Butler's Folly" and "Butler's Toy."[18]

Porter then determined to reduce Fort Fisher the old-fashioned way—by naval bombardment. The *New Ironsides* "opened the ball" at 12:40 P.M. on Christmas Eve, firing a big eleven-inch shell at the imposing sand fort. Colonel Lamb answered with a ten-inch Columbiad from one of his sea-face batteries. This rather prosaic exchange opened the largest naval bombardment of the Civil War, with Porter's warships firing 20,271 shot and shell at the sand bastion on December 24–25. Fort Fisher responded with a total of 1,272 projectiles from its low stock of ammunition.[19]

Bursting Union shells set wooden barracks and buildings on fire and knocked down Colonel Lamb's brick headquarters, but otherwise caused surprisingly little damage to the fort's sand ramparts and few casualties among the garrison. As Lamb and Whiting had anticipated, both the stout defenses and defenders held their own. Assisting Lamb inside the fort was General Whiting, who was there as an adviser to his protégé and as a volunteer combatant. His presence inspired the gray-uniformed soldiers, who greatly admired and respected the diminutive commander whom they endearingly called "Little Billy."

Butler's transports finally returned from Beaufort late in the afternoon on December 24, but after the failure of his powder boat experiment, the general was in no mood to cooperate with Porter. He was convinced that his rival had deliberately sabotaged the project to make him look foolish. Consequently, Butler sent ashore only about one-third of his 6,500 troops near Fort Fisher on Christmas Day. A reconnaissance force, led by General Weitzel, marched down Federal Point toward the fort but soon reported that, despite the intensity of Porter's naval bombardment, neither Fort Fisher nor its armament had been damaged enough to warrant a ground assault. Weitzel concluded that a frontal attack against the still-imposing defenses would be suicidal. In receipt of Weitzel's report, and still seething with anger at Porter, Butler decided to abort the mission altogether. He withdrew his troops from onshore and sailed back to Virginia on December 26.[20]

The failure of the Union effort at Fort Fisher led to a lot of finger-pointing in Washington. Porter laid the blame entirely on the army, and especially on Butler. "There never was a fort that invited soldiers to walk in and take possession more plainly than Fort Fisher," the admiral complained to Welles. Grant was inclined to believe Porter and consequently relieved Butler of his command, sending him packing to his home in Lowell, Massachusetts. Then, while Butler's Democratic supporters huffed and puffed and a formal investigation began in Washington, Grant got serious about renewing military operations at the Cape Fear. Though he had been indifferent toward the first expedition, Grant now took a keen interest in not just sealing the harbor to blockade-running, but taking Wilmington itself. As it turned out, the Fort Fisher debacle had been offset by a concurrent victory on the Georgia coast. After capturing Atlanta in early September 1864, Major General William T. Sherman led a sixty-thousand-man legion virtually unopposed across the state and into Savannah. He presented the city to President Lincoln as a Christmas gift.[21]

Glad to see Sherman safe on the coast, Grant was now eager to transfer his army by sea to Virginia to reinforce his own armies along the Petersburg-Richmond front. But Sherman had an audacious plan in mind instead. He proposed to march to Virginia by way of the Carolinas, destroying supply depots and railroads along the way. If need be, he could strike Wilmington from the rear. Sherman believed that his advance would force Robert E. Lee to abandon his entrenched positions and into open ground where Grant and Sherman together stood a better chance of defeating him. Sherman's plan and his confidence in it greatly encouraged Grant. The crowning achievement might well be the defeat of the Confederacy and the end of the four-year war. At the very least, the commanding general hoped that a successful campaign would keep the South and its armies in disarray. Grant authorized Sherman to begin his "Northern expedition without delay."[22]

Having agreed to Sherman's bold plan, Grant determined to guarantee its success by furnishing his trusted ally with fresh reinforcements and adequate supplies, or, if necessary, a haven on the seacoast halfway between Petersburg and Savannah where he could retreat in case he got into trouble. Wilmington suddenly took on a whole new meaning for Grant. Possession of the Cape Fear River and the city's railroads would enable him to forward men and supplies to Sherman once he reached North Carolina. Grant now put Wilmington squarely in his crosshairs.[23]

As Sherman prepared for his grand march into the Carolinas, Grant renewed the campaign against Wilmington, with the city itself now the principal target. Grant replaced the deposed Butler with the affable Brevet Major General Alfred H. Terry, First Division commander in the 24th Army Corps, and he instructed Terry to work harmoniously with the difficult but steadfast David D. Porter. "It is exceedingly desirable that the most complete understanding should exist between yourself and the naval commander," Grant informed his new appointee. Terry's Provisional Corps, as it was officially designated, comprised the same troops from Butler's failed attack plus one brigade from the First Division, 24th Army Corps, and support personnel for a total of about 9,600 men.[24]

This time there was genuine cooperation between the services. Porter's warships and Terry's transports reached Fort Fisher late on the night of January 12, 1865. Braxton Bragg, ensconced with Hoke's division in Wilmington, was unprepared to contest the landing of Union troops on Federal Point early the following morning. By the time Bragg and his soldiers reached the area, the enemy had already established a beachhead. Union warships provided covering fire for Terry's troops as they were ferried ashore, while, at the same time, they kept up a fierce bombardment of Fort Fisher. For two and a half days, January 13–15, Porter's slightly scaled-down task force of fifty-eight ships pummeled the bastion with 19,682 projectiles. Porter instructed his gunboat commanders to concentrate their ships' fire on the fort's northward-facing artillery that swept the ground across which the army planned to advance. The admiral also determined to share in the army's ground assault by putting ashore a contingent of sailors and marines from various ships in the fleet.[25]

The intense shelling soon drove most of Fort Fisher's defenders into their underground bombproofs. During the height of the bombardment on January 15, Lamb counted 100 shells exploding in his fort in one minute's time. About 350 of Lamb's 1,550 defenders were killed or wounded, and all but one of the fort's cannons on the land face were destroyed or dismounted from their carriages. Whiting sent repeated messages to Bragg, now dug in with Hoke's division at Sugar Loaf Hill four miles north of Fort Fisher, pleading for reinforcements. Not until after sunrise on January 15 did Bragg act in response to Whiting's appeals, landing a troop transport along the riverfront in plain view of the Union fleet. Only several hundred South Carolina soldiers had disembarked before some of the enemy's warships redirected their cannon fire toward the Confederate vessel and drove it off.[26]

After three days of heavy naval bombardment, the Union ground assault began late on the afternoon of January 15. In a symbolic gesture of interservice cooperation, the warships simultaneously blew their steam whistles to signal the advance. But the cooperation was more than symbolic, for in addition to the 3,200 blue-uniformed soldiers of General Ames's division who charged Fort Fisher's battered ramparts near the riverfront, a column of more than 2,200 sailors and marines, which had been landed earlier that morning, stormed down the sea beach. The seamen met blistering musketry from hundreds of Confederate soldiers directed by both Colonel Lamb and General Whiting. They attempted to mount the fort at the Northeast Bastion where the land and sea faces intersected. In less than thirty minutes, however, almost three hundred sailors and marines lay dead and wounded along the oceanfront, while the stunned survivors fled back up the beach.

Although Porter's shore party failed to breach the defenses, its efforts distracted the attention of a large portion of the fort's garrison and enabled the Union army to establish a foothold on the land front's weakly defended west end. The courageous Whiting personally led a counterattack in an attempt to drive the Federal troops out of the fort, but he was severely wounded in the action and removed from the battlefield.

The battle for possession of Fort Fisher now became a soldiers' fight. Hand-to-hand combat and firefights of rifle musketry raged for hours. Colonel Lamb rallied his men for one last counterattack late in the afternoon, but he too was dangerously wounded and taken to the post hospital. Neither Lamb nor Whiting returned to the battle. By 9:00 P.M. the remnants of Fort Fisher's vastly outnumbered and exhausted garrison abandoned the defenses and retreated toward Battery Buchanan, an auxiliary work at the tip of Federal Point. There they hoped to be reinforced by General Bragg or evacuated by boats to the safety of the west side of the Cape Fear River. But frightened Confederate sailors and marines stationed at Battery Buchanan had surreptitiously abandoned the site, taking all the boats with them. Fort Fisher's garrison, including the badly wounded Lamb and Whiting, now had no choice but to await their fate. Union troops caught up with them around 10:00 P.M. on January 15. General Terry personally accepted the fort's surrender from General Whiting, who was lying on a stretcher in the sand. This time there was no finger-pointing on the part of the victorious Union leaders, only praise. "[Terry] is my beau ideal of a soldier and a gentleman," Porter informed Welles. Terry evinced a similar statement of respect for the admiral.[27]

Having sacrificed Fort Fisher to save Wilmington, Bragg now believed he had to abandon the forts at the mouth of the Cape Fear River and withdraw their garrisons to a new northern defensive line anchored at Sugar Loaf on the east side of the waterway and Fort Anderson directly opposite on the west bank. Bragg's evacuation of the defenses south of Fort Fisher allowed Federal forces to quickly gain control of the estuary, which effectively sealed off Wilmington from the sea and ended blockade-running there.[28]

The city of Wilmington, however, was the Federals' primary target. Excited by his corps' success at Fort Fisher, Terry was eager to push upriver at once. Porter, however, cautioned against a premature advance. While he respected the general's audacity, he thought it best to wait until reinforcements arrived to replace the army's casualties from the battle at Fort Fisher. The navy's ammunition also needed replenishing. For a time, conditions were unfavorable for campaigning anyway. Blustery winds, freezing temperatures, and incessant rains in late January and early February kept both armies huddled in their entrenched encampments. Despite the inclement weather for military operations, Grant was so intent on capturing Wilmington that he traveled from Virginia to the Cape Fear to confer with Porter and Terry. Accompanying him were Gustavus V. Fox and Major General John M. Schofield, commander of the 23rd Army Corps, Army of the Ohio. During the night of January 28, the commanders studied maps and charts on board Porter's flagship *Malvern* on the Cape Fear River, perhaps jogging memories of the frequent and productive meetings Grant, Sherman, and Porter enjoyed on board Porter's flagship *Blackhawk* during the Vicksburg Campaign. Grant was now determined to hammer out a strategy to open the railways between the seacoast and Goldsboro, North Carolina, so as to meet Sherman with reinforcements and supplies.

Sherman was ready to invade the Carolinas, targeting Columbia, South Carolina, first, and then Fayetteville, North Carolina, where there were Confederate armories. Sherman's real objective, however, was Goldsboro, the capture of which would be advantageous for two main reasons. First, it was the junction of two coastal railroads: the Wilmington and Weldon, and the Atlantic and North Carolina, both of which could be used to aid Sherman. Second, from Goldsboro, Sherman could easily strike the state capital of Raleigh, where Confederate supplies from Wilmington were being sent, or continue his march up the Wilmington and Weldon line to attack Lee's army from the south. With Fort Fisher now in Union hands, Sherman saw little reason to advance on Wilmington, whose fall, he believed, was now inevitable.

At their Cape Fear meeting, Grant agreed with the advice of his subordinates that Wilmington was the best point from which to move toward Goldsboro with support for Sherman. Although New Bern possessed a deeper harbor more favorable for a supply base, the Atlantic and North Carolina Railroad needed extensive repairs. Grant assumed that the presence of Bragg's army at Wilmington was an indication that the city's railroads were still operational. A bold strike might capture the rail lines and rolling stock before the Confederates could destroy or remove them. Moreover, while Union possession of Fort Fisher gave Sherman a safe haven on the seaboard, he might still need Wilmington as a place to concentrate troops south of Goldsboro in case he met heavy resistance during his advance. Grant therefore deemed "the capture of Wilmington of the greatest importance."[29]

Having studied the defenses guarding Wilmington's approaches, Porter and Terry recommended an advance by way of Fort Anderson on the west side of the Cape Fear River. Even if Fort Anderson's river obstructions slowed the navy's efforts to get upriver, the mainland in Brunswick County would offer the army much more space to maneuver than narrow Federal Point. In a true combined operation, the navy would bombard Fort Anderson and the army would attack the fort from below or attempt to outflank its west end. As was the case at Fort Fisher, cooperation between the U.S. Navy and Army would be crucial. Grant approved the plan, stating emphatically, "It is the best and only thing to be done."[30]

Porter believed that the Wilmington Campaign would require at least thirteen thousand troops, about four thousand more than Terry commanded on Federal Point after suffering heavy losses at Fort Fisher. Grant had foreseen such a contingency, and planned to bring General Schofield's 23rd Army Corps from Tennessee by way of Washington to support Terry's efforts to take Wilmington or reinforce Sherman's army in Georgia. Grant now concluded that there was greater need for Schofield's corps in the proposed move against Wilmington, and he ordered the general to transfer his force to the Cape Fear as soon as possible. Schofield's seniority would elevate him to overall command in the Wilmington Campaign. The vanguard of Schofield's troops, six thousand musket bearers of Major General Jacob D. Cox's Third Division and one brigade of the Second Division, 23rd Army Corps, reached Fort Fisher by early February 1865 and prepared for battle.[31]

The massive Union build-up on Federal Point worried Braxton Bragg, who informed North Carolina governor Zebulon B. Vance that he believed the concentration of enemy troops indicated a movement against Wilmington and then Raleigh at an early date. Bragg urged the state's chief executive to promptly forward all the volunteers he could muster for Wilmington's defense. At the same time, the commanding general began removing government property from the city, and threatened to destroy privately owned commodities—cotton, tobacco, and naval stores—that could be of use to the enemy. And then, as if turning his back on Wilmington as he did Fort Fisher, Bragg relinquished temporary command to General Hoke and departed for Richmond on February 10, 1865. From a public relations standpoint, the trip was an untimely blunder that only reinforced Bragg's lousy reputation. The general's explanation for his absence at such an inopportune time was that he had been summoned to Virginia by the high command to reorganize his staff.[32]

The day after Bragg left Wilmington, Schofield launched his attack against the city, pushing Terry's corps toward Hoke's entrenched camp at Sugar Loaf. After a heavy firefight, General Charles J. Paine's U.S. Colored Troops established a new line to hold Hoke in check and prevent him from reinforcing Fort Anderson. On February 16, Cox's division was transported across the Cape Fear River to Smithville, a small fishing village near the mouth of the river. Early the following morning, Cox began his advance against Fort Anderson ten miles upstream. Porter's gunboats, including the light draft monitor *Montauk*, which had been transferred from the Charleston blockading squadron in late January for operations against Wilmington, also moved up the Cape Fear River so as to cover both Terry's corps demonstrating on the east side of the waterway and Cox's division on the west bank.[33]

Porter's bombardment of Fort Anderson on February 17 enabled Cox to approach the stronghold from the south with little resistance, but failed to silence the Confederate artillery. The gunboats' deployment was restricted by the narrow river channel, which forced them to line up single file and fire their bow guns, placing the brunt of responsibility for capturing Fort Anderson on the army.

A reconnaissance of the fort by Cox and Schofield early on the morning of February 18, however, dissuaded the officers from attempting a frontal assault against the imposing earthen defenses. Instead, as the navy intensified its shore bombardment and Schofield demonstrated in front of Fort Anderson with two of Cox's brigades, Cox led his two remaining brigades on a forced march around Orton Pond, a six-mile-long lake on the fort's west end. By nightfall on February 18, Cox's rapidly moving column had brushed aside a small unit of Confederate cavalry and positioned itself to strike the rear of Fort Anderson early the following morning. Making Cox's force even more menacing, General Ames's division was brought over from Federal Point and joined Cox that evening.

Fort Anderson's commanding officer, Brigadier General Johnson Hagood, faced a desperate situation. His garrison of 2,300 soldiers was much too small to oppose Cox's large flanking force, the blue-uniformed brigades in front of the fort, and the flotilla of gunboats on the Cape Fear River. Hagood believed that he should abandon his defenses, but such a drastic move would require the authorization of his superior officer. General Hoke, however, was reluctant to order the evacuation of Fort Anderson because of standing orders that his positions must be held except in an emergency. A retreat from Fort Anderson would allow the Union navy to move further upriver and threaten Hoke at Sugar Loaf by naval bombardment or amphibious landing. Moreover, the evacuation of both Fort Anderson and Sugar Loaf would greatly compromise the security of Wilmington itself. Under the circumstances, however, Hoke had little choice. As one of Fort Anderson's defenders observed: "Having a very small force there to oppose [the enemy], with Anderson torn up so badly, and no heavy guns on our left [near the river], and a flanking force on the right with nothing to oppose them, we could do nothing but fall back." Both Hoke and Hagood were in full retreat toward Wilmington before sunrise on February 19, 1865.[34]

Federal forces occupied both Fort Anderson and Sugar Loaf early that same morning. Remarked one Unionist: "Fort Anderson is ours. The river is ours. Wilmington is virtually ours." Federal troops on both sides of the Cape Fear River closely pursued the Confederates, who fought a series of delaying actions to the outskirts of the city. After clearing the river of mines and obstructions off

Fort Anderson, Porter's flotilla advanced too, keeping pace with and providing covering fire for the army wings. The navy exchanged cannon fire with a series of Confederate water batteries, known collectively as Fort Strong in Union accounts, on the east bank of the Cape Fear River three miles south of Wilmington on February 19–21. By the afternoon of the twenty-first, Cox's brigades had advanced to the Brunswick River, within sight of church spires in Wilmington to the east. His light artillery responded to Confederate cannon fire from the city's streets, placing a few well-directed shots into the downtown business district, frightening local citizens and quickly ending the duel.[35]

With Union troops poised on the edge of the city, Braxton Bragg, who had finally returned to Wilmington on February 21, ordered its evacuation. Before sunrise the following morning, despondent Confederate forces retreated northward toward Kinston. Following in their wake, Union troops occupied Wilmington early on February 22, 1865. As it was George Washington's birthday, they considered their victory a good omen.

The Union capture of Wilmington severed the Confederacy's last lifeline of supply from overseas and helped assure the success of Sherman's Carolinas Campaign. The fall of the South's strongest fort and its most important seaport was of immense importance. "We had some very important naval victories during the war," Porter boasted, "but none so important as Fort Fisher. It's fate sealed the fate of the Confederacy." Though the Federal amphibious assault on Fort Fisher during Christmas 1864 ended in failure, the combined operation to capture the fort and then Wilmington in early 1865 was a model of cooperation, execution, and efficiency between the U.S. Navy and the U.S. Army. Here, as elsewhere during the war, success was the result of real cooperation between the two services' commanders and forces. The combination of Butler and Porter had failed because neither trusted nor liked the other; the partnership of Terry and Porter succeeded because both commanders respected each other and worked harmoniously to accomplish their mission. As Porter observed: "Our cooperation has been most cordial. The result is victory, which will always be ours when the Army and Navy go hand in hand."[36]

Notes

1. A Late Confederate Officer, "Wilmington During the Blockade," *Harper's New Monthly Magazine* (September 1866), 497.

2. Chris E. Fonvielle Jr., *Historic Wilmington and the Lower Cape Fear River* (San Antonio: Historical Publishing Network, 2007), 35, 39.

3. Chris E. Fonvielle Jr., *The Wilmington Campaign: Last Rays of Departing Hope* (Campbell, Calif.: Savas Publishing, 1997), 15–16, 20–22.

4. Charles L. Webster, *Entrepot: Government Imports into the Confederate States* (Roseville, Minn.: Edinborough Press, 2008).

5. William Lamb, "The Defense of Fort Fisher," in Robert U. Johnson and C. C. Buel, eds., *Battles and Leaders of the Civil War* (New York: Century, 1884–87), 4:642–43; Fonvielle, *Wilmington Campaign*, 34–45.

6. Robert M. Browning Jr., *From Cape Charles to Cape Fear: The North Atlantic Blockading Squadron During the Civil War* (Tuscaloosa: University of Alabama Press, 1993), 8–9.

7. Welles to Goldsborough, May 11, 1862, ORN, 7:341; Browning, *From Cape Charles to Cape Fear*, 274–75.

8. Lee to Welles, December 24, 1862, Lee to Sands, December 21, 1862, Lee to Welles, December 28, 1862, Drayton to Lee, December 27, 1862, Bankhead to Lee, December 27, 1862, and Lee to Foster, December 28, 1862, all in ORN, 8:317–19, 325–29; Browning, *From Cape Charles to Cape Fear*, 277–84.

9. Enclosure A in report of John G. Foster, January 3, 1863, ORN, 8:399–400; Naglee to Halpine, February 11, 1863, OR, 14:399; Welles, *Diary of Gideon Welles*, edited by Howard K. Beale (New York: Norton, 1960), 1:216; Browning, *From Cape Charles to Cape Fear*, 277.

10. Marcus W. Price, "Ships That Tested the Blockade of the Carolina Ports, 1863–1865," *American Neptune* 8 (July 1948): 196–241; Lee to Sands, December 21, 1862, ORN, 8:318; Welles, *Diary of Gideon Welles*, 2:127.

11. Stanton to Grant, September 1, 1864, OR, 42 (part 2): 624; Fonvielle, *Wilmington Campaign*, 57–58.

12. Rowena Reed, *Combined Operations in the Civil War* (Annapolis, Md.: Naval Institute Press, 1978), 331; Fonvielle, *Wilmington Campaign*, 60–61.

13. Welles to Farragut, September 5, 1864, ORN, 10:430.

14. Welles to Lee, September 17, 1864, and October 7, 1864, both in ORN, 10:467, 530; David D. Porter, *The Naval History of the Civil War* (New York: Sherman Publishing, 1886), 684–85; Welles to Farragut, September 5, 1864, ORN, 10:430.

15. *Richmond Enquirer*, October 26, 1864; William Lamb, "The Battles of Fort Fisher," *Southern Historical Society Papers* 21 (1893): 266.

16. *Wilmington Messenger*, June 15, 1893; Porter to Welles, January 20, 1865, ORN, 11:620; Porter, *Naval History of the Civil War*, 756.

17. Benjamin F. Butler, *Butler's Book* (Boston: A. M. Thayer, 1892), 775–76; Fox commission report, November 23, 1864, ORN, 11:215–16; Fonvielle, *Wilmington Campaign*, 97–103.

18. Rhind to Porter, December 26, 1864, ORN, 11:226–27; A. C. Rhind, "The Last of the Powder Boat," *United States Service Magazine* (April 1879), 230–31; Thomas O. Selfridge Jr., *Memoirs of Thomas O. Selfridge Jr.* (New York: Knickerbocker Press, 1924), 122.

19. *New York Herald*, December 31, 1864; Lamb to Hill, December 27, 1864, OR, 42 (part 1): 1004.

20. Fonvielle, *Wilmington Campaign*, 139–40, 145–49, 153–61, 171–72.

21. Porter to Welles, December 27, 1864, ORN, 11:262; Fonvielle, *Wilmington Campaign*, 192.

22. Grant, *The Papers of Ulysses S. Grant*, edited by John Y. Simon (Carbondale: Southern Illinois University Press, 1984–2008), 13:168–69.

23. Fonvielle, *Wilmington Campaign*, 192–94.

24. Grant to Terry, January 3, 1865, OR, 46 (part 2): 25; organization of U.S. forces at Fort Fisher, January 13–15, 1865, in OR, 46 (part 1): 403–4.

25. Porter to Welles, January 17, 1865, ORN, 11:436–42.

26. Lamb, "Defense of Fort Fisher," 649–50.

27. Ibid., 652–53; Terry's report, January 25, 1865, OR, 46 (part 2): 398–99; Porter to Welles, January 15, 1865, ORN, 11:433–34.

28. Fonvielle, *Wilmington Campaign*, 302.

29. Grant to Sherman, March 16, 1865, *OR*, 47 (part 2): 859; Fonvielle, *Wilmington Campaign*, 331–32.

30. David D. Porter memoir, David Dixon Porter Papers, Library of Congress, Washington, D.C., box 2.

31. Grant to Sherman, February 1, 1865, Sherman to Grant, January 29, 1865, and Grant to Sherman, March 16, 1865, all in *OR*, 47 (part 2): 155–56, 193; David D. Porter memoir, Library of Congress; Fonvielle, *Wilmington Campaign*, 331–32.

32. Fonvielle, *Wilmington Campaign*, 340.

33. Schofield to Porter, February 9, 1865, *OR*, 47 (part 2): 371; abstract from journal of Jacob D. Cox, February 11, 1865, *OR*, 47 (part 1): 927–28.

34. Chris E. Fonvielle Jr., *Fort Anderson: Battle for Wilmington* (Mason City, Iowa: Savas Publishing, 1999), 57–80; Ellis to his mother, March 1, 1865, Zaccheus Ellis Papers, Southern Historical Collection, University of North Carolina, Chapel Hill.

35. *New York Herald*, February 23, 1865.

36. David D. Porter memoir, Library of Congress; Porter to Welles, January 15, 1865, *ORN*, 11:434.

9

"The Absence of Decisive Results": British Assessments of Union Combined Operations

Howard J. Fuller

Well before the Civil War erupted in 1861, military professionals in both Britain and the United States had sought to learn lessons from one another about the changing nature of modern war. The Duke of Wellington is said to have regarded Winfield Scott's successful campaign in Mexico as "unsurpassed in military annals." Whereas the famed victor of Waterloo had relied completely on British sea power to support his operations on the Iberian Peninsula, Scott had deliberately cut his line of naval supply from Vera Cruz to strike quickly (before his army withered away from yellow fever) deep into the Mexican interior against the enemy capital itself. While this was a calculated gamble, Scott had demonstrated the full potential of modern "power projection." A potentially long war was kept politically limited yet militarily decisive.[1]

American officers, likewise, sought to observe what their European counterparts were doing, and in that respect the lessons of the Crimean War (1853–56) were crucial. The British army could muster only twenty-six thousand troops for this campaign, though that force was backed by the world's largest battle fleet. The admiralty in London, as well as the popular press, expected a naval coup de main to knock out the dockyard at Sevastopol in the Crimea, and thereby eliminate in a stroke Russian naval power in the Black Sea. Peace was sure to follow.

But their enemy was not so obliging. Facing annihilation in an open sea battle, the Russians stripped their fleet of its heavy guns and reinforced the surrounding harbor fortifications. Then they sank their own ships to obstruct the outer channel. The allied coalition was consequently forced to engage in a massive combined operation, landing troops—and then supplying them—3,000 miles from home, eventually digging in for a long and bitter siege of trench warfare and disease. One year and 230,000 lives later, Sevastopol fell. Present at the scene was the American army observer George B. McClellan, then a captain, who in 1861 predicted that "those who have the longest range guns and the heaviest artillery will succeed."[2]

One thing was certain: a full-scale combined operation was much more complicated, and more costly, than a direct naval bombardment. This caused considerable concern in London; while the British Navy had plenty of blue-water battleships, it had few brown-water gunboats. Russia was a continental power, not a maritime empire whose vital interests depended on command of the sea. Consequently a massive coastal-assault flotilla for what today would be called littoral warfare had to be hastily built from scratch at enormous wartime cost and almost entirely dependent on private industry (presaging the Union navy's troubled mobilization during the Civil War). Hermetically sealing the enemy navy in its own bases was only the first phase. When British and French steam ships of the line finally attempted to silence the granite forts protecting Sevastopol on October 17, 1854, they found themselves easy targets of exploding shell fire and red-hot shot. The British and French ran out of ammunition before any of the enemy guns could be disabled, and the allies suffered over five hundred casualties to the Russians' fifty. This was "not surprising," as one naval authority has commented, "since shallow water prevented any ship getting closer than 750 yards and most were much farther away."[3]

How much of this European experience affected the U.S. Navy at the time is unclear. In 1852 Samuel F. Du Pont reported to the Senate his belief that "whatever may be decided in relation to the national defense by fortifications," it would be "ill-suited . . . to the spirit of this nation to retain its naval forces in its own waters during a war, especially if that war was with a naval power."[4] Steam had opened up the high seas to American naval power. By early 1862, speculating on what would be required to reduce Fort Pulaski, Commander Percival Drayton wrote to John Dahlgren (then still commandant of the Washington Navy Yard) that "the fact is we got to carry on this war as others have always been, through the means of armies":

> The moment we will move away from our ships, take possession of the Rail road and threaten Charleston and Savannah, where they can only be threatened, the coastline of defenses becomes of very little importance, and even in our hands without the power of offensive operations, they do not amount to much. As I said before no war was ever yet finished by even the most successful desultory naval expeditions. The army has first or last to occupy its legitimate sphere of action. To bring matters to an issue, we might hold very prominent points on the enemy's coast and blockade every port and yet not finish the war in twenty years. The proper way to take Pulaski is to take Savannah, but the converse of this is not true by any means.[5]

And yet within eight weeks of Drayton's dour predictions, Fort Pulaski surrendered after a thirty-hour, long-range, artillery bombardment, and Savannah itself was effectively cut off from the outside world. Before the end of that same month, New Orleans fell to a Union naval coup de main led by Flag Officer David Farragut. It seemed the North might manage to avoid costly sieges after all. Certainly Gideon Welles and Gustavus Fox thought so.[6]

To be fair to Drayton, it was doubtful that the loss of its port cities, by itself, would induce the South to lay down its arms and embrace the Union. Blockade, isolation, and a good measure of strategic humiliation, if not public despair, might undermine the Confederate war effort—as it surely did—but critics of an all-embracing Northern "Anaconda" not only wanted the Southern rebellion quickly beheaded rather than slowly strangled, but they also expected more "continental" than "maritime" campaigns. In this context, the navy would have to support the army, not vice versa.

This was a notion unpopular with some U.S. naval officers and was entirely alien to British observers of the Civil War. Since at least the eighteenth century, the first line of both defense and offense for Britain had been her "wooden walls" at sea. Being an island nation helped. This British way of war, as naval historian Nicolas Rodger has observed, was "the use of sea power as a strategic lever to multiply the value of small bodies of troops." Funding European coalitions against continental threats, such as those represented by France, was politically more expedient at home than a large British Expeditionary Force abroad, especially since "coastal raids against a major power were not a war-winning strategy by themselves."[7]

These lessons were not lost on British war planners during the "Pax Britannica" that followed the American Civil War. One prominent British naval historian has argued that the "strategy of imperial defense" used throughout this era ultimately rested not so much on Trafalgar-like decisive battles at sea, or even the successful defense of global trade routes, but on the explicit threat of coastal assault. In this strategic construct, bombarding an enemy dockyard (such as Cronstadt or Cherbourg) "would facilitate the most complete application of maritime power to the problem of defeating a self-sufficient continental state." The same went for thriving commercial targets, such as New York City—holding them hostage to high-tech, naval mass destruction was "the key to victory."[8]

Or was it? A naval sword of Damocles, while it may have been decisive in various diplomatic crises between stronger and weaker powers, was always double sided. One nation's show of strength—one prime minister's bluff and bluster—was another's raison d'etre for renewed if not eternal defiance on land and sea. Naval power was always a short-term solution with potentially long-term consequences and political side effects for both sides. It was thus in an attempt to understand the nature of modern war itself that European professionals—

especially the British—took an express interest in the U.S. Civil War. As British military historian Brian Holden Reid has written, "It is the American Civil War, marked by a conspicuous lack of technique and organization at its outbreak . . . that signals the increasing social dimension accorded to warfare by the Industrial Revolution." Or as Rowena Reed asserted in *Combined Operations in the Civil War*, the massive but time-consuming mobilization of Northern resources for full-scale war on both land and sea represented "unsound military logic" when Southern civilization might be "paralyzed" by skilful combined operations rather than brutally crushed and eradicated through total, attritional warfare.[9]

British assessments of Union combined operations in the Civil War were liable to be inaccurate simply because few people in the United States, North or South, were certain how ultimately effective they could be. The nature and course of the Civil War itself was difficult to comprehend. British officers were subject to some of the worst propaganda and bias both from the Confederates inside Charleston and from Union officers commanding the blockading vessels outside it. Lieutenant Colonel Arthur Fremantle of H. M. Coldstream Guards observed that despite the "deserted state of the wharves" in the place where secession began, the people "all seem happy, contented, and determined." At any rate, Confederate general Joseph E. Johnston had assured him that "ninety-nine out of a hundred" people in the South "would sooner become subjects of Queen Victoria than return to the Union."[10]

British observers questioned the relevance of Civil War precedent; because of their suspected sympathy for the Confederacy, Union authorities barred the British from a number of opportunities to observe the consequences of battle. British military and naval observers were ordered to maintain their own strict neutrality: "to avoid all party discussion . . . [and] . . . to study rather general systems and principles, such as are usually considered open to all the world, and in which nations take a pride in offering their improvements to others; and to avoid prying into any details in which the authorities desire to maintain any degree of mystery or reserve." Even so, Union authorities remained suspicious. British officers were not allowed to board the monitors off Charleston to examine the damage inflicted on them in the April 1863 attack, and Edwin Stanton revoked passes for British observers to accompany the Army of the Potomac before it crossed the Rapidan into the wilderness in May 1864. All this tended to leave British professionals in the dark. "The attack and defense [of Charleston] are pregnant with instruction," concluded the commander in chief of the North American and West Indies Station, Vice Admiral Sir Alexander Milne, "but from the not unnatural reluctance of the U.S. authorities to admit of communication while the attack is actually in progress we are not enabled to profit as much by this lesson as is desirable."[11]

Moreover, British conviction that the Union Navy was hardly the equivalent of the vaunted Royal Navy influenced their conclusions. Just because the Americans were unsuccessful in battling their way into Charleston did not mean that British forces would also fail. One British report even claimed that the fall of Fort Pulaski at the mouth of the Savannah River was more indicative of "the wretched inefficiency of the defence made by the Confederates" than the skill of Union engineers. The cover of the June 18, 1864, issue of the *Illustrated London News* depicted a staged exercise of "Siege Operations at Chatham" observed by the royal family and crowds of Victorian civilians from decorative box-stands. The first act in this drama was the planting of charges "under the supposed cover of night" against a boom backed by mines in St. Mary's Creek. "In as little time as it took them to get fairly out of harm's way," the paper reported, "a pillar of water shot up, carrying with it the scattered timbers of the obstruction." Here was combat engineering made easy. Though the display was meant to demonstrate the latest combined coastal assault and defense techniques, the overall impression was that, thanks to a combination of high technology and spirited enthusiasm, such battles could be decided fairly quickly and neatly.[12]

Not so in the American Civil War. In describing General Quincy A. Gillmore's long-range bombardment of Fort Sumter in Charleston Harbor, the colonel of the 7th Connecticut reinforced Gideon Welles's preconceptions that lengthy sieges would allow defenders to regroup and make repairs. The Connecticut colonel could not understand why Dahlgren's naval squadron did not simply rush past Sumter and into the harbor. The colonel concluded that Dahlgren must be "feeble in health, vacillating in purpose and to all appearance wholly without that exultant courage which knows that these things *must* cost life, and having weighed well all the chances, casts soul and body into the struggle." But the confidential British *Report upon the Military Affairs of the United States of America*, printed for the War Office and the British cabinet in August 1864, sided with Dahlgren (and by implication with Du Pont before him) by declaring that "in order to reduce a well constructed casemated fort, it is now generally conceded that a force must be landed, and siege batteries (armed with heavy guns) erected"—in other words, that a combined operation would be needed.[13]

Of course most if not all professional officers of the British army (and navy) were making these reports not only to benefit from American experience and improve on their own practices, but also to gauge the Union's ability to wage war, and specifically to wage war against Britain. Episodes like the *Trent* Affair of late 1861 had demonstrated to Lincoln's administration that Lord Palmerston's ministry was not above making the most of U.S. weaknesses when it came to settling questions of international maritime law. If the government in Washington didn't like it, the British were perfectly prepared, it seemed, to defend Canada from another Yankee invasion, while sweeping the Northern blockade of the South and replacing it with a British blockade of the North.

The most ominous long arm of British power projection, of course, was direct naval coastal attack—a descent on relatively defenseless American port cities from Maine to Washington, the biggest prize being New York City. If modern forts could not stop modern warships—specifically ironclads—from steaming past them, subjecting the city to shellfire, and then repeating the process someplace else, then larger strategic mandates like the imperial defense of Canada could rest assured. The British were also concerned how coastal defense issues might affect their own sense of security—that is, how they could prevent French ironclads from doing the same to them. Yet given the state of New York City's defenses by 1864, the British *Report* concluded that "if an iron-clad fleet can run past one or more forts, and take up a position between them and the place defended, with impunity from attack, and further be a match for any auxiliary floating defences, it can only be said that that particular system of defence is defective, and not that forts are not a match for ships." This only confirmed the bitter lesson of the Crimean War: "that ships cannot contend with forts when the conditions are anything like equal." Indeed, "running past" forts was an ironclad's best chance of survival.[14]

The same could be said for the Union Navy in its several attempts to overcome Charleston's defenses from 1863 until the end of the war, the only campaign, according to Rowena Reed, that was "seriously studied in Europe" (see Chapter 6). If monitors could be physically obstructed, then the army would be needed after all for a combined operation and a lengthy siege. This was a startling conclusion for it implied the end of much of Britain's offensive leverage against the United States. A naval coup de main would no longer be sufficient; instead it might require something more akin to the costly siege of Sevastopol—or Charleston. Even then, as the siege of Charleston was making plain, the results were far from certain. "Notwithstanding the immense amount of metal expended by the Federal naval and military forces," wrote Lieutenant Colonel T. L. Gallwey of the Royal Engineers and Captain H. J. Alderson of the British army, "Fort Sumter still holds out, and at the time of our visit in April 1864, we were told that the channel faces were still heavily armed, so that for the purpose of reciprocal defence of the entrance of the harbour with Fort Moultrie, and other adjacent works, it is as strong as ever."[15]

Nevertheless, the *Philadelphia Inquirer*, for one, was quite content with Gillmore's display of heavy gunnery before Charleston. Just as the British watched Civil War engagements with one eye on a possible future war with America, Americans watched with half an eye toward a possible future war with Britain. If nothing else, the bombardment of the Charleston forts demonstrated to the British how much technology had changed since the siege of Sevastopol. In addition to battering the rebel forts, it kept the British "deterred by our successes, not knowing but that just as they put in their oars we may have the Rebellion on its back, and be ready to pitch into them with tremendous force." Because most of the British observers of Union combined operations focused on the efficiency of long-range American gunnery, it was significant that "the artillery of the Federal States is superior to that which has been used against them," and they concluded that "it would be therefore advisable to watch the future progress of the U.S. in the manufacture of Heavy Artillery."[16]

Of course, there were more British interests at stake than strictly the defense of the empire. Palmerston himself noted to the Duke of Somerset, the First Lord of the Admiralty, how the American Civil War had demonstrated "the value of Gun Boats in assisting Troops in a Country intersected by Rivers which communicate with the Sea and are navigable for Gun Boats, and China seems in that Respect to resemble America." This might ensure that the Taiping Rebellion could be kept "away from the seats of our Commerce." Parliament was also unusually divided over the prime minister's insistence on a whole new series of expensive coastal fortifications. The Union's inability to take Charleston seemed to attest to the power of forts in stopping even armored steamships.[17]

Likewise, Union failures in protracted combined operations supported the prevailing notion that the Civil War was terribly mismanaged by incompetent leaders who had been elected by the enfranchised Yankee mob, and was likely to end in a Northern defeat after years of unnecessary and "barbaric" warfare. The *London Times* declared that "the long delay on Federal preparations, their reliance upon mechanical ingenuity, rather than upon bulldog courage, have given their opponents time to turn Charleston, Savannah, Mobile, Wilmington, Vicksburg, Port Hudson, and Richmond into almost impregnable fortresses, which could not be carried by any soldiers upon earth without fearful loss." The *Times* attributed the Union's inability to seize Charleston to the fact that it was assailed by "men fighting with so little heart as is everywhere exhibited by the mercenaries of Mr. Lincoln." *Punch* likened Union frustrations before Charleston to a "Great American Billiard Match," where "Abe Lincoln may have skill, but he has not shown much of it: and certainly he more than once has shown himself out-generalled." Even Rowena Reed wrote of the "pernicious effect of government interference on operations," while Brian Holden Reid, in an article for the *Journal of Military History*, argued more charitably that "the points expounded by Victorian and Edwardian writers about the Civil War were developed within an understanding of the overall democratic context in which they would have to work."[18]

Presumably that "context" included what Lieutenant Colonel Gallwey described to Lord Lyons, the British envoy in Washington, D.C., on May 27, 1864, as Union losses were piling up in Grant's Overland Campaign. In relation to the "probable operations of the United States Forces in case of a war with this country," he was certain "the absence of decisive results which has hitherto been apparent in all the Campaigns of this civil war is a proof of the inferiority of the U.S. troops as maneuvering bodies and serve to show that the great mass of the armies can only be regarded in the light of irregular forces." This was to be blamed on the "general inefficiency of the officers (many of whom are nevertheless excellent, especially those of the regular army) and the spirit of independence which governs the men and renders them impatient of control." In short, as the historian Edward Hagerman put it, the problem was not Union reliance on machinery, but "a Civil War fought by citizen soldiers," and "public expectations on both sides for quick and dramatic victory through the test of battle."[19]

These contemporary observers suggested that if successful combined operations were a matter of well-planned, fully supported, pinpoint strikes, then victories in the Civil War could be attributed to military and naval professionalism in the highest (i.e., European) sense; while defeats were the obvious result of political intrusions responding to relentless pressure from the masses. By 1864 a popular and recurring theme in the British press, as expressed by *The Standard*, was that "the war has become one merely of vengeance, in which New England preachers and orators purchase the delight of torturing Southern women and children with the blood of tens of thousands of rowdies from New York, ruffians from the West, and mercenaries from Ireland and Germany, but in which the original purpose has not merely been forgotten but rendered utterly and forever unattainable." The ensuing mess was surely a "total war" if not necessarily a genuinely "modern war."[20]

Yet what of the impact of iron-armored warships in this strategic environment? Should Fort Sumter have surrendered as easily as Fort Pulaski? Would the burning of New York City by a British fleet have meant the end of the United States? Would the loss of Charleston have meant the end of the Civil War? According to Lieutenant Colonel Fremantle, the "official orders, both from the Government and from the Town-Council ... was to allow Charleston to be laid in ashes sooner than surrender it; the Confederates being unanimous in their determination that, whatever happened, the capital of South Carolina [*sic*] should never have to submit to the fate of New Orleans." With their predominant focus on Union military and naval technologies, contemporary British observers often overlooked the proverbial forest to focus on the trees. To them, the *science* of warfare was more readily digestible than its *art*, which often defied calculation. British leaders were surprised that the Confederacy lost, and historians ever since have been prone to explain the defeat in material terms.[21]

This tradition began with none other than Jefferson Davis himself, who reduced his explanation for Southern defeat to a simple inferiority of numbers. "The efforts which were put forth to resist the operations on the Western rivers, for which the United States made such vast preparations," he wrote after the Civil War, "were ... necessarily very limited. There was a lack of skilled labor, of shipyards, and materials for constructing ironclads, which could not be obtained or prepared in a beset and blockaded country." But this only begged the question of why the South lacked these resources to begin with; why cotton and slaves were anachronistic to victory in modern warfare by land and sea. It also said little for the defense of Charleston, which, Captain John Rodgers wrote to his wife in April 1863, was saved by the "obstructions ... not the batteries formidable as they were." In his opinion, obstructions had also stopped his former command, the ironclad *Galena*, from reaching Richmond the year before (see Chapter 4). His only consolation was that "the lesson is worthy of being remembered should we in a foreign war have our own harbors to defend." That same month, Boston industrialist John Murray Forbes wrote Gustavus Fox from London that British Captain Theophilus Alexander Blakely had admitted to him that "one ironclad ... can take Plymouth[,] where the channel is too wide to obstruct[,] or any other Port depending on Guns without obstructions."[22]

Such a prospect seemed not at all impossible in 1863. Transmitting a report by Royal Navy Captain John Goodenough on the "Naval Establishment of the United States" to Foreign Secretary Lord John Russell, Lyons considered "that in the present temper of the American people, advantage would be eagerly taken of any conjuncture of circumstances which would enable a declaration of War against England to be made with tolerable safety." Moreover, Lyons complained, such anti-British feelings were "utterly unreasonable and utterly regardless of facts ... the result of the annoyance caused by the civil commotion, which is the first check which has been given to a previously uninterrupted course of progress and prosperity." Reflecting on "the American Navy in the late War," the *Edinburgh Review* in 1866 considered it a lesson in how such "progress and prosperity" had actually worked against Union victory:

> Some will say . . . the chief thing shown is the possibility of creating, from private resources during actual war, all that a great contest at sea may require without that elaborate preparation and vast expenditure to which in this country we dedicate millions yearly in time of peace. The example of the Great Republic and the precepts of the successful statesmen which have carried her safely to a triumphant re-union, prove, when studied closely, the very contrary. It cost them years of toil and uncertainty and oceans of expenditure before the naval predominance to which the North had full right was completely asserted.[23]

Even so, the millions that British taxpayers paid were largely for the upkeep of a blue-water battle fleet, which counted for very little during the Crimean War, or against China, or Japan, or New Zealand, or against the African slave trade in the mid-Victorian era. Such a force arguably would have counted for very little against the Confederate States—and certainly for combined operations in shallow waters. In 1871, when asked whether "auxiliary vessels" could be quickly produced during a wartime emergency, Laird Brothers of Liverpool confirmed that "although a large fleet of wooden gunboats at the time of the Crimean War was turned out with great rapidity, the more complicated type of vessel involved in an ironclad would take a much longer time to get ready for service." The Royal Navy "could not place much reliance on extemporising a fleet of ironclad turret vessels after war was declared, and it does not appear in the present state of political matters that much time is allowed to elapse between the occurrence of the complications that may ultimately lead to war and the declaration which leads to action being taken."[24]

Indeed, the uncertain position of Britain greatly complicated Union naval power during the Civil War. Ships needed for commerce protection—British-built cruisers such as the CSS *Alabama*—were ships that could have bolstered the blockade, whose squadrons might have then spared more ships for in-shore work. The whole issue of "sacrificing" the monitors in a sort of mad dash against Charleston's obstructions, simply on a point of U.S. naval attrition, hinged on having sufficient reserves of such vessels (and their precious fifteen-inch guns) in case of a foreign war, or to meet foreign-built ironclad rams such as the CSS *Stonewall*. Seeking to bolster the contribution of his beloved monitors in the South Atlantic campaign, the general inspector of Union ironclads, Alban C. Stimers, wrote to Fox in 1864:

The great function which [the monitors] have already performed of preventing European intervention is of more value to the country than several times their total cost, alterations and improvements included, and really when you look at the subject aside from your strong desire and ambition that the Navy shall be constantly adding lustre to its fame I think you must agree with me that beyond maintaining the blockade the Navy can do very little toward shortening the present war even if all our iron clads were done. As soon however as this War is over, if not before, we shall have ships to fight and we may yet be thankful that we did not impair the efficiency of these new and powerful vessels by attempting to enter with them into those torpedo snares—the Southern ports.[25]

The message of the navy was that despite their disappointing performance at Charleston, monitors might still serve as war-winning "silver bullets," but only against the right targets. The same could be said for Union combined operations in general. As Robert E. Lee admitted to Arthur Fremantle, "The South was obliged to keep large bodies of men unemployed, and at great distances from each other, awaiting the sudden invasions or raids to which they were continually exposed."[26]

What helped define the American Civil War as "modern" was that popular politics and propaganda were becoming as important, and as decisive, as military professionalism. It is curious that British military historian Paddy Griffith's analysis in *Battle Tactics of the American Civil War* (1987) ends on the assumption that, save the stultifying effect of training programs, tactical doctrine, staff work, and engineers, "the Civil War could have shown us decisive results as dazzling as anything seen in the days of Napoleon." After all, Napoleon himself was defeated after Moscow was occupied in 1812; even then victory in war was not as simple as winning decisive battles.[27]

In recounting the events surrounding the *Trent* Affair, John Abbott's *History of the Civil War in America* (1863) emphasized that the "turbulence of democratic communities has been a favorite bug-bear with the possessors of aristocratic power. . . . The mob, it was said, always ruled in America; and now the mob was organized in five hundred regiments . . . and the administration must do as their soldiers bid them." On the contrary, American citizens were deeply disappointed "of knowing that those who wield the power in such an empire as Great Britain, should be so unwilling to believe that the common people would consent to sacrifice feeling, to the performance of what might be calmly deemed right, in the administration of their affairs." Instead, "the leading presses of London declared . . . that war was for her advantage, since she might then adjust the boundaries of her colonies at her own will, open the southern ports, and teach a lesson to the United States. The first steamers which hurriedly sailed from England, loading with troops for Canada, left the docks with the band playing 'I wish I was in Dixie's Land,' amid cheers of an enthusiastic multitude ashore."[28]

In any case, British assessments of American capabilities had to acknowledge that something vital had changed as a result of the Civil War; that pivotal events such as the Confederation of Canada in 1867 (the British North America Act) were a direct response to the perceived inability of imperial forces to resist the rising tide that the United States represented, ably or not, in world history. As Kenneth Bourne has argued, "The end of the Civil War in America confirmed the achievement of Manifest Destiny without presenting to Great Britain the expected consolation of a permanent disruption of the Union. The reduction and withdrawal of the garrisons from Canada was a clear recognition of this fact by the Derby and Gladstone governments alike."[29]

One of the most important observers in this process of assessment—a key player in any potential war with the United States—was Sir Alexander Milne. In October 1863, having completed a guided hospitality tour of the new defenses at New York and Washington, the vice admiral reported to the admiralty how he was "much struck with the 15 inch Guns of large size, intended for the Monitors and likewise for Harbour Defences; a considerable number already in position on the Eastern side of Fort Tomkins for the defence of the narrows at New York, and others are being placed on the opposite shore at Fort Hamilton; other are again being mounted on the new Forts on the Potomac for the defence of Washington and they have become the most powerful Gun for this purpose in the United States." Actually, within the year, the most powerful gun would be the twenty-inch-caliber, fifty-two-ton Rodman, firing one-thousand-pound shot with effectively twice the hitting power of even the fifteen-inch cast-iron smoothbore. John Ericsson had meanwhile devised plans for mounting twenty-inch navy varieties on the oceangoing monitor *Puritan*—with possibly twenty-inch guns for the *Kalamazoo*-class double-turreted monitors designed by the navy's Bureau of Ship Construction and Repair—had the war continued another year, or had the threat of war with Great Britain loomed larger than it did after 1863.[30]

Even more important than ordnance for defending New York (or indeed most other ports) were simple obstructions backed by minefields and guarded by forts. In many ways, obstructions were quicker and easier to construct than heavy artillery, and more reliable in keeping enemy warships out. A relatively low-tech line of ropes strung between Forts Sumter and Moultrie was enough to unnerve Union ironclad commanders in their abortive attack on Charleston on April 7, 1863. Another well-known fact of the Civil War is that far more

Federal warships, including ironclads, were lost to rather crudely fashioned "torpedoes" or mines than to enemy gunfire. (Indeed no monitor was ever sunk by gunfire.) In March 1866, on the request of Gideon Welles, a special Joint Board of Army and Navy Officers met to discuss the new role of ironclads, obstructions, and mines in relation to harbor and coastal defense. Torpedoes, the board admitted, "were more dreaded than any other sunken obstacles, more perhaps than shore batteries themselves." But the board's conclusion was that these would continue to serve as auxiliaries to forts, and that a reliable system of obstructions should be hammered out in peacetime experiments, however expensive, rather than hastily improvised during hostilities. Since it was obvious that Congress was not about to make these types of appropriations, Welles could only dissolve the board in July.[31]

Time, therefore, worked two ways. If the British were to carry out their "strategy of imperial defense"—characterized by a series of quick and lethal blows against an enemy coast—then they would have needed to attack major U.S. ports such as New York while they were still more or less soft targets. Offensive operations, indeed, would have to be rather meticulously preplanned (and prepaid) if they were to be suddenly sprung on a distinctly unprepared antagonist. By the beginning of 1865 the controller of the navy, Rear Admiral Robert Spencer Robinson, noted to Somerset and Sir Frederick Grey, the First Sea Lord, that "the Northern States would suffer little material injury by hostilities with Great Britain," and that "very little damage it is apprehended could be done by Great Britain to the coastal towns of America by hostile operations. They are well defended now by land fortifications and the war with the South has called into existence a large fleet of vessels adapted for purposes of defence." Likewise—and this is important—the British were distinctly not prepared to do this with the force they had available during the Civil War. Only the partially armored HMS *Warrior* was ready for high-speed trials by the spring of 1862. Further, she could not be docked in Bermuda because of her excessive size, especially her draft (twenty-seven feet), yet her remarkable iron hull attracted marine growth and therefore required frequent docking. In the meantime, even the original USS *Monitor*—constructed in a fraction of the time of the *Warrior*, the smaller *Defence* and *Resistance*, or even the emergency ironclad conversions of British wooden-hulled ships of the line—could close with and penetrate the five armored batteries left over from the Crimean War.[32]

All this severely complicated matters for British planners. As Robinson observed as late as 1869, "No great naval battle will be fought at very high speeds. Two fleets meeting each other, however anxious both sides may be to fight it out, will find it necessary to keep together and maneuver with precision. . . . The great maritime powers with whom alone we should enter on a contest for Life or Death, would be France and Russia. A war with America would be of so different a nature that the Navy required for that purpose is altogether a thing apart." In discussing the "essential" primacy of an armored, blue-water battle fleet, Grey in 1876 reflected, "When I was taking part in the administration of the Navy at the Admiralty twelve years ago, I brought the question seriously before my Chief, and pointed out that unless we did take measures to increase the number of our unarmoured ships and cruisers, we should be driven to the necessity of repairing old worn-out vessels in order to meet the demands of the day." This, too, said nothing for a coastal assault flotilla. Writing on the eve of U.S. entry into the Second World War, naval theorist Bernard Brodie maintained that the "fundamental purpose of sea power is to retain seaborne communications for oneself and deny them to the enemy.... Fleets may also be utilized for other purposes, particularly as a very mobile heavy artillery in support of land forces operating near the coast." But it was "the power to dominate transportation at sea and not the ability to function as an occasional adjunct to land forces that justifies the existence of a great fleet."[33]

Thus, despite the triumph of British diplomacy during the *Trent* Affair of late 1861, by the summer of 1862 Gideon Welles was writing in his diary, "We are not, it is true, in a condition for war with Great Britain just at this time, but England is in scarcely a better condition for a war with us." As reported by the *National Intelligencer*, the British bill for the *Trent* reinforcements was £973,000, which Radical leader John Bright typically condemned since it had inflicted "a sting" between the two nations "that it would take centuries to remove," but which Palmerston just as characteristically defended as "calculated to insure the continuance of peace." Though Palmerston later recommended to Queen Victoria that her minister to the United States, Lord Lyons, be decorated with a Knight Grand Cross of the Civil Order of the Bath, Lyons himself observed to Lord Russell that the ultimate reason the captured Southern emissaries were given up "was nothing more nor less than the military preparations made in England." He had been "sure from the first that [the Americans] would give in, if it were possible to convince them that war was really the only alternative." It was left to him only to present such an ultimatum politely. As Palmerston noted to a friend after the *Trent* crisis, "If we had not shewn that we were ready to fight, that low-minded fellow [Seward] would not have eat the leek as he has done."[34]

The critical side effect was how this loosened the purse strings of Congress. The original $1.5 million appropriated for three experimental ironclads—including John Ericsson's unlikely *Monitor*—had already been increased by another $10 million for the construction of "20 ironclad gunboats," and after the *Monitor* had proven herself in combat in March 1862, this was increased still more to $30 million. Within a month Ericsson was drawing up plans at the request of the chairman of the Lake Defense Committee (and the New York Chamber of Commerce) for a Great Lakes monitor "drawing 8 feet fully loaded; 6 feet 6 inches without stores, ammunition or ballast for canals." Meanwhile, a further $10 million was set aside for improved coastal fortifications and armaments, with bills leaping on the security-crisis bandwagon to propose a new, "strategic" canal network that would link the Mississippi River to the Great Lakes. As one congressman argued, "The enlargement of the Illinois and Michigan canal has, by the conduct of Great Britain, been rendered a clear, absolute, military necessity. A failure on our part to construct it would now be sheer stupidity. England has, by her canals, made the lakes as free to her navy as the ocean. . . . The paw of the British lion is rather too plainly in sight on these peaceful lakes."[35]

This was more true than members of Congress realized—but neither was it what they had in mind. A Royal Navy captain with the wonderful name of John Bythesea, who was attached to the Defence Commission of Canada, toured American naval, maritime, and industrial facilities on the lakes in the autumn of 1862, followed by a quick look at "the fortifications of Portland, Portsmouth, Boston, Newport, New York—the Navy Yards"—and "such iron clad ships as were accessible." The enlargement of the Erie Canal was still incomplete after twenty-six years, but more crucially, the necessary human and natural resources to effect a rapid change when called for were already in place at thriving port cities like Cleveland and Toledo, Ohio; some six thousand experienced shipwrights were employed along the lakes alone. "Foundries and machine work shops of every description exist at all the important places, many of which," Bythesea noted, "now employed in the manufacture of Agricultural implements and Railway rolling stock, could, in the event of hostilities, be employed in the construction of Marine Engines and iron cased Vessels."[36]

Indeed, by the beginning of 1864, Union military and naval powers had multiplied at an alarming rate, as war against the rebellion dragged on and on. Anglo-American relations, meanwhile, had soured. Lincoln's administration argued that the South was being sustained in no small degree by violations of Britain's neutrality, perpetrated by British subjects building, manning, and supporting Confederate blockade-runners, commerce raiders, and even an ironclad or two. Though the British clamped down on these activities before they became a fatal casus belli, Lyons wrote from Washington that "a War with a European Power, and especially a War with Great Britain is a contingency never absent from the minds both of men in power and the Public at large; and some of the measures taken, such as those for the defence of the Northern Ports, have little reference to the present struggle with the Southern States." Whitehall and the admiralty accordingly dispatched formal missions to openly gather intelligence. For the most part, with a sort of flattered pride, Union military and naval officers were happy to oblige them.[37]

The conclusion of their reports might have been expected. Captain James Goodenough of the Royal Navy confirmed that the Union states were "preparing for war against a maritime power by aiming at destroying its commerce and protecting its [own] ports with vessels of a peculiar construction, and by breaking a blockade of any its ports with [the] aid of swift manageable invulnerable vessels." To be sure, the Yankee monitors had obvious defects, namely a slow rate of fire, slow speed, and a severely restricted operational range, but Goodenough admitted that their cast-iron fifteen-inch guns were "perhaps superior to those cast in Europe," and it was "difficult to substitute an exact comparison between their endurance and that of similar guns in England." Perhaps even more important, the U.S. Congress had passed an act increasing enrollment at the Naval Academy to "nearly 800 students and the annual addition to the Navy on the same percentage will be from 70 to 80; which," he noted, "when the difference of age at the time of entry is taken into account is as great as the annual addition to the lists of Officers of the British Navy."[38]

Colonel Gallwey's analysis "on the probable operations of the United States Forces in case of a war with this country" also discerned that "having thus provided for the defence of the principal ports against attack, the attention of the U.S. Government would be directed (in case of war with England) to two main points—viz.: the destruction of our commerce, and the conquest or occupation of Canada." For the latter objective, Gallwey "assumed that there could be no difficulty in raising a sufficiency both of men and material, as the war would be a popular one with the masses, and there would not be that disinclination to enlist in either the military or naval forces which exists at present." Even with other ongoing strategic concerns, the Union might still unleash an invasion of Canada with 150,000 soldiers, though presumably better-officered British regulars and modern fortifications might still offset superior numbers, leaving the decisive burden of offense, once again, to the Royal Navy.[39]

At the same time, Palmerston and William Gladstone, the chancellor of the exchequer, were hotly engaged in a momentous debate over defense expenditures and the upcoming national estimates. "We must keep Pace with France, America and Russia," insisted the aging prime minister, "& we must not forget that the Fleets numerically smaller of the lesser Maritime Powers will tell more effectively than in the olden Time because of their modern Construction." The new race between armor-piercing ordnance and thicker iron-armor plating was also adding to Britain's insecurities. "With respect to Batteries," Palmerston wrote, "we are as yet unprovided with Cannon of sufficient power. There is little use in firing at an Iron Clad Ship unless you can send your Shot or your Shell through her Armour Plating—and I believe that at present with the exception of some [experimental] Armstrong Guns, and they are few, our Land Batteries and our Ships of War are not provided with guns that will send a shot through Iron Plates." Gladstone privately noted this interpretation of events held out "a dark prospect," and he replied "in a rather decisive tone, for I feel conscious of right & of necessity."[40]

The bigger strategic problem was that until Britain could overcome the Union's new coastal defenses—the power of which was demonstrated at Charleston, Wilmington, and elsewhere—she could not apply the same political leverage that she had achieved in 1861 by threatening to pounce on the American coast with her naval power alone. By the end of 1864, Palmerston again complained to George Robinson, now Earl de Grey, who was war secretary, that the Royal Navy still had no heavy guns "which would smash and sink the Monitors" and thereby keep the St. Lawrence open. Somerset had already reminded Palmerston that the "cost of providing guns of the description now required will be great. The guns and projectiles for the navy will be nearly half a million. Our forts also must be supplied with the new armaments. Bermuda should not be left without some of the heaviest ordnance, and Malta requires some for the sea-defences. Bermuda I consider to be the most urgent, and perhaps Halifax should follow." Milne's replacement as the North American Station commander, Vice Admiral Sir James Hope, meanwhile held little confidence that Britain could win a naval war on the Lakes. "The real question" he wrote, "is, can we in the face of the great natural advantages possessed by the Americans, obtain this superiority—and if so would the cost both in men and money not be so great as to render it much more serviceable to the Country to spend it elsewhere. I should view any such attempt as a drain and a most unwise one on the resources of the Country in no degree inferior to that occasioned to Russia by the siege of Sebastopol." As always, it was a question of balance between political ends and military means. "The one great dread of the prime minister, as it regards American affairs," the U.S. minister to Britain, Charles Francis Adams, wrote to William H. Seward in March 1865, "is that of appearing to be bullied." The same, of course, could be said for everyone.[41]

Thus, British scrutiny of Union combined operations in the Civil War led to a reconsideration of the empire's entire defense establishment. While many whistled in the dark by attributing Union failures at Charleston and elsewhere to inferior soldiery and poor leadership, many more recognized that the lessons of Sevastopol—and of Charleston—compelled a reassessment of Britain's historical reliance on blue-water battleships. In the end, however, the reconsideration stopped short of revolution. Coastal flotillas, even ironclad flotillas, might be the key to victory at places like Charleston, but *only* in places like Charleston; for most British strategic thinkers, the blue-water battle fleet remained the sine qua non of naval power.

Notes

1. Quoted in Kevin J. Dougherty, "Logistics Lessons Learned by Lieutenant Grant in Mexico," *Army Logistician* 35 (January–February, 2003): 34–36.
2. Clark to Benjamin, August 10, 1861, *OR*, 51 (part 2): 342.
3. David K. Brown, "Shells at Sevastopol," *Warship* 3 (1979): 75.
4. Samuel Francis Du Pont, "Report on the National Defenses," November 1, 1852, U.S. Naval Historical Center Archives, Washington Navy Yard, Washington D.C., 28.
5. Drayton to Dahlgren, February, 1862, John A. Dahlgren Papers, Library of Congress, Manuscript Division, Washington, D.C., box 5.
6. See, for example, Welles to Fox, August 16, 1864, Gustavus Fox Papers, New-York Historical Society, New York, box 9. At a Confederate Court of Inquiry on the fall of New Orleans, General Pierre G. T. Beauregard stated that Farragut's threatened bombardment of New Orleans "would have been a mere empty bravado, a wanton destruction of an immense amount of private and public property, which would have shaken at the time the Confederacy to its very foundations and thrown upon its Government a helpless population of about 160,000 non-combatants (men, women, and children) to feed and provide for when already overburdened to supply the wants of the armies in the field." Beauregard noted that Federal guns could sweep every street. "Without the command of the Mississippi River," New Orleans was "not worth holding as a military or strategic position." *OR*, 6:600–601.
7. N. A. M. Rodger, *The Command of the Ocean* (London: Norton, 2004), 270–71, 575–77. See also C. J. Bartlett, "Statecraft, Power, and Influence," in C. J. Bartlett, ed., *Britain Preeminent: Studies in British World Influence in the Nineteenth Century* (London: Macmillan, 1969), 174.
8. Andrew Lambert, "Politics, Technology, and Policy-Making, 1859–1865: Palmerston, Gladstone, and the Management of the Ironclad Naval Race," *Northern Mariner/ Le Marin du Nord* 8 (July 1998): 16; Andrew Lambert, "Australia, the *Trent* Crisis of 1861, and the Strategy of Imperial Defence," in David Stevens and John Reeve, eds., *Southern Trident: Strategy, History, and the Rise of Australian Naval Power* (Crow's Nest, New South Wales, Australia: Allen and Unwin, 2001), 112.
9. Brian Holden Reid, *The American Civil War and the Wars of the Industrial Revolution* (London: Cassell, 1999), 210; Rowena Reed, *Combined Operations in the Civil War* (Annapolis, Md.: Naval Institute Press, 1978), xxviii–xxxi.
10. See the report of acting consul Henry P. Walker to the Foreign Office, April 11, 1863, Admiralty Papers, 1/5851, British National Archives, Kew, United Kingdom; Arthur Fremantle, *Three Months in the Southern States* (London: William Blackwood and Sons, 1863), 181–82, 120–21.
11. *Report upon the Military Affairs of the United States of America by Lieutenant-Colonel T. L. Gallwey, R.E., and Captain H. J. Alderson, R.A.*, 1864, British National Archives, 33–34, ix–x (hereafter *Report on Military Affairs*); "Memorandum Relative to the Civil War in America," MLN/125/1, in Milne Papers, National Maritime Museum, Greenwich, United Kingdom. On July 17, 1863, the *Chicago Tribune* complained that "the London *Times*, with its nose in the air, talked learnedly of the Northern States being like Prussia, small in territory, but populous and prosperous, doing well in a small way, while the Empire had passed to the Great Slave Oligarchy."
12. *Illustrated London News*, June 18, 1864; *Report on Military Affairs*, 33–34, ix–x.

13. Hawley to Welles, August 31, 1863, Gideon Welles Papers, Library of Congress, Manuscript Division, box 22, reel 21–22.
14. *Report upon the Military Affairs*, 23.
15. Rowena Reed, "The Siege of Charleston," in William C. Davis, ed., *The Image of War, 1861–1865* (New York: Doubleday, 1983), 4:177; *Report on Military Affairs*, 23.
16. *Philadelphia Inquirer*, September 28, 1863; Lieutenant Colonel T. L. Gallwey, confidential report "on the probable operations of the United States Forces in case of a war with this country," July 19, 1964, No. 467, Admiralty Papers, 1/5902.
17. Palmerston to Somerset, July 29, 1862, Somerset Papers Collection, Buckingham Record Office, Aylesbury, United Kingdom.
18. "Ships vs. Forts," June 8, 1863, in Palmerston Papers (Broadlands), Southampton, United Kingdom ND/D/25 (enclosed *Times* clipping dated June 1, 1863); "Great American Billiard Match," *Punch*, May 9, 1863; Reed, *Combined Operations*, 386; Brian Holden Reid, "'A Signpost That Was Missed?' Reconsidering British Lessons from the American Civil War," *Journal of Military History* 70 (April 2006): 413.
19. "Confidential Report"; Edward Hagerman, *The American Civil War and the Origins of Modern Warfare: Ideas, Organization, and Field Command* (Indianapolis: Indiana University Press, 1988), 234.
20. *The Standard*, July 16, 1864, quoted in Alfred Grant, *The American Civil War and the British Press* (Jefferson, N.C.: McFarland, 2000), 57.
21. Fremantle, *Three Months in the Southern States*, 203–4.
22. Jefferson Davis, *The Rise and Fall of the Confederate Government* (New York: Da Capo Press, 1990), 2:20; John to Anne Rodgers, April 1863, Rodgers Family Papers, Library of Congress, Manuscript Division, box 22; Forbes to Fox, April 29, 1863, Fox Papers, New-York Historical Society, box 6. For the nature of the Forbes-Aspinwall secret mission to England, see Richard S. West Jr., *Gideon Welles: Lincoln's Navy Department* (New York: Bobbs-Merrill, 1943), 264–65.
23. Lyons to Russell, April 25, 1864, in James J. and Patience P. Barnes, eds., *The American Civil War Through British Eyes: Dispatches from British Diplomats* (Kent, Ohio: Kent State University Press, 2005), 3:157; "The American Navy in the Late War," *The Edinburgh or Critical Journal* 124 (July–October, 1866): 227.
24. "Birkenhead Iron Works," March 4, 1871, in Sir Thomas Brassey, *The British Navy: Its Strengths, Resources, and Administration* (London: Longmans, Green, 1883), 3:73–75.
25. Stimers to Fox, February 29, 1864, and Gillmore to Fox, October 20, 1863, both in Fox Papers, New-York Historical Society, box 9 and box 6.
26. Fremantle, *Three Months in the Southern States*, 211.
27. Paddy Griffith, *Battle Tactics of the American Civil War* (Ramsbury, UK: Crowood Press, 1987), 192. Brian Holden Reid refers to this as the "residual belief in short wards" (*American Civil War*, 65–66).
28. John S. C. Abbott, *The History of the Civil War in America* (New York: Ledyard Bill, 1863), 1:310–11.
29. Kenneth Bourne, *Britain and the Balance of Power in North America, 1815–1908* (London: Longmans, Green, 1967), 300; Bartlett, "Imperial Britain," in Bartlett, *Britain Preeminent*, 154.
30. Milne to Admiralty, October 18, 1863, Admiralty Papers, 1/5821.
31. Board to Welles, March 1, 1866, March 2, 1866, April 12, 1866, and July 14, 1866, and Welles to Board, July 14, 1866, all in record group 45, entry 367 ("Harbor Defense Board," letter book), U.S. National Archives, College Park, Md.
32. Memo, Robinson to Board, September 1, 1865, Admiralty Papers, 1/5931.
33. Robinson to Board, February 3, 1869, Admiral Papers, 1/6138; Grey's observations are in an 1876 session of the Institute of Naval Architects, quoted in Brassey, *British*

Navy, 2:267; Bernard Brodie, *Sea Power in the Machine Age* (New York: Greenwood, 1941), 91–92.

34. Gideon Welles, diary entry of August 11, 1862, in Welles, *The Diary of Gideon Welles*, edited by Howard K. Beale (New York: Norton, 1960), 1:79; *National Intelligencer*, March 6, 1862; Norman B. Ferris, *The Trent Affair: A Diplomatic Crisis* (Knoxville: University of Tennessee Press, 1977), 194, 197–98; Palmerston to Sullivan, January 26, 1862, in Kenneth Bourne, ed., *The Letters of the Third Viscount Palmerston to Laurence and Elizabeth Sullivan, 1804–1863* (London: Royal Historical Society, 1979), 319.

35. *Congressional Globe*, 37th Congress, 2nd session (June 30, 1862), 3026–27.

36. Bythesea's "Report on the Lakes of Canada, on Some of the U.S. Ports and Their Defenses and on Some Ships of the U.S. Navy and Their Armaments—with Plans," November 8, 1862, is in Admiralty Papers, 1/5791 (from Captains, B–D, 1862).

37. Lyons to Russell, November 3, 1863 (from FO, September–December, 1863), Admiralty Papers, 1/5852.

38. J. G. Goodenough, "Report on Ships of United States Navy, 1864," Admiralty Papers 1/5879. Goodenough's enclosed report to Lyons is dated April 12, 1864, and is accessible in Richard M. Basoco, William E. Geohegan, and Frank Merli, eds., "A British View of the Union Navy, 1864: A Report Addressed to Her Majesty's Minister at Washington," *American Neptune* 27 (January 1967): 30–45.

39. "Confidential Report."

40. Palmerston to Gladstone, October 19, 1864, Palmerston Papers, private letter book, April 1862–March 1865; diary entry of October 21–22, 1864, in William Gladstone, *The Gladstone Diaries*, edited by H. C. G. Matthew (Oxford: Oxford University Press, 1978), 6:308; Gladstone to Palmerston, October 22, 1864, in Philip Guedalla, ed., *The Palmerston Papers: Gladstone and Palmerston: Being the Correspondence of Lord Palmerston with Mr. Gladstone, 1851–1865* (London: Victor Gollancz, 1928), 305, 310–13.

41. Palmerston to de Grey, September 11, 1864, and Somerset to Palmerston, September 9, 1864, both in Palmerston Papers, private letter book; Hope to Somerset, December 27, 1864, Somerset Papers Collection; Adams to Seward, March 30, 1865, in *Papers Relating to Foreign Affairs Accompanying the Annual Message of the President*, 39th Congress, 1st session (Washington, D.C.: Government Printing Office, 1866), 298. For the contemporary British debate on ordnance, see Captain E. G. Fishburne, "Naval Ordnance," *Journal of the United Service Institution* 8 (February 1, 1864): 1–51. See also Bourne, *Britain and the Balance of Power*, esp. 281.

10

Union Combined Operations in the Civil War: Lessons Learned, Lessons Forgotten

Edward H. Wiser

The foregoing essays demonstrate that American joint land-sea operations, and in particular amphibious assaults, did not originate in the twentieth century as the U.S. Marine Corps prepared for war in the Pacific. Still, there was little formal study of U.S. combined operations doctrine and methodology prior to the landing on Guadalcanal in August 1942. This oversight is unfortunate, because to some degree every major American war has witnessed a measure of army–navy cooperation. The essays in this volume show that there was ample precedent for the massive amphibious operations of 1942–45, but there were also numerous antecedents for the combined operations of the Civil War era.

The first strictly American combined arms endeavor was Esek Hopkins's March 1776 descent on Nassau in the Bahamas. Hopkins has been both praised and maligned for his actions by contemporaries and historians, but he made history leading the first amphibious assault by the new republic. He exercised unity and clarity in command, established definitive, obtainable objectives, and possessed excellent intelligence of the harbor, terrain, and capabilities of his opponents—factors that would elude many Civil War commanders.[1]

In the years after the Revolution, cooperation between the services remained a small but dynamic aspect of U.S. overseas activity. The first years of the new navy found sailors and marines engaged in terrestrial adventures on the North Africa coast on several occasions, specifically against the piratical Barbary States on "the shores of Tripoli" in 1804–5. The U.S. Army and Navy cooperated to prosecute the war against the Seminole Indians in Florida between 1836 and 1842, and they teamed up again to penetrate the coast and rivers of Mexico during the Mexican-American War (1846–48). There were numerous other overseas landing operations by U.S. forces, mostly sailors and marines, prior to the Civil War. Marine Corps Captain Harry Ellsworth has documented thirty-nine Marine Corps landings between 1800 and 1861. To be sure, these were mostly small affairs and none involved the army. They did, however, provide a mild catalyst within the navy for consideration of a combined operations doctrine, "a set of principles based on the analysis of past experience as it applies to the roles, missions, and objects in the current operational milieu."[2]

The most important pre–Civil War American amphibious operation was General Winfield Scott's landing at Vera Cruz, Mexico, in March 1847. It was unprecedented in size, scope, and objective and broke new ground for the army and the navy. It was the nation's largest combined operation until Roanoke Island in February 1862, and remained unsurpassed in complexity until the second attack on Fort Fisher in January 1865. Scott's campaign was a near-perfect example of a well-conceived and -executed nineteenth-century amphibious landing, and was in many ways superior to several of the Civil War efforts described in the foregoing essays. It was the United States' first significant joint overseas operation and was executed almost flawlessly—despite the dearth of accurate combat intelligence and the decision to land nearly ten thousand men at night.[3]

In particular, the Vera Cruz landing was characterized by excellent liaison between the army and navy commanders. Scott initiated communications with naval component commander David Connor as soon as the former was designated to lead the Army Expeditionary Forces. Connor made coastal reconnaissance patrols and conducted intelligence-gathering activities at Scott's request, quickly passing the results along to his military counterpart. Since neither the civilian nor military structures delineated spheres of command and control, the on-scene commanders settled matters amicably between themselves without oversight or interference from higher authorities. In other words, it was the good sense and resourcefulness of Scott and Connor that abetted success. It would have made for a different outcome had they not been such consummate professionals, ready to consult and compromise. In some ways, however, this effective cooperation was unfortunate, for the success they achieved through voluntary collaboration prevented the development of any institutional doctrine for amphibious operations.[4]

The efficiency of the American landings at Vera Cruz benefited from the skills of an unsung naval officer who designed the landing boats so that three of them could be stacked one inside the other for an efficient use of deck space. Though he was under no mandate to do so, Scott deferred to Connor on the selection of "rendezvous areas, landing beach, fire support plan, and control of shipping." Scott recognized that his counterpart's experience leading the Gulf Blockading Squadron gave him superior and intimate knowledge of terrain, hydrography, and weather, and he was wise to avail himself of the expertise.[5]

The Americans also benefited from superior staff work. Men like Pierre Beauregard, Joseph E. Johnston, Robert E. Lee, and George Meade served on

Scott's staff and demonstrated their readiness for bigger things to come. It was a model of professionalism, coordination, and cooperation the American services would not equal or surpass until 1943, and it was far superior in every respect to the bungled Anglo-French invasion of the Crimea a decade later.[6]

The final word on the value and relevance of the Mexican experience comes from no less an authority than General Holland M. Smith, who commanded the U.S. Marine amphibious force in World War II. In *The Development of Amphibious Tactics in the U.S. Navy,* Smith devoted two and a half times as much text to the Mexican War as he did to the entire Civil War. He concluded of Vera Cruz and smaller operations, "Amphibious tactics reached a new level of development, which was little improved in the next seventy-five years."[7]

American soldiers, sailors, and civilian leaders learned much from all these antebellum examples of combined operations, but as the foregoing essays in this volume indicate, there was no effort to institutionalize a combined arms doctrine. Instead these incidents of combined operations were perceived as ad hoc alliances for limited objectives considered to be outside the norm, an activity that was (as Antoine Henri Jomini noted) "rare" and to be avoided if possible. As a result, Americans were politically, culturally, institutionally, and professionally disinclined and unprepared to execute combined arms campaigns in 1861. Interservice rivalry and cultural animosity were stronger elements than cooperation in the bureaucracy of the era, and the men at the top were noted for their egos and zealous guardianship of prerogatives of rank and place. The same rivalries and personalities persist today, but established institutions and doctrine have made them less dominant.[8]

Historian George Buker's comments about the leaders of the Second Seminole War era are applicable to those of the Civil War: "Many naval officers misunderstood the military role, and army officers failed to understand the seagoing functions of the navy." They were occasionally willing to work as a team "but unable to grasp the modern military concept of joint operations," and declined to devise appropriate doctrine, organization, and tactics to meet the situation. Generally, nineteenth-century American naval officers opposed the development and implementation of doctrine because of its perceived constraint on commanders. They preferred a more individual, intuitive approach that sufficed for *guerre de course* but was an invitation to chaos in the context of complex, large-scale operations.[9]

More than thirty years ago, Rowena Reed published *Combined Operations in the Civil War,* and despite its shortcomings and controversial conclusions, it remains the only full-length scholarly examination of joint army–navy activity between 1861 and 1865. Unfortunately, few scholars followed up on her pioneering work. Therefore, it behooves current scholars to examine the spectrum of

Civil War combined operations in search of common denominators that will help reveal why some succeeded and some did not—and what, if anything, in the way of doctrine, strategy, and tactics the two armed forces took with them into the decades following Appomattox.[10]

Not all combined operations were amphibious landings. They included raiding parties bent on destruction of local infrastructure and supplies, and naval gunfire support of an independent land force such as at Shiloh or during the Petersburg Campaign. Navy and army transports played an active, even ubiquitous role in mutual support. General intelligence gathering and reconnaissance was a function of both services, and they routinely shared their findings, especially toward the end of the war. Army forces garrisoned and protected naval installations, and the navy returned the favor with vessels posted to protect army outposts at places like Bermuda Hundred, Plymouth, and New Bern. The sea service also filled the blockade and siege functions in conjunction with the army on the western rivers at places like Vicksburg and Port Hudson.[11]

In examining the conduct and results of these encounters, one thing becomes evident: the longer a campaign lasted, the more likely it was to expose fissures along the army–navy fault line. Despite a determination to work together, sustained activities lasting more than a few days tended to wear away the initial goodwill of the cooperating commanders and expose the preexisting service distrust or even hostility. This led to rivalry, bickering, and disappointment. As Robert Sheridan and Mark Snell demonstrate, the Peninsula Campaign was rife with lost opportunity, and as Francis DuCoin shows, the interminable Charleston campaign eventually broke down the determination of the Union commanders to cooperate.

Successful sustained partnership went awry for many reasons. First, and most important, was the lack of a single overall commander or a clear command structure to resolve conflicts and allocate resources and responsibilities. There was no government mandate that compelled a naval officer to confer, plan, or act with army forces, or vice versa. Such arrangements were normally ad hoc. The appointment of an overall commander armed with a presidential order could charge his subordinates with certain tasks, as happened in the Union capture of Norfolk; without this directive, however, the two services blundered about without strategic direction or tactical oversight, and many procedures had to be invented anew with each undertaking.

All along the South Atlantic coast, the navy often devised ambitious plans only to find that troops were not available to cooperate, or the army sought to follow up a victory only to find that naval capabilities were lacking. Even when the two services had significant forces in a given sector, and shared both a concept of operations and an axis of advance, there was no guarantee they would work well together. Sometimes the Federals were fortunate, as with the pairing of Ulysses S. Grant and Andrew H. Foote or the team of David Farragut and Gordon Granger. And sometimes they were not so lucky, as in the combination of David Porter and General Nathaniel Banks in the Red River Campaign. The absence of unambiguous control at these levels made for ongoing uncertainty—a very dangerous state of affairs in the presence of a determined enemy.

Each plan and engagement was extemporaneous, dependent on local personalities, and often lacked clearly delineated areas of responsibility. Either service commander was free to depart from the plan at any time and without prior notice to his counterpart. Porter and Nathaniel Banks did well on the Red River until Banks decided to depart from the planned axis of advance and head inland toward a fateful engagement at Mansfield, Louisiana. This diversion of forces gave the outnumbered rebels a slender chance and they seized it vigorously.

Operational details were properly the province of the commanders and their limited staffs, and the outcome was dependent on their foresight and ability. Often with little or no experience, these officers had to improvise, and inevitably some issues went unresolved. Sometimes they managed to work together effectively in spite of the absence of an overarching protocol. At other times, simple functions like "combat loading"—the stowing of gear and supplies in the reverse order in which it will be needed ashore—were ignored and the mission needlessly endangered. Resolution via the evolution of doctrine, methods, and techniques—that is, standard operating procedure—would not be devised for another seventy years. This lack of an institutionalized amphibious/joint ops doctrine greatly hindered the Union war effort.[12]

Conflicts, real or potential, went unresolved or were decided through procedures that led either to amiable settlement or argument and hostility. Contingencies such as when to lift or shift naval gunfire support, how and when to direct tactical movement ashore, when to withdraw a fleet because of weather changes, and myriad other possibilities were often left unaddressed. Indeed, the vagaries of wind and weather were often ignored. Such moves could have repercussions, and often only Confederate weaknesses or the fog of battle allowed the attackers to escape disaster. This happened more than once, but the landing of artillery at Fort Fisher is particularly illustrative of the danger. Brigadier General Henry L. Abbot, supervising the siege artillery train, reported that on January 13 and 14, 1865, "the sea was too rough to land the guns." He finally got three thirty-pounder Parrotts ashore on the fifteenth before Fisher fell to infantry assault and the disembarkation was suspended. Abbot's guns were unloaded in the following manner:

They were raised from the hold and slung overboard, by using purchases from the masthead and the yards strengthened by a preventer brace. They were carefully lowered overboard, and placed on the launch (one at a trip), with very considerable risk, owing to the rolling of the ship. The launch was then pulled along the warp to the edge of the surf, and the gun rolled overboard. It was then dragged up by about 200 men upon a rope secured to it. It was a slow and dangerous process, and only possible in a very smooth sea.

There are very few days in a North Atlantic winter when a thirty-pounder Parrott rifle, weighing 4,200 pounds and spanning 11 feet, can be landed from a surfboat on an open beach. "On January 20," Abbott continued, "a storm drove my vessels to sea where they remained on the following day." Res ipsa loquitur—the thing speaks for itself.[13]

Perhaps that is why the parties involved realized their limitations and often chose to focus on less ambitious undertakings where both commanders and most of their forces remained within sight of one another. The doctrine and technology of the time and the characteristics of the mission affected the scope of operations, and in such a dynamic tactical environment, commanders could generally only control what they could see.

The composition of forces also left much to be desired. Apparently, most army commanders other than George McClellan and Ambrose Burnside believed that any infantry unit could be stuffed aboard transports, in stinking, crowded, unhealthy conditions, taken to sea, held in a floating prison for days, dumped over the side into small boats, taken through dangerous surf, plopped with uncertain support on an open beach, and still assemble, organize, and fight as though in a set-piece battle on a Virginia tobacco field. It was an unreasonable expectation, and several times only strained Southern resources prevented a Union setback. The navy suffered the same kinds of assumptions in trying to convert jack-tars to line infantry. Sailors traditionally make poor strike troops, but Porter and others were blissfully indifferent. At Fort Fisher, the Union admiral created new martyrs for the naval pantheon, and a long casualty list, by sending a battalion of sailors, armed like the Pirates of Penzance with pistols and cutlasses, against the most powerful fortification on the North Carolina coast.[14]

On at least two occasions the Union had the makings of a true amphibious force. Mark Snell outlines the success of William B. Franklin's division on the York River, and David Long describes the actions of Ambrose Burnside's Rhode Island division in the North Carolina Sounds. The familiarity of many of Burnside's soldiers with small boats allowed them to play a role similar to that of John Glover's Marblehead regiment in the Revolution, which safely transferred

Washington's army from Brooklyn. Instead of continuing to take advantage of their expertise, however, these men were sacrificed to the chaos of the Peninsula and never replaced. It was a huge policy blunder by the War Department.[15]

Taken collectively, it is evident that the Union harvested little from the past and had to relearn the lessons of combined operations the hard way. Early successes in North Carolina owed considerably more to Confederate weakness than Federal prowess. For years Charleston defied Union combined efforts at capture. Fort Fisher fell only after the first assault was easily repulsed. Surprisingly, only the much-maligned Ambrose Burnside enjoyed the luck and good fortune to produce cheap, useful, repeated victories along the coast. Their strategic potential was squandered by withdrawal of his force to Virginia and abandonment of the Carolina coastal offensive.

The failure to use combined operations and amphibious warfare to its full potential reflects adversely on the Union's wartime leaders and administrators, but blame also falls on the prewar service academies and strategists. Neither the army nor the navy bothered to examine and codify the lessons of the early U.S. wars, especially the Mexican conflict, a fact that indicts the institutions as well as the individuals.

If Civil War leaders learned little from prewar examples, postwar leaders seemed to have learned little from the experiences between 1861 and 1865. Instead, those who stayed on active duty and served in the decades that followed the war quickly adapted to the new realities of their service. They cast off the tactics of massed fire and giant flanking maneuvers that characterized "the late unpleasantness," and returned to the duties of the antebellum era: policing the frontier. It was a reflection of political and popular desires, and a task they performed well.

Manifest destiny—filling up the continent—was the popular postwar call to action, and Americans were more concerned with westward expansion and internal development than crafting a doctrine for amphibious operations. Consequently, there was no inclination or foreseeable need to evolve combined operations doctrine or training. Nor was there an external threat from across the sea. The United States remained a continental power, with no overseas possessions or vital commercial interests to protect. The "flight from the flag" occasioned by the Confederate raiders had decimated the American merchant marine and reduced the apparent need to maintain a significant naval presence overseas. Expeditionary warfare was again an aberration, ignored by the army and rarely discussed in the navy. Though much of the army was tied down garrisoning a recalcitrant, reactionary South from 1868 through 1877, this was considered an anomaly of the policing function that was not so different from keeping watch over settlers and plains Indians.

The navy retrenched and languished under the leadership of David Dixon Porter and the inept administration of the Grant years until its spiritual rebirth under James R. Soley, Stephen B. Luce, and Alfred T. Mahan in the 1880s and 1890s. Before the appearance of this scholastic trinity, the establishment of the United States Naval Institute in 1873 had demonstrated evidence of intellectual vigor. While the navy might have been in the doldrums physically, there were clearly signs of progressive thought within the officer corps, though power projection was not foremost among their concerns.[16]

The *Virginius* Incident of 1873 showed what a paper tiger the U.S. Navy had become. *Virginius* was a former Confederate blockade-runner that was employed running guns and supplies to Cuban rebels. The Spanish seized the ship in 1873 and hanged some of the crew, thereby raising a cry of protest from the United States. President Grant directed the navy to mobilize, and ordered elements to Key West as a show of strength. It was a sad affair. Most of the ships were Civil War veterans that had been built quickly, on a tight budget, and with little oversight. They consequently had short service lives, and in the malignant climate of the Grant years, with indifferent maintenance and repair, they deteriorated rapidly. Having gathered the "fleet" at Key West, it was thought a propitious moment to hold maneuvers. Alas, those maneuvers revealed that the ships and skills of the U.S. Navy were so poor that the sea service was unable to defend the American coastline, much less initiate an offensive against the moribund Spanish. The only bright spot was a landing party exercise by seven hundred sailors and marines that was lauded in an article by naval officer and author Foxhall Parker, who concluded, "Taking into consideration the fact that at least one-half the men were greenhorns, recently shipped, the affair was an exceedingly creditable one."[17]

A few years later, Lieutenant John R. Soley penned a comprehensive history of American naval landing parties, which he termed "naval brigades." Soley went beyond a simple narrative to discuss in detail desired features of organization, equipment, support, and tactics. The experiences of the Spanish-American War, specifically the amateurish landing at Daiquiri, showed that no one in power was listening to Soley and his colleagues, or was willing to act against the prevailing blue-water culture. Decades later, Holland M. Smith would condemn the 1898 Santiago landings, writing that the transports were kept too far offshore: "This operation was notable for the lack of cooperation. . . . Naval gunfire was not extensively employed. . . . The beaches chosen for the landing were unsuitable. . . . The Army had no organic field artillery."[18]

In fact, the operation was flawed to its core. Troops were landed farther from the objective than necessary and thus needlessly exposed to delaying actions. There were no provisions for landing livestock; instead, horses and mules were simply shoved over the side. Many of the poor animals, dropped unceremoniously into the water, swam out to sea and were never recovered. Fortunately for the attackers, the indolent enemy was not sufficiently organized, creative, or aggressive enough to take advantage of the opportunities presented. Otherwise, the landings at Daiquiri and Siboney could have become major disasters. Smith later commented: "This failure to apply the lessons of the Civil War undoubtedly emphasized the need in the Navy for trained specialists in ship-to-shore operations."[19]

A few other voices anticipated the United States' growing role as a global power and called for renewed consideration of expeditionary warfare. One was Admiral Luce, who, upon the establishment of the Naval War College in 1885, wrote that the graduate school would have eight dominate themes taught under the heading of "the Science and Art of War." Listed in the order used by Luce, they include: "1, Strategy and Tactics; 2, Military Campaigns; 3, Joint or apposed Military and Naval operations, treated from a *military* standpoint; 4, Disposition and handling of seaman, landed for military service; 5, Elements of Fortifications and Intrenchments; 6, Naval Strategy and Tactics; 7, Naval Campaigns; 8, Joint or apposed Military and Naval Operations, treated from a *naval* stand-point."[20]

Luce was clearly a creative thinker and prophet, but Mahan's narrower vision triumphed. It was one where the primary goal was sea power and control of the shipping lanes, and it remained strictly blue water in nature. Mahan argued for construction of a battle fleet, not patrol, escort, and landing craft, and in this the United States was not alone. Despite their imperial ambitions, the major European powers took little serious interest in combined operations beyond the occasional punitive expedition against poorly armed and organized opponents.[21]

Amphibious warfare, joint operations, and brown-water/green-water warfare had no place in the permanent military and naval policies of the late nineteenth century. The philosophy of power projection, of moving forces across the oceans to place them on hostile foreign shores, evolved slowly as the United States moved toward the status of imperial power. But military and naval doctrine based on force projection was still generations away—it would not be officially incorporated until 1954 with the establishment of the Armed Forces Staff College, now the Joint Forces Staff College.

World events in the first decades of the twentieth century transformed the national security picture. The United States obtained possessions in the Caribbean and Pacific, as well as worldwide commercial and diplomatic interests. Power projection, security of sea lanes, and establishment of advanced operating bases were suddenly worthy topics for discussion and war planning. The rise of the Japanese Empire, its success in wars against China and Russia, and its acquisition of the former German islands of the western Pacific led U.S. naval and military interests to view Japan as the most likely threat in Asia. Plans proceeded accordingly, and of necessity expeditionary warfare lay at the heart of the matter. The result was the development of War Plan Orange, the specialization of the Marine Corps as the national expeditionary strike force, and the first serious considerations of how to place an armed force on a defended beachhead.[22]

By this time, many of the lessons of 1861–65 had become technologically dated and largely irrelevant. As the navy and especially the marines began serious consideration of what might lie ahead, they looked for illustrative and illuminating examples from the experience of overseas powers. Japanese landings in Korea, Allied efforts at Gallipoli, and German excursions in the Baltic were seen as far more relevant and valuable than the blunders of commanders from seventy years prior. Thus the value of lessons learned from the Civil War had been depreciated by the passage of time, technical developments, and political events. The writings of pioneers such as Earl "Pete" Ellis, Holland Smith, and Victor Krulak document that the amphibious doctrine that served the United States and its Allies so well in World War II was drawn from twentieth-century sources, not the Civil War.

There were still a few lessons to be learned from the nineteenth-century bloodbath, had the new commanders cared or needed to consider them. Lack of unity of command or clear designation of areas of authority and responsibility bedeviled Porter, Farragut, Banks, and their peers. The new maritime doctrine accepted these tenets as so self-evident they were probably at a loss to explain why such simple questions had not been resolved by their predecessors.

The need for timely, accurate combat intelligence—which had been discounted by many Civil War commanders, who evidently assumed they could adapt to whatever the South, nature, or the elements threw at them—was fully accepted by 1920. Neither Burnside at Roanoke Island nor Benjamin Butler and Alfred Terry at Fort Fisher landed a scouting party to reconnoiter the terrain they would fight over.[23]

Burnside belatedly sent Lieutenant W. S. Andrews to make a cursory survey of the shoreline at Ashby's Harbor after he had already made the decision to land there and placed his transports and boats in position to disembark. Yet he did not order any soundings, simply trusting that the water depth was adequate—hardly a shining example of planning and leadership. Depth of water was not the only unknown. Marshy areas such as found on Roanoke have soft, mushy bottoms, and Burnside dumped ten thousand men in the water without knowing if they could make it ashore to dry ground with or without knapsacks, weaponry, and enough ammunition for battle. The most elementary knowledge of the area would have given warning of the possible problems, but the commanding general remained either unaware or unconcerned. Burnside was not alone, of course. Admiral Samuel Phillips Lee was disgusted by the refusal of army leaders at Cape Fear in the fall of 1864 to send scouting parties ashore to determine enemy dispositions, fortifications, roads, and the consistency and gradient of the landing beach.[24]

The twentieth-century warriors knew better and planned accordingly. Generally, the naval and military institutions had matured to the point where their leadership, staff abilities, and brain trusts were professionally and intellectually far superior to that of the Blue and Gray. What had been a vexing administrative and intellectual challenge in 1862 was solved (finally) in 1943, though only after many of the these same problems marred the U.S. Marine landing on Betio Island in Tarawa Atoll in November of that year.

The single most important factor that determined success or failure in Civil War combined operations was the personality of the two commanders. If they got on well, they had a high probability of success; if not, the operation generally failed. It evidently did not occur to anyone in power that an overall commander would have made the cult of personality less important and would have helped resolve other problems. Had the concept of a supreme commander been considered it would likely not have been accepted unless imposed by presidential authority. The institutional conflicts of the nineteenth century were fully as ingrained as they are today, and as usual, senior leaders tended to be creatures of ego, jealous of their power and prerogatives.

Most of these major shortcomings could have been resolved by political will or by soldiers with the independence of thought to escape convention. Significant Union errors of omission and commission can be traced to leadership at the highest levels, from President Lincoln on down. It might be argued that it is unreasonable to expect Lincoln and his cabinet to conceive and create a modern system of command and control, only recently established in Prussia, and years away from realization in Britain, France, or Russia. After all, as Craig Symonds points out, Lincoln did attempt to overcome the barriers between the services by inserting himself at critical moments in the decision-making process. Even he, however, failed to establish protocols for other combined operations, relying instead on the willingness of the commanders to get along.

It is not unreasonable to expect that the brain trust that brought about emancipation, radically reworked the Federal financial apparatus, established the first conscription act, and permanently interjected government into the daily lives of all Americans, could have designed and produced a better command structure had it so desired. There was even some precedent for such action: the secretaries of the army and navy codified command arrangements on the Great Lakes during the War of 1812, and the delineation of responsibilities facilitated American victories at York and Fort George in 1813.[25]

An examination of the president and his cabinet—in the political, military, economic, and social spheres—reveals a willingness to conceive and take radical action if it could further the Union war effort. The logical conclusion may be discomfiting to his admirers. Lincoln was, is, and forever shall be one of America's greatest presidents. He was a great American because of his unswerving tenacity and political brilliance in maintaining the republic. As a man he is an unsurpassed humanitarian because of his deep compassion and the manner in which he personally shouldered the ordeal of the Union. But as a military impresario, judge of military talent, and leader of the chief belligerent in America's bloodiest war, he fell woefully short more than once.

There is no reason why the war effort was not headed by a joint commander or committee similar to the Joint Chiefs. Lincoln seems to have had this in mind when he named Henry W. Halleck as his chief of staff, and army combatant forces were finally united under Grant in March 1864. But even this modern command structure was undone by Halleck's unwillingness to command and Grant's decision to travel with the Army of the Potomac. And in any case, this structure did not embrace the navy. Finally, Grant soon found, as many senior officers do today, that giving an order and having it followed in both spirit and letter are often two different things. Even after the army reached this state, the navy, though run by men of commendable administrative abilities like Gideon Welles and Gustavus Fox, lacked a chief of naval operations or naval staff to give its far-flung operations continuity, efficiency, and mutual support. A system to prioritize resources and goals was never established or refined. What existed was ad hoc, uncertain, and inherently unstable. With both services unable to fully organize and control their own houses, it is unsurprising they were powerless to suppress their institutional differences and agree on an overall command structure. This was the factor that confined successful combined operations to the tactical level.

The second restraining factor was the stunted development of tactical innovations and refinement of procedures. Union field commanders frequently showed daring and initiative in envisioning combined arms assaults, notions too often untempered by reflection, planning, and overall concepts and goals.

In training, structure, and doctrine, many commanders and their forces were too professionally immature to realize their objectives. Hindsight can be a valuable instructor, but it is difficult to justify the unsupported night assault on Fort Sumter (an objective that could not be used even if it had been taken) and the naval brigade advance at Fort Fisher. Had the chain of command been willing to nurture a culture of professionalism and expertise, well-trained, experienced staff officers might have made for better results by delegating more of their authority to practitioners of the complex endeavor of amphibious attack. Considered together with the persistence of frontal attacks against fortified positions held by well-armed veterans, the student of military matters could argue that the army was intellectually moribund—a state of affairs that would not change until the early twentieth century.[26]

Third was a lack of communication—not communications as in signaling, though that was vital, but communication as in liaison and understanding of elements peculiar to each service, its organization, structure, and technical capabilities. The near absence of meaningful liaison between the services was sometimes appalling. When it was present and involved officers with initiative, it could have decisive results, as at Forts Henry and Donelson, in naval gunfire support of Grant's hard-pressed troops at Shiloh, or between John Dahlgren and his army counterparts in the last year at Charleston. When it was absent, the Union courted trouble. One of the most egregious examples was the misunderstanding between Grant and the James River Squadron in late January 1865 at the Battle of Trent's Reach. Had there been close liaison between the two commanders, Parker would have been able to respond to Grant's concerns about his supply base by assuring him that the Union squadron was in place to protect City Point and the army's rear, and that his initial withdrawal was simply an adjustment to conform to the tactical situation. Instead, Grant's unfamiliarity with the situation (and with naval matters generally) created misunderstanding. He became alarmed that the rebel flotilla was about to smash his supply depot, and he contacted Porter, Welles, and Edwin Stanton in a manner that grew increasingly emotional, abrasive, and strident. Those gentlemen responded in similar tones and acted strongly and quickly, but with little accurate knowledge of the circumstances in the field.[27]

Porter in particular, always ready to pontificate, judge, and condemn, sounded nearly hysterical. The correspondence that passed among these leaders reflects poorly on them in a moment of crisis. Meanwhile, Parker sat cautiously but confidently on the river while his seniors suffered the equivalent of an emotional command breakdown. It was not a proud moment for either service, and it all could have been avoided—if Grant had sent a trusted young officer to serve alongside Parker, explaining his needs, desires, and concerns, and had

Parker reciprocated with an officer who could listen attentively and explain the intricacies of naval maneuvers and deployments.[28] As it was, Grant showed his prejudices along with a sense of denial and an impulsive rush to judgment that first appeared in the West. Porter revealed himself as the often-malignant politico he was throughout his career. Welles, a basically competent administrator and the most stable character in Lincoln's cabinet, temporarily seems terribly uninformed, no longer in charge, and overwhelmed by his position—and at that moment, to a degree, he was.

In the end, although the Union possessed a capability the gray coats could only dream of—the ability to lift an army from its base, place it intact and en masse anywhere along the South's three-thousand-mile shoreline, and keep it supplied—it is challenging to understand why it was not used more often and on a larger scale. This question goes to the heart of overall Union strategy. Lincoln's desire to sever ties between the agricultural south and European industry, mining, and finance makes excellent sense. The instrument he chose, the blockade, was cumbersome, slow to come into place, needed time to make its presence felt, and was grossly inefficient. The Union never had enough ships or men to satisfy the squadron commanders or completely shut off the flow of supplies and cotton, and the ships they did have were largely ill-suited to the task: they were often absent, going home for repairs and provisioning, undergoing those tasks, or en route returning from them. And all the while the money flowed out of the U.S. Treasury. The blockade became considerably more effective with time, but it was never an efficient use of naval resources.[29]

It need not have been this way. Nothing closed a Southern harbor more effectively, efficiently, or permanently than a garrison of coast artillerymen and a battery of thirty-two-pounders. This point was proven repeatedly early in the war at Cape Hatteras, Fort Macon, Port Royal, Beaufort (N.C. and S.C.), New Orleans, Fort Pulaski, and Fort Clinch on Amelia Island. Each of these places was seized and resourcefully garrisoned by the Union army after a combined operation. The principle of economy of force has seldom been so well employed. They permanently and efficiently shut off contraband commerce and ended the Confederate presence in each area of occupation.

The bottom line is that the North, with all its naval might and overwhelming resources, failed to use combined operations and amphibious assaults in the manner best fitted to the time, technology, and task—to occupy the Southern coast and make the blockade redundant, thus freeing men, ships, and myriad resources for offensive operations elsewhere. To do so was well within its power, involving as it did biting off parts of the rebel perimeter one readily digestible piece at a time. From there they could have used the extensive river system as a highway to invade the interior or raid at will. As shown by other contributors to this book, it must be remembered and acknowledged that the Union leadership conceived, attempted, and achieved much in the use of combined operations. Yet had they chosen to professionally organize, train, and plan for such actions, they could have accomplished much more while expending fewer human and material resources. Had the same men chosen to embrace combined operations on a *strategic* scale along the littoral periphery as they did on the Mississippi River, the war might well have progressed toward its just conclusion more efficiently and with fewer casualties.

Notes

1. William J. Morgan et al., *Naval Documents of the American Revolution* (Washington, D.C.: Government Printing Office, 1969), 4:133, 152, 403; Nathan Miller, *Sea of Glory: A Naval History of the American Revolution* (Charleston, S.C.: Nautical and Aviation Publishing, 1974), 107–12; Charles R. Smith, *Marines in the Revolution* (Washington, D.C.: Government Printing Office, 1975).

2. Harry A. Ellsworth, *One Hundred Eighty Landings of the United States Marines, 1800–1934* (Washington, D.C.: U.S. Marine Corps History and Museums Division, 1974), 157–59; George E. Buker, *Swamp Sailors in the Second Seminole War* (Gainesville: University of Florida Press, 1997); James C. Bradford and Gene A. Smith, "Foreword," in R. Blake Dunnavent, *Brown Water Warfare* (Gainesville: University Press of Florida, 2003), xiv.

3. General intelligence concerning the coast, landing sites, hydrography, and nearshore terrain was excellent, having been gathered by the blockading forces under David Connor. What was lacking was timely knowledge of Mexican dispositions, capabilities, intentions, and details of the terrain beyond the beach.

4. Robert S. Henry, *The Story of the Mexican War* (New York: Da Capo Press, 1950), 262–63; John F. Polk, "Vera Cruz, 1847," in Merrill Bartlett, ed., *Assault from the Sea: Essays on the History of Amphibious Warfare* (Annapolis, Md.: Naval Institute Press, 1983), 76.

5. Henry, *Mexican War*, 262; Polk, "Vera Cruz," 76–78.

6. Polk, "Vera Cruz," 78; John Sweetman, "British Invasion of the Crimea, 1854," in Bartlett, *Assault from the Sea*, 79–87.

7. Holland M. Smith, *The Development of Amphibious Tactics in the U.S. Navy* (Washington, D.C.: U.S. Marine Corps History and Museums Division, 1992), 9.

8. Antoine Henri Jomini, *The Art of War* (Philadelphia: J. B. Lippincott, 1862), 248–52.

9. Buker, *Swamp Sailors*, 4, 33; Dunnavent, *Brown Water Warfare*, xiv.

10. Rowena Reed, *Combined Operations in the Civil War* (Annapolis, Md.: Naval Institute Press, 1978). Reed's book is the only one to examine this aspect of the war. She offers several controversial conclusions, including the notion that George McClellan was the most insightful thinker of the Union army and that his successor, Henry Halleck, disliked joint operations and sought to eliminate combined arms efforts.

11. See the reports of Lieutenant Gwin, April 8, 1862, in *ORN*, 22:762–66, and that of May 8, 1862, in *ORN*, 23:90.

12. Brigadier General Thomas W. Sherman gave specific instructions regarding combat loading in preparing for the 1861 attack on Port Royal, but they were ignored. Porter's fire support plan for the second attack on Fort Fisher was a model for its time. See *Annual Report of the Department of the Navy*, National Archives Microfilm Publication M1099, reel 8, p. 179.

13. Abbott's report is in *OR*, 46 (part 1): 167–68.

14. Kidder's report is in *ORN*, 11:446–47; James R. Soley, "The Naval Brigade," *Proceedings of the United States Naval Institute* 6 (1880): 271–94. Soley seems to have been one of the few to give serious consideration to the organization, training, and equipping of naval brigades for combined operations.

15. Robert W. Daly, "Burnside's Amphibious Division, 1862," in Bartlett, *Assault from the Sea*, 88–94.

16. Lance C. Buhl, "Maintaining 'An American Navy,' 1865–1889," in Kenneth J. Hagan, ed., *In Peace and War* (Westport, Conn.: Greenwood Press, 1984), 145–73.

17. Ibid., 147, 154–55; Foxhall A. Parker, "Our Fleet Maneuvers in the Bay of Florida, and the Navy of the Future," *Record of the United States Naval Institute* 1 (1874): 163–64.

18. Soley, "Naval Brigade"; Smith, *Development of Amphibious Tactics*, 15.

19. Frank Freidel, *A Splendid Little War* (New York: Bramhall House, 1958), 81; Alfred A. Nofi, *The Spanish-American War* (Conshohocken, Pa.: Combined Books, 1996), 120–23; Smith, *Development of Amphibious Tactics*, 15. The number of animals lost remains a matter of dispute. Lieutenant (later Admiral) Joseph Taussig wrote of being assigned to tow animal carcasses away from the landing areas at Siboney. See diary entry for June 25, 1898, manuscript collection 97, Joseph Taussig Papers, Naval War College. Naval gunfire was employed at Daiquiri but failed to strike anything of value. In any case, the Spanish evacuated before the first American came ashore.

20. *Annual Report of the Secretary of the Navy, 1898* (Washington, D.C.: Government Printing Office, 1898); Stephen B. Luce, "United States Navy War College," *United Service* 12 (January 1885): 88.

21. See Roger Thompson, *Lessons Not Learned: The Navy's Status Quo Culture* (Annapolis, Md.: Naval Institute Press, 2007).

22. Robert D. Heinl, "The U.S. Marine Corps: Author of Modern Amphibious Warfare," *United States Naval Institute Proceedings* 73 (November 1977): 1310–23; Hans G. von Lehmann, "Japanese Landing Operations in World War Two," in Bartlett, *Assault form the Sea*, 195–96. See also Brian Linn, *Echo of Battle* (Cambridge, Mass.: Harvard University Press, 2008).

23. Daly, "Burnside's Amphibious Division," 93. Shallow-water operations are inherently risky for small craft as well as ships. A strong, sustained wind can blow water in or out of a bay, river, or sound in less than twenty-four hours. The author has witnessed the depth of confined waters alter by as much as six feet above or below normal during such events, and wind-induced fluctuations of two to four feet are routine. Shallower bodies of water can be rendered closed to navigation in a very short time. The broad shallow sounds of North Carolina, where depths of ten to fifteen feet prevail, are notoriously susceptible, especially in winter. Burnside was a lucky man at Roanoke. At Fort Fisher, Brigadier General Geoffrey Weitzel commanded the landing force and spent three days studying the Confederate works from offshore. He interviewed naval officers, captured Confederates (and at least one spy), but never put a party ashore to examine the terrain. See Chris Fonvielle Jr., *The Wilmington Campaign: Last Rays of Departing Hope* (Campbell, Calif.: Savas Publishing, 1997), 69–71.

24. Daly, "Burnside's Amphibious Division," 93; Joseph E. King, "The Fort Fisher Campaign, 1864–65," in Bartlett, *Assault From the Sea*, 102.

25. "Agreement Concerning Joint Operations," April 13, 1813, in William S. Dudley, ed., *The Naval War of 1812: A Documentary History* (Washington, D.C.: Naval Historical Center, 1985), 2:434–35; Isaac Chauncey to Secretary of the Navy Jones, April 28, 1813, and May 15, 1813, both in Dudley, *Naval War of 1812*, 2:449–52, 163–64.

26. Brian Linn, *The Echo of Battle* (Cambridge, Mass.: Harvard University Press, 2007), 28 (for a review of the limits of nineteenth-century American military and political thinking, see Chapter 1, "Fortress America," 10–39).

27. For Shiloh, see the report of Lieutenant Gwin, April 8, 1862, in *ORN*, 22:762–66; for Charleston, see Commander USS *Vermont* to Dahlgren, November 28, 1863, Gordon to Turner, December 31, 1863, Dahlgren to Welles, March 22, 1865, and Dahlgren to Welles, March 24, 1865, all in *Area Files of the United States Navy*, National Archives Microfilm Publication M625, reel 205.

28. See Parker's report in *ORN*, 11:632–33. Porter's comment is dated January 26, 1865, and is in *ORN*, 11:644.

29. The efficacy of the Union blockade is still a matter of contention among historians. The nineteenth-century historian James R. Soley argued that it was decisive (*The Blockade and the Cruisers* [New York: Charles Scribner's Sons, 1883]), and others such as E. Merton Coulter and Francis Bradlee have agreed. More recently critics like Frank Owsley, Stephen Wise, and William N. Still Jr. have argued that it was of little importance.

Contributors

Francis J. DuCoin, a native of Philadelphia, earned his masters in biomedical engineering at Drexel University and attended the University of Pennsylvania's School of Dental Medicine. When he is not running his dental practice in Stuart, Florida, he is an avid Civil War collector and historian with special interest in Civil War photography and naval history.

John P. Fisher is an adjunct assistant professor of history at the University of Cincinnati and director of the Southeast Ohio Educational Opportunity Center. He holds a Ph.D. in history from Texas A&M University, and is the author of an article on Texas and the Union blockade, as well as articles in the *International Encyclopedia of Military History*.

Chris E. Fonvielle Jr. is an associate professor of history at the University of North Carolina, Wilmington, where he teaches courses on the American Civil War. He holds a Ph.D. from the University of South Carolina and is the author of *Last Rays of Departing Hope: The Wilmington Campaign*. He was the curator of the exhibit on "The Blockade-Runners" at the Museum of the Confederacy.

Howard J. Fuller is Senior Lecturer of War Studies at the University of Wolverhampton in the United Kingdom, where he teaches courses on the American Civil War, the British Empire, and naval warfare of the nineteenth century. He is associate editor for the *International Journal of Naval History*, and the author of *Clad in Iron: The American Civil War and the Challenge of British Naval Power*.

David E. Long is an associate professor of history at East Carolina University, where he teaches courses on the American Civil War. He holds a Ph.D. in history from Florida State University and a J.D. from the Ohio State University Michel E. Moritz College of Law. He practiced law for twelve years before turning to full-time study as an historian. He is the author of *The Jewel of Liberty: Abraham Lincoln's Re-election and the End of Slavery*.

Robert E. Sheridan is Professor Emeritus at Rutgers University and one of the discoverers of the wreck site of the USS *Monitor*. In his most recent work, *Iron* *from the Deep: The Discovery and Recovery of the USS* Monitor, he combines his perspective on the *Monitor*'s discovery with a history of the ship, including its role in the Battle of Drewry's Bluff.

David C. Skaggs is Professor Emeritus at Bowling Green State University, where he taught for more than thirty years. He holds a Ph.D. in history from Georgetown University, and was a fellow at the U.S. Arms Control and Disarmament Agency and a visiting professor at the Air War College at Maxwell Air Force Base in Alabama. He is the author of several books on nineteenth-century naval history, including biographies of Thomas MacDonough and Oliver Hazard Perry.

Mark A. Snell is an associate professor of history at Shepherdstown University and the director of the George Tyler Moore Center for the Study of the Civil War. He is a retired army officer and former assistant professor at the U.S. Military Academy at West Point. He is the author or editor of several books, including *From First to Last: The Life of Major General William B. Franklin*.

Craig L. Symonds is Professor Emeritus at the U.S. Naval Academy, where he taught courses on the American Civil War and naval history for thirty years. He is the author of twelve books, most recently *Lincoln and His Admirals: Abraham Lincoln, the U.S. Navy, and the Civil War*, which won the Barondess/Lincoln Prize, the Daniel and Marilyn Laney Prize, the John Lyman Book Award, and the Lincoln Prize in 2009.

Edward H. Wiser is an army captain with a Ph.D. from Florida State University, where he wrote his dissertation on Civil War torpedo boats. He is an adjunct professor of strategy and war at the Naval War College extension.

Index

Abbot, Henry L., 139–40
Adams, Charles F., 131
Afghanistan, U.S. war in, 6
Agawam (U.S.N. gunboat), 104
Alabama (C.S. raider), 64, 124
Alamo (Texas State gunboat), 67
Albemarle Sound (North Carolina), 25
Alexander, Barton Stone, 32–33, 34–35, 41–42, 43*n*
Ames, Adelbert, 103
Anaconda Plan, 56, 117
Anderson, H. J., 120
Anderson, Joseph Reid, 27
Andrews, A. S., 144–45
Annapolis, Maryland, 11, 13
Antietam, battle of, 100
Aransas Bay, Texas, 66, 68
Arizona (side-wheel steamer), 63–64
Arnold, Richard, 37
Aroostock (U.S.N. gunboat), 45

Bache, A. D., 56
Bancroft, George, 12
Banks, Nathaniel P., 60, 62, 67–68, 139
Barbary Wars, 135
Barhamsville, Virginia, 38, 43*n*
Barnard, John G., 37–38, 56
Bayou City (C.S. gunboat), 60
Beaufort, North Carolina, 12, 20, 25, 29, 104
Beauregard, P. G. T., 83, 92, 132*n*, 136
Bee, Hamilton, 66, 68
Bell, Henry H., 61, 62–64, 65, 71
Benham, Henry, 76, 79
Bermuda Hundred, Virginia, 88–89
Betio. *See* Tarawa, battle for
Bienville (U.S.N. gunboat), 74, 77
Blackhawk (U.S.N. river gunboat), 109
Blair, Francis P. (Frank), Jr., 88
Blair, Francis P., Sr., 88
Blair, Montgomery, 88
Blakely, Theophilus A., 123

blockade, 56, 96–97, 101, 117, 148
Blockade Board, 56, 99
Boardman (army steamer), 37
Boggs, William R., 70
Bourne, Kenneth, 126
Bragg, Braxton, 103, 107–8, 110, 112
Branch, Lawrence O'Bryan, 19, 27
Bright, John, 128
Brodie, Bernard, 128
Brown, S. K., 67
Brownsville, Texas, 68
Bryant, William Cullen, 12
Buker, George, 137
Bull Run, battle of, 10, 97
Burnside, Ambrose E., 8, 10–21, 23, 26, 100, 140–41, 144
Burnside, Molly, 13
Butler, Benjamin F.
  and the Bermuda Hundred, 87–90
  and Texas, 58–59
  and Wilmington, North Carolina (Fort Fisher), 103–8
Bythesea, John, 129

Catskill (U.S.N. monitor), 82
Charleston, South Carolina, 74–85, 99, 101; map, 78
  British assessment of, 118–19, 120–23, 131–32
  combined attack on, 82–85
  ironclad attack on, 81
Chase, Salmon P., 2, 4–5
City of New York (army supply ship), 16
City Point, Virginia, 45, 88–89
Clifton (U.S.N. side-wheel steamer), 63–64
Cold Harbor, battle of, 91
Colonel Satterly (army transport), 15
Colorado (U.S.N. steam frigate), 102
Columbia, South Carolina, 109
combat loading, 139

Commodore Jones (U.S.N. river gunboat), 89
Connor, David, 136
Cooke, Augustus P., 70
Corpus Christi, Texas, 57, 66
Cox, Jacob D., 110–12
Crescent (army supply ship), 65
Crocker, Frederick, 63–65, 71

Dahlgren, John A., 81–85, 116, 119
Dana, Napoleon Jackson Tecumseh, 68
Davis, Edmund J., 59
Davis, Jefferson, 103, 123
De Grey, Earl. *See* Robinson, Robert S.
Delaware (army troopship), 19
Diana (Texas State gunboat), 66
Dowling, Richard, 65, 71
Drayton, Percival, 77, 79–80, 116–17
Drewry's Bluff , 5, 44–52
  casualties, 51
  described, 45–46
  in the 1864 campaign, 89–90
Dismal Swamp Canal, 20
Du Pont, Samuel F., 13, 25, 51, 116
  and the Blockade Board, 56
  and Charleston, 74–81

Eastern Queen (army transport), 14
Elizabeth City, North Carolina, 20
Ellis, Earl "Pete," 144
Ellsworth, Harry, 135
Eltham's Landing, Virginia, 32–42, 44, 65; map, 34
Esposito, Vincent, 23
Ericsson, John, 126
Erie Canal, 129
Estrella (U.S.N. side-wheel steamer), 70

Farragut, David Glasgow, 6, 46, 93
  at Mobile Bay, 101, 139
  at New Orleans, 88, 117
  and the Texas coast, 57–60, 61, 62–63, 70
Farrand, Ebenezer, 46
Fayetteville, North Carolina, 97, 109
Fisher, Charles F., 97
Flora (army transport), 74, 77
Foote, Andrew Hull, 51, 139
Forbes, John Murray, 123
Fort Anderson (N.C.), 99, 108–9
  surrendered, 111
Fort Bartow (N.C.), 17
Fort Campbell (N.C.), 97
Fort Caswell (N.C.), 97, 100
Fort Clark (N.C.), 11
Fort Darling (Va.), 89. *See also* Drewry's Bluff
Fort Donelson (Tenn.), 51
Fort Esperanza (Tx.), 69
Fort Fisher (N.C.), 25, 88, 139; map, 98
  attempt to blow up, 104
  bombardment of, 105, 106
  described, 97, 98–99
  infantry attack on, 107–8, 140
Fort Griffin (Tx.), 64–65, 71
Fort Henry (Tenn.), 51
Fort Holmes (N.C.), 97
Fort Johnson (S.C.), 74
Fort Macon (N.C.), 20, 25, 29
Fort Monroe (Va.), 2–3, 45
Fort Moultrie (S.C.), 84
Fort Pulaski (Ga.), 79, 116, 119, 122
Fort Strong (N.C.), 112
Fort Sumter (S.C.), 82–83, 84, 120–21, 122
  combined attack on, 82–85
  ironclad attack on, 81
  See also Charleston, South Carolina
Fort Thompson (N.C.), 19
Fort Tomkins (N.Y.), 126
Fort (Battery) Wagner (S.C.), 82–83
Foster, John G., 17, 26–29, 100
Fox, Gustavus Vasa, 5, 44, 74–75, 93–94, 101, 108, 117, 123, 146
Franklin, William B.
  in the Peninsular Campaign, 32, 34–41, 43n, 140
  on the Texas coast, 63–65, 71
Fredericksburg, Battle of, 10, 21, 100
Fremantle, Arthur, 118, 122–23, 125

Galena (U.S.N. ironclad)
  at Charleston, 75
  at Drewry's Bluff, 35, 45, 46–47, 123
  weaknesses of, 50–51
Gallwey, T. L., 120, 122, 130
Galveston, Texas, 56–57
  re-captured by Confederates, 60–61
  Union capture of, 57–58
Gatlin, Richard C., 27
Geer, George S., 47
George Peabody (army transport), 14
Gillis, John P., 67
Gillmore, Quincy Adams
  at Charleston, 81–85, 119
  on James River, 91

Index

Gladstone, William, 130
Glover, John, 140
Goldsboro, North Carolina, 11, 24, 26, 109
Goldsborough, Louis M., 13, 26, 35, 45, 53
   in Hampton Roads, 2–3, 5–6
   in Pamlico Sound, 17, 19, 20
   and Wilmington, North Carolina, 99–100
Goodenough, James, 130
Goodenough, John, 123
Granger, Gordon, 139
Granite City (U.S.N. gunboat), 63–64, 69, 70
Grant, Ulysses S., 6, 51, 62, 139, 146
   and the James River, 89–94, 147–48
   Overland Campaign, 87, 89
   and Wilmington, North Carolina, 102, 108–9
Greeley, Horace, 24
Grey, Frederick, 127–28
Griffith, Paddy, 125

Hagerman, Edward, 122
Hagood, Johnson, 111
Halleck, Henry, 1, 62, 66, 100, 146
Hampton, Wade, 39–40
Hampton Roads, Virginia, 2
Hardee, William J., 1
Harriet Lane (U.S. revenue cutter), 60
Harrison's Landing (Va.), 45
Hartford (U.S.N. screw sloop), 61, 93
Hatteras Inlet, expedition to, 14–21, 25, 27–28
Hawkins, Rush, 11–12, 16–18
Hay, John, 87
Helper, Harvey H., 19
Helper, Hinton R., 19
Hempstead, N.Y., 10
Henry Andrew (U.S.N. gunboat), 77
Henry Janes (mortar schooner), 58
Hill, Daniel Harvey, 27
Hoke, Robert F., 103–4, 110–12
Hood, John Bell, 39
Hooper, Quincy, 61
Hope, James, 131
Hopkins, Esek, 135
Huger, Benjamin, 27
Hunter, David, 75–80
Huron (U.S.N. gunboat), 104

Iraq, U.S. war in, 6

J. H. Bell (Texas State gunboat), 66
Jeffers, William N., 3, 48

John F. Carr (Texas State gunboat), 66–67
Johnson, Amos, 63
Johnston, Joseph E., 24, 36, 52, 118, 136
Jomini, Antoine Henri, 1, 137
Jones, Archer, 24
Kalamazoo (projected U.S.N. ironclad), 126

Kensington (screw steamer), 57–58
Keokuk (U.S.N. ironclad), 81
Krulak, Victor, 144

Laird Brothers (shipbuilders), 124
Lamb, William, 97–98, 104–8
Lamson, Charles W., 63
Lanman, Joseph, 94
Laurel Hill (army transport), 65
Law, P. L., 60
Lee, Elizabeth Blair, 88
Lee, Robert E., 15, 89, 100, 106, 125, 136
Lee, Samuel Phillips, 87–92, 100, 102, 145
Lee, Stephen D., 40
Lincoln, Abraham, 1, 93, 101–2, 104, 145–46
   and the blockade, 56
   British opinions of, 121–22
   and grand strategy, 87, 148
   at Hampton Roads, 2–6
   and the North Carolina Sounds, 12–13, 16, 25, 29
   and the Peninsula Campaign, 33, 42*n*, 45, 53–54, 100
   re-election, 102
logistics
   in North Carolina, 16, 23–24
   in Virginia, 51–52
   on Texas coast, 62
Louisiana (U.S. bomb vessel), 104
Lowe, Thaddeus, 42
Luce, Stephen B., 142–43
Lynch, William F., 28
Lyons, Lord (Richard B. Pemell), 122, 123, 128–29

Mackie, John, 49
Maffitt, John, 69–70
Magruder, John B.
   and the Peninsular Campaign, 33
   and the Texas coast, 60, 66, 67, 69–70
Mahan, Alfred T., 142
Malvern (U.S.N. gunboat; D. D. Porter's flagship), 91, 109
Marchand, John B., 75

Mary Hill (Texas State gunboat), 66–67
Mason, Charles M., 67
Matamoros, Mexico, 59–60, 61–62
McClellan, George B., 1, 2, 7–8, 23–24, 25, 115, 140
   and the North Carolina Sounds, 10–13, 16, 26–27, 29
   and the Peninsula Campaign, 32–42, 42*n*, 45, 51–54, 100
   and Texas, 62
McDowell, Irvin, 33–34
McPherson, James M., 23
Meade, George G., 87, 136
Meigs, Montgomery, 76
Merrimack (as ironclad). See *Virginia*
Mervine, William, 57
Miami (U.S. revenue cutter), 2, 4
Milne, Alexander, 118–19, 126, 131
mines. See torpedoes
Minnesota (U.S.N. steam frigate), 2, 93–94, 102
Missroon, John S., 33–35
Mobile Bay, Alabama, 101
Monitor (U.S.N. ironclad), 3, 75, 100, 127, 128–29
   attack on Drewry's Bluff, 44–45, 47
   weaknesses of, 49–50
Monongahela (U.S.N. screw steamer), 68–69
Montauk (U.S.N. monitor), 83, 100, 110
Morehead City, North Carolina, 24, 29
Morning Light (U.S.N. gunboat), 61
Myer, Albert, 80

Naugatuck (U.S.N. gunboat), 45, 48
Neptune (C.S. gunboat), 60
New Bern, North Carolina, 11, 18–19, 24, 26, 100
   capture of, 19–20, 28–29
New Ironsides (U.S.N. ironclad), 81, 83, 102, 105
New Orleans, Louisiana, 88, 117
New York City, 117, 120
Newton, John, 35, 37, 39
Norfolk, Virginia, 3–4, 45
Normandy, allied invasion of, 6, 42

obstructions. See torpedoes
Onondaga (U.S.N. ironclad), 92–93, 94
ordnance, 126, 140
   at Fort Fisher, 104
   on James River, 47–48
Owasco (U.S.N. gunboat), 60, 68

Pacific (mail steamer), 60
Paine, Charles J., 103, 110
Palmerston, Viscount (Henry John Temple), 121, 128, 130–31
Pamlico Sound, North Carolina, 10–21, 25, 27–28, 104; map, 18
Parke, John G., 20, 26, 28–29
Parker, Foxhall, 142
Parker, William A., 92–94
Passaic (U.S.N. monitor), 100
Passaic-class monitors, 81
Pender, Dorsey, 40
Peninsula Campaign, 2, 24, 29–30, 32–41, 45, 100
Petersburg, Virginia, 87, 91
Pettigrew, James J., 30
Pickett (U.S. Army gunboat), 14
Pierce, Leonard, 62
Pilot Boy (army steamer), 17
Planter (pilot boat), 74–75
Pocahontas (army transport), 15
Port Royal, South Carolina, 11–12, 25, 80
Port Royal (U.S.N. paddle steamer), 45
Porter, David Dixon, 28, 51, 92, 94, 139, 142
   and Wilmington, North Carolina, 102–12
Powhatan (U.S.N. steam frigate), 102
Puritan (U.S.N. monitor), 126

Rachel Seaman (U.S. schooner), 57–58
Radford, William, 93–94
Red River Campaign, 62
Reed, Rowena, 1, 7–8, 11, 23, 29, 32, 41, 118, 120, 122, 137
Reid, Brian Holden, 118, 122
Reilly, James, 40
Reno, Jesse, 26, 28–29
Renshaw, William, 57–58, 60
Rhind, Alexander C., 104
Roanoke Island (N.C.), 15–18, 25–26; map, 18
Robinson, Robert S., 127–28, 131
Rodger, Nicholas, 117
Rodgers, C. R. P., 76
Rodgers, John, 5, 35, 45, 47, 49, 51, 123
Rowan, Stephen, 19–20, 26, 28
Rucker, Daniel, 33
Russell, Lord John, 123

Sabine Pass, Texas, 56–57
   Confederate counterattack, 61
   reasons for failure, 71
   Union attack on, 57–58

Index

Union attack, second, 63–64
Sachem (U.S.N. gunboat), 63–64
Saluria, Texas, 66–67
Savannah, Georgia, 116–17
Schofield, John M., 108, 110–12
Scotia (U.S.N. gunboat), 70
Scott, Winfield, 1, 115, 136
Secessionville, Battle of, 74–75, 79
Sedgwick, John, 40–41
Selfridge, Thomas H., 104
Seminole Wars, 137
Semmes, Raphael, 69–70
Sevastopol, campaign for, 115–16, 121
Seward, William H., 5, 62, 128, 131
Shawsheen (U.S.N. river gunboat), 89
Sheridan, Philip, 102
Sherman, Thomas W., 11–12
Sherman, William T., 30, 74, 88, 102, 106
Shufeldt, Robert W., 61
Sigel, Franz, 87
Signal Corps (U.S.), 39
signaling, 80
Slocum, Henry, 37, 39
Smalls, Robert, 75–76
Smith, Edmund Kirby, 66, 70
Smith, Gustavus, 38
Smith, Holland M., 137, 142
Smith, Leon, 60, 67, 69
Smith, William, 32, 35–36, 42, 49
Soley, James R., 142
Spanish-American War, 142–43
Spotsylvania Court House, Battle of, 89, 91
Stanton, Edwin M., 2, 33, 77, 118
Stevens, Isaac, 74–75, 80
Stevens, Thomas H., 40
Stimers, Alban C., 124–25
Stonewall (C.S.N. ironclad), 124
Strategy Board. *See* Blockade Board
Stringham, Silas, 25
Stuart, J. E. B. ("Jeb"), 53
Susquehanna (U.S.N. paddle steamer), 102

Taiping Rebellion, 121
Tarawa, battle for, 145
Tattnall, Josiah, 45
Taylor, George, 37
Taylor, Marble Nash, 12
Tennessee (U.S.N. side-wheel steamer), 68
Terry, Alfred H., 106–12
Tibbits, Howard, 63
torpedoes, 84, 126–27

Trent Affair, 120, 125, 128
Trent's Reach, battle of, 92–93

Uncle Ben (C.S. gunboat), 61, 66
USS *Monitor* Center (Mariners' Museum), 6, 8

Vance, Zebulon B., 110
Velocity (U.S.N. gunboat), 61
Vera Cruz, Mexico (U.S. landing), 136
Virginia (C.S. ironclad), 3, 5, 32, 44, 46
    destroyed, 45, 75
Virginia (U.S.N. steamer), 68
Virginius Incident, 142

Wabash (U.S.N. steam frigate), 102
Wachusett (U.S.N. steam sloop), 35, 49, 51
War Department, U.S., 1
Warrior (R.N. ironclad), 127
Washburn, Cadwallader C., 69
Washburn, Samuel, 48
Weitzel, Godfrey, 64, 92
    at Fort Fisher, 103–5
Weldon, North Carolina, 97
Welles, Gideon, 13, 56–57, 91, 93, 117, 128, 146, 148
    and the blockade, 62
    and Charleston, South Carolina, 74, 79
    and ironclads, 44, 99
    and relations with the army, 65, 79
    and Wilmington, North Carolina, 101
Wellington, Duke of, 115
Westfield (U.S.N. gunboat), 60
Whiting, William Henry Chase (W.H.C.), 38, 97–98, 103, 105–7
Williamsburg, Virginia, 5
    battle of, 36, 37–38
Wilmington, North Carolina, 11, 25, 96–112; map, 98
    described, 96
    land campaign against, 108–12
    See also Fort Fisher
Wise, Henry A., 27
Wood, John Taylor, 46, 51
Woodbury, Daniel, 33
Wool, John E., 3, 45
Wright, Horatio G., 77, 79

Yates, Frank, 39
Yorktown, Va., 2

Zouave (army gunboat), 15

The North's Civil War
Paul A. Cimbala, series editor

1. Anita Palladino, ed., *Diary of a Yankee Engineer: The Civil War Story of John H. Westervelt, Engineer, 1st New York Volunteer Engineer Corps.*

2. Herman Belz, *Abraham Lincoln, Constitutionalism, and Equal Rights in the Civil War Era.*

3. Earl J. Hess, *Liberty, Virtue, and Progress: Northerners and Their War for the Union.* Second revised edition, with a new introduction by the author.

4. William L. Burton, *Melting Pot Soldiers: The Union's Ethnic Regiments.*

5. Hans L. Trefousse, *Carl Schurz: A Biography.*

6. Stephen W. Sears, ed., *Mr. Dunn Browne's Experiences in the Army: The Civil War Letters of Samuel W. Fiske.*

7. Jean H. Baker, *Affairs of Party: The Political Culture of Northern Democrats in the Mid–Nineteenth Century.*

8. Frank L. Klement, *The Limits of Dissent: Clement L. Vallandigham and the Civil War.* With a new introduction by Steven K. Rogstad.

9. Lawrence N. Powell, *New Masters: Northern Planters during the Civil War and Reconstruction.*

10. John A. Carpenter, *Sword and Olive Branch: Oliver Otis Howard.*

11. Thomas F. Schwartz, ed., *"For a Vast Future Also": Essays from the* Journal of the Abraham Lincoln Association.

12. Mark De Wolfe Howe, ed., *Touched with Fire: Civil War Letters and Diary of Oliver Wendell Holmes, Jr.* With a new introduction by David Burton.

13. Harold Adams Small, ed., *The Road to Richmond: The Civil War Letters of Major Abner R. Small of the 16th Maine Volunteers.* With a new introduction by Earl J. Hess.

14. Eric A. Campbell, ed., *"A Grand Terrible Dramma": From Gettysburg to Petersburg: The Civil War Letters of Charles Wellington Reed.* Illustrated by Reed's Civil War sketches.

15. Herbert Mitgang, ed., *Abraham Lincoln: A Press Portrait.*

16. Harold Holzer, ed., *Prang's Civil War Pictures: The Complete Battle Chromos of Louis Prang.*

17. Harold Holzer, ed., *State of the Union: New York and the Civil War.*

18. Paul A. Cimbala and Randall M. Miller, eds., *Union Soldiers and the Northern Home Front: Wartime Experiences, Postwar Adjustments.*

19. Mark A. Snell, *From First to Last: The Life of Major General William B. Franklin.*

20. Paul A. Cimbala and Randall M. Miller, eds., *An Uncommon Time: The Civil War and the Northern Home Front.*

21. John Y. Simon and Harold Holzer, eds., *The Lincoln Forum: Rediscovering Abraham Lincoln.*

22. Thomas F. Curran, *Soldiers of Peace: Civil War Pacifism and the Postwar Radical Peace Movement.*

23. Kyle S. Sinisi, *Sacred Debts: State Civil War Claims and American Federalism, 1861–1880.*

24. Russell L. Johnson, *Warriors into Workers: The Civil War and the Formation of Urban-Industrial Society in a Northern City.*

25. Peter J. Parish, *The North and the Nation in the Era of the Civil War.* Edited by Adam L. P. Smith and Susan-Mary Grant.

26. Patricia Richard, *Busy Hands: Images of the Family in the Northern Civil War Effort.*

27. Michael S. Green, *Freedom, Union, and Power: The Mind of the Republican Party During the Civil War.*

28. Christian G. Samito, ed., *Fear Was Not In Him: The Civil War Letters of Major General Francis S. Barlow, U.S.A.*

29. John S. Collier and Bonnie B. Collier, eds., *Yours for the Union: The Civil War Letters of John W. Chase, First Massachusetts Light Artillery.*

30. Grace Palladino, *Another Civil War: Labor, Capital, and the State in the Anthracite Regions of Pennsylvania, 1840–1868.*

31. Andrew L. Slap, *The Doom of Reconstruction: The Liberal Republicans in the Civil War Era.*

32. Christian B. Keller, *Chancellorsville and the Germans: Nativism, Ethnicity, and Civil War Memory.*

33. Robert M. Sandow, *Deserter Country: Civil War Opposition in the Pennsylvania Appalachians.*